When Oberlin Was King
of the Gridiron

Oberlin Victorious

Dedicated to the Champions of the State

Don't you see our foot ball booters as they're lined up for the fray?
Don't you see our pig-skin punters nerved and braced to win the day?
Don't you hear the horns a tooting, don't you hear the welkin ring?
Don't you hear the rooters rooting, don't you hear the songs they sing?
Don't you see the pig-skin flying toward the other fellows' goal?
Look! to run it back they're trying; but see how our stone wall holds? . . .
It's our nerve and brain and science, with a dash and vim that's great,
Bids all other teams defiance, and defeats Ohio State. . . .
And when victory is certain; when we shout "Good boys, well done,"
With the Gold and Crimson floating proudly o'er the men who won,
When we tear the heavens open with our mighty Hi-O-Hi,
When we cheer our mole-skin heroes to the dark November sky,
When we cheer for those defeated, as we cheer for those who win,
Then is college life worth living, if it's lived in Oberlin.

   —M. B. Jewett (Class of '00), *Oberlin Review*, December 19, 1901

When
OBERLIN
Was King of the Gridiron

The Heisman Years

Nat Brandt

Published by Oberlin College

Library of Congress Catalog Card Number 00-010265
ISBN 0-87338-684-1
Manufactured in the United States of America

Produced and distributed by The Kent State University Press,
Kent, Ohio 44242

06   05   04   03   02   01   5   4   3   2   1

Unless otherwise noted, illustrations are courtesy of
the Oberlin College Archives.

Library of Congress Cataloging-in-Publication Data
Brandt, Nat.
When Oberlin was king of the gridiron: the Heisman years / Nat Brandt.
p.   cm.
Includes bibliographical references (p.   ) and index.
ISBN 0-87338-684-1 (alk. paper) ∞
1. Oberlin College—Football—History.
2. Heisman, John W. (John William), 1869–1936.
I. Title.

GV958.024 B72   2001
796.332'63'0977123—dc21   00-010265

British Library Cataloging-in-Publication data are available.

To Roland Baumann, archivist of Oberlin College, who has made the labors of research the most pleasant and rewarding experience possible and without whose guidance this, and my two earlier books dealing with Oberlin, could not have been written.

OTHER BOOKS BY NAT BRANDT

The Man Who Tried to Burn New York
The Town That Started the Civil War
The Congressman Who Got Away with Murder
Con Brio: Four Russians Called the Budapest String Quartet
Massacre in Shansi
Harlem at War: The Black Experience in World War II
Mr. Tubbs' Civil War

With John Sexton
How Free Are We? What the Constitution Says We Can and Cannot Do

With Yanna Brandt
Land Kills
A Death in Bulloch Parish

CONTENTS

ILLUSTRATIONS

ACKNOWLEDGMENTS

The dedication of a book of mine to Roland Baumann is long over-due. This is the third book I have written dealing with Oberlin, and none would have been possible without his assistance and guidance. As archivist of Oberlin College, he has always been helpful, encouraging, and patient with my seemingly endless inquiries. As a friend, he has been supportive, and both he and his wife, Phyllis, have made my stays in Oberlin especially enjoyable ones.

I also wish to express my gratitude for this book to Ken Grossi, assistant archivist; Tammy Martin, departmental secretary; Whitney Pape, Special Collections librarian; and Martha Staehlei, student assistant.

A number of other individuals at Oberlin College were kind enough to share their thoughts and, in some cases, their materials with me. I am grateful to them, too. Among them were Vince Rosenthal, a member of the Heisman Club; Ira Steinberg, professor of philosophy; Tom Reed of the Class of 1939; Don Hunsinger, former director, and his secretary, Edna Christopher, of the Department of Physical Education; and George Andrews, professor of mathematics, whose father was on Oberlin's undefeated football team of 1921 and who was himself a member of the team in 1950.

I am especially indebted to Geoffrey Blodgett, who has also been generous in support of my research in Oberlin, both for this book and for the other two as well. Like Professor Andrews, he once played football for Oberlin; as an end on the varsity, he set six records, was the top receiver in the Ohio Conference in 1952, and that same year was selected by the Associated Press to its All-Ohio Conference first team. Blodgett, a professor of history, graciously shared his notes, his thoughts, and his enthusiasm. He was kind enough to read early versions of my manuscript and made insightful recommendations for changes and additions. Any errors or misconceptions, however, are mine.

Finally, I am, as usual, indebted to my wife, Yanna, whose editorial acumen has sharpened every word in every sentence. She has always been my most demanding and sagacious editor.

PROLOGUE

The day is damp, chilly, blustery. Flurries of wet snow—unusual for northern Ohio so early in the autumn—continue to fall throughout the afternoon. An inch or so of snow covers the field, except for the five-yard markers, where groundskeepers have cleared it away so the white lines are visible. There are maybe fifty people in the stands on the home side, huddled under umbrellas; actually a few more are across the field in the visitors' bleachers. Some thirty-five Oberlin players are suited up in the team's new red jerseys. Twice that number wear their opponents' colors. There are no cheerleaders, no marching band. By halftime, Oberlin is scoreless and trailing by twenty-five points, on the way to a 45–0 drubbing and its thirty-ninth straight loss.

On the field, football stirs little excitement at Oberlin College. Off the field, though, in the halls of academe, a raging controversy has grown in intensity in recent years, raising a legion of questions and a host of answers for and against the game. What can be done to make a small liberal arts school competitive? New, unprecedented financial enticements to lure high school athletes? More personnel to assist in recruiting? Lower academic standards? How can Oberlin remain in the North Coast Athletic Conference without a viable football team? Some supporters of the game have proposed instead a nationwide league of similar, small, academically oriented schools. But does it make sense to continue to sponsor a sport that attracts so little campus attention? Should Oberlin simply abandon football?

Nowadays it is popular among scholars to analyze football according to one's field of interest. Historians trace the sport to a ball game called *harpastum*—an outlet for youthful vigor in Hellenistic times. To some sociologists the game is an exercise that mirrors the Industrial Age because of its reliance on planning, precision, and teamwork. Others liken it to the unique experience of the American frontier in the nineteenth century, when the boundary of civilization was relentlessly pushed westward, much as a scrimmage line presses against an opponent. Those of a military bent point to its similarities to an army at war, a team divided by function into infantry, cavalry, and artillery. Contemporary observers see in it another kind of American experience, as a leveler of economic classes that has witnessed athletes that first were chiefly Anglo-Saxons, then immigrant groups from Europe, and now African Americans.

Ever since modern football's popularity spread like wildfire across America in the latter part of the nineteenth century, there has been a constant: Moralists have wondered whether the courage, strength, and endurance that the game requires build character, or whether the violent clash of two opposing teams condones brutality and leads to unnecessary, serious injuries. It is this quandary that was very much in the forefront of the controversy over football in the 1890s when Oberlin College first fielded a team. Those same moralists soon had other ethical questions to ponder, because football increasingly took on the aspects of a commercial venture, one in which winning became synonymous with prestige, stimulating enrollments and providing a new, lucrative source of revenue for schools. At many schools, the game led to the corruption of academic values: Youths were recruited for their physical ability, not their learning potential. College play became, in a short time, the training ground for professional sport.

At the turn of the century, as football grew in popularity and its rules and strategies evolved, every issue it evoked, from philosophical to trivial, was raised, argued, endlessly debated. For unlike sports of a tamer nature, football raised passionate emotions, pro and con, and those issues have persisted for more than a hundred years.

1

IN THE BEGINNING

*The athletic field is about the best laboratory known where
the young man can get the training, the discipline, the experience
that will systematically and inevitably turn the trick.*
—*John W. Heisman*

One afternoon in early October 1892, when the first chill of autumn was being felt and students strode briskly under still-green elms by the lecture halls and across Tappan Square, an uninspiring-looking young man walked onto the playing field of Oberlin College. He wore eyeglasses, the result of a freak football accident. His nose was slightly misshapen, also the result of a freak football accident. A few weeks shy of his twenty-third birthday, the "bespectacled, stoop-shouldered" young man exuded a "dejected, hands-in-pocket kind of air," one of the players recalled.[1] Dejected because Adelbert College in Cleveland had the day before turned down his proposal to coach its football team, he had, instead, accepted an offer to coach Oberlin's squad, though the student-run athletic association had no money to offer him a salary.

The awkward-looking fellow was actually a lawyer by training, but was unable to practice because of his poor vision. He was toying now with another vocation. A football enthusiast and a player since his own high school days, he thought he could do what a number of other athletes, veterans of the game from the East, where football developed, were doing: coach the sport they had played in college. There was a growing demand for experienced players as school after school expanded their sports programs to include the game.

3

The young man who appeared on the Oberlin playing field was a University of Pennsylvania graduate. His name was John Heisman. He was enrolled at Oberlin as a postgraduate student in its arts department. On paper, that is, for his matriculation was a figment of someone's imagination. He never, so far as it is known, attended a single class, and never, it *is* known, earned a single mark or grade.[2] As a postgraduate, however, he was—according to the lax rules of the day—eligible to play football as well as coach the school team, and play for Oberlin he would, his poor eyesight notwithstanding.

That Oberlin even had a football team seems surprising at first glance, considering the school's beginnings. There was little time for frivolity of any kind when the Christian colony and its college were established in the early 1830s. Its founders purposely chose an isolated, primitive forest, away from the evil temptations of an urban environment, to train missionaries and teachers, male and female, who would spread the Gospel throughout the West. The school's first presidents, as well as its teachers, were unorthodox—heretics in the eyes of Presbyterians and Congregationalists. They rejected sacraments, believing wholeheartedly that an active, moral life and deeds governed the way to salvation.

The school's motto, "Learning and Labor," was no mere bromide. The students, farm youths in the main, had to work every day, Sundays excepted. But many of the jobs they toiled at—clearing the forest and erecting buildings—evaporated as the land was cleared and the campus slowly evolved. As the school grew, the jobs that provided work for students, once plentiful, were either too few or no longer existed; both a sawmill and a farm, for instance, proved unprofitable. Cautiously, Oberlin, which once frowned on sports, embraced the idea that physical activity in itself was healthy both for the body and the soul. It was a philosophy new not only to Oberlin's leaders but to Protestant theologians as a whole. It was called Muscular Christianity.

The phrase first surfaced in an 1858 magazine's description of Thomas Hughes's novel *Tom Brown's Schooldays*. Muscular Christianity was akin to a similar phrase, "healthy animism," used seven years earlier to describe the work of Hughes's friend, clergyman Charles Kingsley. Kingsley considered the old Calvinist taboo about discussing the body and its functions "maundering" and leading to "effeminate shavelings."[3] Hughes himself spoke of "the manliness of Christ."[4]

America was fertile ground for the thoughts of the two Englishmen, especially after Hughes toured the country in the early 1870s. Shortly after his visit to Cornell, where he played football with students, the Cornell Football Association was formed.[5] At the time, critics believed too many clerics were dying of "nervous diseases" because they failed "to take proper care of their bodies," and there were too many Christians of the "weak, womanish, watery-eyed type."[6] Ministers were too often considered "mama's boys" whose health was "fragile." They were individuals whose "delicate" and "tasteful" attributes might appeal to women, but whom men found "especially repulsive."[7] Many concerned congregants found it troubling that "strong men" did not enter the ministry. A study of the nation's students over a thirty-six-year period from 1870 on showed that the number of divinity students increased by 137 percent—on the surface a substantial total. But the increases in secular professions were enormous in comparison: the number of medical students rose by 302 percent, that of law students by 848 percent, and the total of business students by a percentage greater than both medicine and law combined.[8]

"Body-as-temple" theologians were quick to argue that physical vigor and spiritual sanctity were not incompatible, that there was a morality of fitness. They attacked sermons that reflected early Victorian Protestantism, which likened women to angels or talked of Christ's feminine characteristics—his sensitivity, refinement, and avoidance of life's coarser aspects. Moses was a "strong man," one religious-oriented magazine declared, "Else the march over the desert would have exhausted him, the anxiety of the exodus crushed him." Others joined in: Jesus radiated "good health," John was a "strong, eager, enthusiastic young man," Paul "one of the great sports lovers of his day." Despite his lack of "personal purity," even Samson, said one author writing on Christian manhood, displayed "mighty strength and . . . healthy and resolute and infectious good humor."[9]

Perhaps the greatest champion of those new devotees of what was called "the Strenuous Life" was Theodore Roosevelt, who criticized the "general tendency among people of culture and education . . . to neglect and even look down on the rougher and manlier virtues."[10] A man cannot be efficient "unless he is manly," Roosevelt declared. "If we lose the manly virile qualities," the nation, he said, would "reach a condition worse than that of ancient civilizations in the years of decay."[11] As a future president of Oberlin put it, just after the turn of the century, it was the obligation of every Christian to "make his body the best instrument that he can make it for the spirit, the very best medium for the spirit to work through."[12]

This radical new notion slowly filtered through Christian intellectual circles, into popular publications and from campus to campus. Students, eager to satisfy their craving for some diversion to their humdrum school routine, pressed college officials to permit them time to relax, to play. One of the first college gyms was erected in Amherst in 1860, the result of the deaths of two seniors reportedly from overstudying. Exercise, it was believed, would have saved them. It was Amherst that subsequently pioneered in the employment of a qualified physician to head its department of physical education. The demands on soldiers of both sides during the Civil War underscored the necessity for physical well-being and stamina; too many recruits showed up at training camp lacking the energy and stamina needed on the battlefield. And, anyway, there was always a thirst among young people for an outlet for their sexual urges. The Civil War had provided an outlet for physical aggression, but a generation later, only exercise and sports met that need. At first, once the war was over, baseball and track events became popular. Physical training, a particular goal of eugenicists, was made mandatory in public schools throughout Ohio in 1892. "The ideal student," said Charles W. Eliot, president of Harvard, was being "transformed from a stooping, weak, and sickly youth into one well-formed, robust, and healthy."[13]

Two phenomena appeared. One was the number of athletes who chose to be preachers, as did the evangelist Billy Sunday, who had played center field for the Chicago Whitestockings in the 1880s. The second phenomenon was the number of athletes from Eastern schools, where most sports developed, who, like John Heisman, became coaches. During the 1890s, for example, according to one enthusiast's count, forty-five former players from Yale, thirty-five from Princeton and twenty-four from Harvard were teaching football in schools other than their alma maters. The need for coaches reflected the growing popularity of the sport. In 1890, Army played Navy for the first time in the East; Minnesota and Wisconsin confronted one another for the first time in the Northwest; and, in the West, Iowa, Kansas, Missouri, and Nebraska formed their own football association.[14]

Some persons believe that as the result of the absence of any major war between 1865 and 1898, football had assumed the role of being the nation's moral teacher. Certainly, football—with its strenuous exertions, bodily punishment, and need for self-discipline—came as close to war as one could get in what was known as the Gilded Age. Like military life, it instilled manly virtues, courage, teamwork, and—loyalty. And not only for the young men who took part. Young women flocked to the games to root for their heroes, to urge them on to greater glories, to cheer their victories, to praise their endeavors. Football, in that sense, was an acceptable way for the sexes— whether player or spectator restrained in an otherwise strict school or social environment—to flirt. The campus role model, the youth who set the style, was no longer the fellow wearing a black suit, stiff collar, and bowler hat. Instead, he wore heavy corduroy pants, a turtleneck sweater, and, for a hat, a heavy stocking cap pulled over his long hair. He was a football player.

One thing was clear. Football was an exciting game. It was a great release from the tensions and grind of the classroom. For a few hours each week, academic routine could take a backseat to the enthusiasm and thrill that the game inspired. No other sport demanded such exertions. Indeed, none other was as dangerous.

The physical rigors demanded by the game had its supporters; indeed, there were many proponents, educators among them, who valued what they called football's virtues. One of them was the Rev. Dr. John Bigham, a professor of philosophy at DePauw University, who had studied and attended games at Amherst, Yale, and Harvard. He declared: "The game does not profess to be a gentle, tame affair, like a church social or afternoon tea. The players . . . must be strengthened by careful and cumulative training during the season: regular habits, sound and sufficient sleep, a scrupulous care in diet, and daily hard, intelligent practice on the field."[15]

Bigham was certain that "greater physical harm, even loss of life, results from over-study or dissipation, tendencies in all student bodies which football counteracts." In fact, the Reverend Doctor Bigham rhapsodized:

As played by college men the game involves some beautiful and even spiritual elements: college spirit, courage, unselfishness—"faith, hope, love: these three." The great apostle to the Gentiles appreciated athletics, and uses them as illustrations of spiritual struggles, aptly and sympathetically. . . . Foot-ball and Christianity have some common factors. Both are decried by scoffers who ignore the beneficial effects of athletics and the superb achievements of the Christian church: who have never studied either foot-ball or the Bible; never seen a game or experienced the great change of heart: in brief, who know not whereof they grumble. Many players in our colleges are earnest christian men. Should a Christian institution have foot-ball? The answer comes from Wesleyan for the Methodists, Princeton for the Presbyterians, and Yale for everybody.

Remembering one particular Yale-Harvard game, Bigham baldly confessed—without saying which team he rooted for: "One of the most fervent prayers I ever breathed was on the field in Cambridge . . . it was indeed a grateful recognition thereof that murmured: 'Praise God from whom all touchdowns flow.' Smile not, *O fratres in ecclesia eruditissimi,* you would have done the same had you been there."

Football, those who agreed with Bigham said, built character, developed personal courage, and stimulated teamwork. Bigham reiterated: "For the players of my own college and university days (great days they were, brethren), are now tackling heavy responsibilities on foreign mission fields, in church work, in professional and business enterprises, with the same undaunted vim and self-control that won our applause on the gridiron field. *Pax, pax vobiscum,* ye venerable ecclesiastics and horrified women, come out and see the boys play."

Bigham's point was well taken. The benefits of the game in building character and leadership were abundantly clear to its supporters well before the turn of the century. The captain of Princeton's eleven in its historic first game with Rutgers in 1869 became chief justice of the Supreme Court of New Jersey. Rutgers's captain was a distinguished clergyman.[16] Those two colleges, as well as others who took up the sport, boasted bankers, lawyers, successful businessmen, diplomats, and educators among the veterans of the game. Those on Yale's championship varsities included the artist Frederic Remington,[17] the mayor of Grand Rapids, Michigan,[18] and the superintendent of banking in New York State.[19] Harvard's teams produced a congressman.[20] The first secretary of Columbia's football association was the university's future president, Nicholas Murray Butler.[21] One of two halfbacks on Princeton's team in 1879 became a missionary in Japan, the other was elected to Congress from Maryland.[22] An end for the University of Pennsylvania became the state's attorney general,[23] a guard later represented the state in the U.S. Senate.[24] Three players on one of Lafayette's first teams became railroad executives.[25]

John Heisman, for one, agreed with Bigham's reasoning. The sport, he believed, developed willpower, self-control, clear thinking, the formation of good habits, discipline, teamwork, memory, and sportsmanship. As he would write in a book on the principles of the game: "That's the time, the place and the way to learn how to govern, to control, to conquer yourself. Will not this help at least a little in the right molding of a boy's character?"[26]

But while the manly and character-building virtues of football were celebrated by individuals such as Heisman and Bigham, the severity of the sport haunted others. Fatalities were not unusual, and injuries were common, attributed in the main to the lack of proper training, especially in schools new to the sport. Reporting on two deaths during the 1886 season, *Century* magazine noted that "both occurred in colleges which were attempting to play the game as it is played by the leading teams, without any of the preparation which they find an essential." When a former "robust" Oberlin student died suddenly, a rumor quickly spread that the youth's "entire system seemed suddenly to break down" after he took part in a football game.[27] The truth was that the youth had never played football, but it was easy to believe the rumor that the game had caused his death, considering the frequency of accidents. A game between Purdue and the University of Michigan lasted only a half hour because so many players were hurt that Michigan could no longer field a team.[28] Even training was dangerous. One Oberlin football prospect said he received "a tremendous crack on the nose from the 'heel of the hand' of a big senior who in practice was trying to teach me (a 140-pound halfback) to keep my head down when making a line plunge. Rivers of fluid spurted from nose and eyes, and I was so blinded that I had to be led to the sidelines."[29]

The fatalities and injuries buttressed arguments against the sport. At the beginning, before the idea of a scrimmage line and a neutral zone or rules against manhandling an opponent, teams stood upright face to face before a play even started, hurling verbal abuses and pushing and shoving to gain advantage. There was an "asserted tendency," said a writer for *Century* magazine, "to degenerate into personal combat."[30] As an example, the writer pictured a ball carrier running downfield, one arm holding the ball "while the other is moving with the rapidity of a steam-engine's piston toward and from his opponent . . . a scandalous case of 'slugging,' as striking has come to be called."[31] Football, the writer insisted, "is as safe as any outdoor game can well be, provided it is played with the careful preparation and training which are the rule in the larger colleges." A successful team, he added, "can no longer afford to indulge in individual combat."

John Heisman thought the game in its early days was so violence prone that it was in serious danger of being outlawed. "Too many boys," he declared, "were being carried to hospitals with broken bones, broken necks and backs, and fractured skulls. And some had died and others were doomed to lives of paralysis."[32]

The argument against football also had its moral side, one that echoed loudly in Oberlin. Its tone was set at the first intercollegiate game, between Rutgers and Princeton (then Nassau Hall), in 1869. A Rutgers professor rode up on his bike to the field, watched the game briefly, then pedaled away, saying for all to hear, "You men will come to no Christian end."[33] Later, after the sport had caught on throughout what was then the West, the Popular Amusements Committee of a Methodist conference gathered in Kansas resolved that it was "more fully convinced than ever" that such games were "dangerous physically, useless intellectually, and detrimental morally and spiritually."[34] As for Oberlin, at one point an anonymous contributor to the town's local newspaper, the *News*, raised the question, "Is it not true that foot ball and salvation do not and can not go together?"[35] Other critics assailed the game's deceptions—fake handoffs and the secrecy of a team's signals, to name two—as unethical. And even after Oberlin entered intercollegiate competition, and was successful, a meeting of deacons and section leaders of the First Congregational Church unanimously adopted a resolution condemning football games. Some of the church officials, the *News* reported, "went so far as to express the conviction that these [games] were the cause of religious apathy and spiritual dearth that is upon the churches, and that they are really blocking the wheels of salvation; that the time, the thought, the interest, the strength, the money and the influence given by the community to secure these games are inimical to the spirit and work of Christ."[36]

Oberlin was one of several colleges that came to regard the sport of football with a jaundiced eye. Even before its first football team took the field, its main struggle was not on the scrimmage line but in the debate about priorities: the classroom vs. the gridiron. No such dilemma stirred similar wrangling at many other schools. At the newly founded University of Chicago, for example, its ambitious president, William Rainey Harper, frankly described football as a "traveling advertising organization of the University."[37] At a time when schools were competing for undergraduates, football, as Harper and many other officials of institutions of higher education discovered, could be instrumental in raising the prestige of their schools, thereby attracting both students and noted teachers. Sports—but especially intercollegiate football and, more especially, a winning team—were becoming major factors in a school's success and reputation.

Always the maverick, Oberlin was on a different tack. It was—has always been—a teaching school, not a research institution. One of the college's underlying principles, as fervent a half century later as it was at its founding, was the education of "the whole man"—to "provide for the body and heart as well as the intellect."[38] Academically, that meant a liberal arts education that included courses in literature, music, art, philosophy, and, above all, religion. And by religion, Oberlin's founders meant both the salvation of the soul and the reform of society. For Oberlin's students were as serious-minded as they came. Which is not to say that sports were anathema. On the contrary, as the college grew from infancy to its teen years, the role of exercise began to play an increasingly important part in a student's life on campus. Football, however, was always the exception. Oberlin's answer to the deeply felt pros and cons about the game, a response that would resonate for more than a century, was perhaps best expressed by an 1869 graduate: "In so far as football may be a recreation for those who participate and an entertainment for those who look on, it may be tolerated or even commended, but no one should feel bound by a sense of duty, either to himself or to others, to expend a large amount of time and energy in training, or to encounter the hazards that inevitably attend the collision of large bodies of heavy and determined men moving in opposite directions; nor should he imagine that the future existence of his college depends upon the success of its football squad, rather than the ability and devotion of its faculty."[39]

When Oberlin finally entered the intercollegiate arena, football was a different game from that first college football game between Rutgers and Princeton in 1869. The changes were revolutionary.

2

THE SPORT

Thy founders bold in time of old
Laid they foundations sure,
That for the right, in noble fight,
Thou ever shouldest endure.
—*Clara Little Simpson, Class of '92*

American football derived from a spirited English kicking sport that began unceremoniously as a hostile reaction to the quarter century that the Danes occupied the British Isles. A few years after the Danes left in 1042, some workmen digging on the site of an old battleground brought up what they thought was the skull of a Danish invader and for fun they started booting it around. Legend has it that a group of barefoot boys saw the workers and dug up a skull of their own, but kicking the hard skull with their bare toes hurt, and one of the youngsters substituted a cow bladder.

The rowdy sport was first called "mellay," which in time became the word "melee"—a near-riot—an apt description of the mob scene and the way the English approached the sport. For some unfathomable reason, it was chiefly played the day before Ash Wednesday as part of the religious holiday of Shrove Tuesday. On that day, it is said, every man, young or old, farmer or laborer, apprentice or journeyman, came out to play. In time, contests between adjoining villages became commonplace. Scores, even hundreds, of locals would try to kick a bladder down the road and into the middle of their neighbor's town. As might be expected, shopkeepers along main street complained, so vacant fields were marked off, boundaries set up, and a primitive set of rules were established that granted a point to every ball kicked over an opponent's goal line. As many as fifty participants were on a team; the only rule was that each side have the same number of players.

"Kicking the Dane's head," or simply "kicking the bladder," eventually became so popular that Henry II, worried that his subjects were ignoring their mandatory archery practice to engage in "futballe," ordered his subjects to "cease playe" or face jail. Henry's ban lasted for more than four hundred years—into the sixteenth century, well after firearms replaced the long bow and arrow. James I revoked the ban, but his decree was simply an acknowledgement of reality. For in the intervening years, English commoners had continued to play the game either clandestinely or openly under more tolerant rulers than Henry.

Football teams now spread across the English countryside. To further define the playing field, goal posts and, later, a crossbar were erected. According to legend, the game was still a kicking game until one afternoon in 1823 when a youth at Rugby College did the unimaginable. The bell in the school tower began ringing the fifth hour, the signal for the boys to quit playing. As the first chime rang out, so the story goes, young William Ellis caught a kicked ball and, instead of heeling it and taking a free kick, suddenly tucked the ball under his arm and ran with it. Ellis's reputed unheard-of act added a new dimension to football, which now became a combination of kicking and running that, in honor of Ellis's alma mater, was called rugby. While Ellis's role is considered a myth, a new wrinkle had been added to the game, which was indeed called rugby. Not everyone, however, liked the innovation; they stuck strictly to the kicking game, which became known as soccer.

The idea of rugby traveled across the Atlantic to America, where it developed in a haphazard, unstructured fashion for nearly half a century. Football in America was mainly a school sport. Its first appearance, or what passed for it, was on college campuses on the East Coast. Sophomores at Harvard and later Yale hazed freshmen in a game they called football. It was basically a kicking game, though; its chief purpose was to ignore the ball and take aim instead at the naive freshmen, who, not unexpectedly, quickly caught on and kicked back.

Before long, regular class-against-class contests were organized at both Harvard and Yale, but the game had become so brutal and unwieldly that authorities at both schools abolished it in 1860. The game was not revived on the campuses until after the Civil War, and by then football was being played at other colleges, as well as at private high schools, in the East. There were on-the-spot games and there were intramural games, but no contests existed between schools even though baseball had already pioneered intercollegiate rivalries. Then, in the fall of 1869, students at Rutgers—in the midst of a hot dispute with their Princeton counterparts over possession of a Revolutionary War cannon and still smarting from an embarrassing 40–2 baseball defeat at the hands of their rival three years earlier—saw an opportunity for revenge. They challenged Princeton to a football game. The rules they agreed on—for each school followed its own set of regulations—limited each side to twenty-five players, forbade the tripping or holding of players, and set up a field that was 120 yards long and 75 yards wide. There was no time limit; whoever scored six goals first would be the winner.

Although it is heralded as the first official intercollegiate football contest, the game between Rutgers and Princeton was essentially a soccer match. Players could advance the ball by using their feet, heads, or shoulders, or even by batting it with their fists or hands, but they were not permitted to run with the ball. On the cold, windy afternoon of November 6, Rutgers won the game by a score of six goals to four. (A week later, in a return match, Princeton won 8–0. Rutgers would not defeat Princeton again until sixty-nine years later, in 1938.)

The following year, 1870, Columbia assembled a team and joined Princeton and Rutgers in a series of games. Yale put together a team in 1872 and in its only game defeated Columbia. Yale played that game under a modification of the "Association Code"—that is, soccer rules. Variations in those rules were so dissimilar that finally representatives of Columbia, Princeton, Rutgers, and Yale got together in 1873 to draft a uniform code of regulations. Basically, though, the ones they decided on still resembled soccer.

Fortunately for American football, Harvard had refused to attend the meeting. It played by a different set of rules called the "Boston Game," which was more like rugby. A player could carry the ball until tackled. In time, Harvard prevailed, and eventually both Yale and Princeton scuttled the soccer-like code and followed Harvard's lead, much, as it ironically turned out, to Harvard's regret. For Yale's varsities became football's champions until well into the twentieth century.

Authorities at many schools were reluctant at first to permit their students to field a team to play other schools. In 1873, a student at Cornell, where informal campus games were played, wrote a friend at the University of Michigan and arranged a game to be played on neutral ground in Cleveland. There were to be thirty men to a side. But when he learned about the pending contest, the president of Cornell quickly rejected the idea, saying, "I will not permit 30 men to travel 400 miles merely to agitate a bag of wind."[1]

"Bag of wind" indeed! Footballs were hard to come by in 1873. The Princeton-Yale game that year, their first meeting, was delayed because neither side showed up with a ball, and it took an hour and a half until one was secured. A second delay followed when the ball burst in the midst of play and had to be repaired.[2]

Harvard's insistence on rugby rules was momentous for football. So, too, was a series of games it played in 1874 with McGill University. The first game, played at Harvard under "Boston Game" rules, with fifteen men to a side, employed a round ball and permitted running with it. The second game, played again at Harvard, employed an egg-shaped ball. Running with the ball was permitted again, but the game was played with only eleven men on a side because at the last minute four members of the McGill team could not make the trip. That game is considered the first actual game of rugby football ever played in the United States.[3]

The game developed in the next years in a helter-skelter fashion. New rules and adjustments were continually made. Harvard reverted to using fifteen men when it challenged Yale to a game. But for the previous two years, ever since it played a visiting Eton team from England, Yale had been playing with only eleven men on a side. It agreed to field fifteen but insisted on certain changes that became known as "Concessionary Rules." Basically, the game was still rugby. The Rutgers-Princeton game six years earlier had drawn two hundred spectators. The Harvard-Yale game of 1875 attracted more than two thousand fans. A sign of the future was the fact that the spectators paid to watch the game; admission was fifty cents.[4]

Until then, what collegians wore while playing was as random as the rules. They donned an assortment of clothing, not one stitch of which had any protective value. They abjured any head covering except perhaps a stocking cap or a skullcap that came down to the ears. In fact, for a while in the 1890s, many players affected long hair, a style started by a Princeton player that eventually went out of fashion when Yale footballers showed up for a game with Princeton in 1895 with their hair neatly and closely shorn.[5] At the initial Rutgers-Princeton game, the Rutgers men wore what was variously described as red turbans or scarlet stocking caps, but otherwise they and the Princeton players simply laid aside their coats, vests, and ordinary hats and went at each other in their street clothes. At the Harvard-McGill games, Harvard's players tied magenta handkerchiefs around their heads and wore white undershirts and dark pants. McGill's team was more suitably attired in rugby-style white trousers and red and black striped shirts, caps, and stockings.[6]

Regular uniforms were introduced at the first Harvard-Yale game in 1875. Harvard players showed up sporting fetching shirts, stockings, and knee breeches that were all crimson. Yale players wore dark trousers, blue shirts, and yellow caps.[7] The Yale uniforms took on a different look at the second meeting with Harvard: each player now wore white pants, blue cap and stockings, and a blue shirt with a white *Y*. University of Pennsylvania footballers came to a game with Princeton in 1876 donned in cricket suits of white flannel.[8] Their opponents had adopted a grim all-black look for their knee pants, stockings, and shirts. The Princeton uniform was relieved only by orange trimming around the neck and wrists and a large orange *P* on the shirt. When a Princeton player named Ledou P. Smock subsequently put on a canvas jacket tightly laced up the front to wear over his jersey, it became de rigeur at most schools, and players were nicknamed "canvasbacks."[9]

The snug fit of the canvas jacket made ball carriers difficult to grab and tackle. But later, when so-called mass-momentum plays were devised, loops were sown on the pants and jackets of ball carriers so that they could literally be pulled, or dragged, forward by their teammates. Teammates were even able to grab hold of a runner and hurl him over an opponent's line until that was outlawed in 1905.[10]

Football fans rooted for their school or class, but, whether male or female, in a rather genteel manner. No one had ever thought of a cheering section. At the first intramural games, before there were grandstands, spectators stood along the sidelines or sat on buggies and buckboards and, if the team they backed made a spectacular play, they might applaud. But in Princeton's return match with Rutgers in 1869, its team used a "scarer," a blood-chilling Civil War yell, every time the ball was put in motion. The only problem was that the yell required a lot of breath and left the players short of oxygen just when they needed it most. By the next game, the team was able to save its wind by schooling some fellow students in the scream. Yells, cheers, and even songs soon became the custom at every school's games.

Two Princeton players who saw the first Harvard-Yale game in 1875 returned to New Jersey and convinced other classmates to switch to the rugby game. Princeton then invited Harvard, Yale, and Columbia to confer about adopting a set of rules everybody would follow. The meeting in late November 1876 resulted in the formation of the American Intercollegiate Football Association and the scheduling of mutual games. There was one change made in the rugby code: A goal equalled four touchdowns and the game was to be decided by a majority of touchdowns. Otherwise, following the English rule, games would consist of forty-five-minute halves, with a ten-minute intermission between them. And the egg-shaped rugby ball officially supplanted the round rubber ball. It became variously and colloquially known as a "pigskin, the windbag, the inflated cushion, the leather ellipse."[11]

There was one notable absence at that meeting: Walter Camp, a veteran footballer who took it upon himself to defend, develop, and promote the game. The man who would become known as the "father of football" and be the final arbiter in disputes represented Yale at every subsequent intercollegiate rules committee meeting until his death in 1925. But at the time of the committee's first meeting in 1876, he was in his second year of playing halfback on the Yale varsity.

Camp's basic ideas were simple: To stimulate more action in the game, to reward both offensive and defensive efforts, to punish infringements, and to promote fair play. But each new wrinkle that he lobbied for seemed to open the door to another loophole, so every year there were—and have been—changes.

At the second meeting of the football association in 1878—the first that he attended—Camp fought for limiting teams to eleven men. He lost that argument. He also was turned down when he suggested that a safety—the touching of the ball behind one's own line in order to get a free kick out—count as points against the kicking team. It wasn't until 1880 that he finally prevailed. Camp was then also able to convince the rules committee to permit a team to retain the ball after a player was tackled and downed. In rugby, after a player was downed, the ball was put into play by a "scrummage."[12]

That same year, the association came up with the idea of turning what had become a seesawing defensive game into one in which each side would have an unhampered opportunity to devise a coordinated offense. It invented the scrimmage line to substitute for the mob-like rugby "scrum." Now each team would be given the opportunity to put the ball into play by a centering operation. The innovation led to the naming of the players on and behind that line. There was the "snapper-back" or, more familiarly, the "center rush" or just plain "center," whose responsibility it was to put the ball into play by heeling it back with his foot. Next to him, on either side, were the men who protected him, the "guards." Next to them were players called "next-to-ends" whose chief duty as tacklers on defense led to their finally being labeled "tackles." At the extreme end of the line were the "end men," or simply "ends." The "quarter back" stood right behind the center. He got the ball from the center but could not carry it himself. He had to hand it off to another player, either another back or any one of the linemen. Or he could "pass" it—that is, toss a lateral sideways or backwards—to a teammate. A forward pass was not permitted. Behind the quarterback were two halfbacks, who did most of the ball carrying, and farther back was the man usually responsible for kicks and line bucks—and invariably the heaviest man in the backfield as well—the fullback. All the footballers, whether linemen or backs, played the same position whether on offense or defense. Substitutions were permitted only when a player was too injured to continue. In addition, the playing field underwent a bit of shrinkage; it was now 110 yards long and 53⅓ yards wide. As with rugby, kickoffs were at the center of the field.

The innovative scrimmage line led, however, to a new strategy that almost doomed the game. In a Princeton-Yale game in 1881, Princeton's captain, in a ploy obviously intended to stymie an aggressive Yale team, decided that, instead of running with the ball or kicking it, his team would just hold onto it—indefinitely—thus forcing the game into a draw. Which is what the Princeton team did for almost all of the first half. Not to be outdone, the Yale eleven did the same for all of the second half and into overtime, until darkness halted the game.[13]

There was no rule against the maneuver, but, needless to say, the game was a bore. Spectators were disgusted. For some benighted reason, several other schools adopted the scheme, retaining the ball as long as they could without advancing it an inch. As the enthusiasm of fans on the sidelines continued to wane, Camp reinvigorated the game by devising a system of downs and yards-to-gain. Under his scheme, which was adopted by the association, each team was given three chances to advance the ball five yards "or lose ten yards." If the ball was not advanced the five yards or more, possession of the ball changed hands. The game's emphasis now shifted to one in which running with the ball to make yardage was more important than kicking it.

There was, however, one difficulty with the new system that cropped up immediately. The referee ordinarily kept track of the ball's progress by dropping a hankie and measuring with his eye how far it was to the next first down. But when the referee wasn't looking, one or the other of the opponents would nudge the hankie backwards or forwards with his foot. The solution was to mark off the field every five yards to help the referee determine whether a team had gained the necessary yardage. The lined field now looked like a gridiron.

Although the scrimmage line defined the offensive-defensive symmetry of the game, and the gridiron pattern made the innovations manageable, other problems now arose. For one thing, there was no neutral zone between the two teams, and players, lined up and waiting for the ball to be centered, stood and wrestled one another. That prompted teams to enlist the biggest players possible, preferably those with pugilistic training, and unsportsmanlike brawling was commonplace at many games. John Heisman recalled that before the rule about tackling was changed in 1888, "You could leap upon the runner's shoulders. You could fetch him down with a strangle hold. You could put a head-lock on him. But you were penalized and put down as a dirty player if you tackled him below the waist."[14]

The new rule allowed tackling below the waist but not below the knees. Despite the restriction, the now-permissable low tackle put a practical end to any effective open-field running and dodging. To replace it, mass-momentum plays, with players formed in close formations to spearhead and protect a runner, became popular. Earlier, Princeton had come up with the idea of having two players act as "interferers," running alongside the ball carrier to make it difficult for their opponents to tackle him. Now, however, the entire team, their arms locked around one another and their legs churning in unison, formed a huge rugby-like mass and bullied forward, the ball carrier tucked safely behind his teammates. Teammates sometimes took up the carrier and literally flung him over their opponents' shoulders. Such plays and off-shoots such as V wedges produced innumerable injuries on both sides. They were "crushers," said Heisman, that "were killing the game as well as the players."[15] At first, explained Heisman, who played end for the University of Pennsylvania, a defensive line played "astonishly wide." Both he and his compatriot at the other end of the line were sometimes as far as a hundred feet from their tackles. The idea was to prevent end runs. If a runner cut between an end and a tackle, "You merely closed in." But a strung-out line did not work against mass plays. It had to contract, and halfbacks were sometimes shifted into the line between an end and a tackle to break up a play.[16]

The new system of downs also led to the problem of how a quarterback informed his teammates what kind of play was next. No one thought of having a huddle between plays. (That wouldn't occur to anyone until the first indoor games, when the noise level inside a crowded arena made verbal signals impossible; even then, it took years before the idea caught on.) In the beginning, a number of alternatives were employed. Hand and foot signals were used at first, but a lineman could not always catch the quarterback's motions without taking his eyes off the man opposite him. Supposedly undecipherable phrases or sentences were used, each one masking plays such as an end run, buck into the center of the line, or punt. "Line up Brown," one of that university's linemen recalled, meant left tackle through right tackle. (Linemen then were allowed to run with the ball.) "Let's get into the game" meant right end around the left end, and "Hit 'em hard, bullies" had the left halfback going around his own end. The quarterback cursing the center signaled a decoy play. Brown's halfback was quite good at imitating a sneeze, and when he did, it meant the fullback was to punt.[17]

As can be imagined, such an assortment of signals was unwieldy and proved difficult for players to remember. Some teams switched to using the first letter of a sentence as a signal. Others tried a numerical system, with, say, the second number in a string of numbers denoting what play the quarterback wanted. But defensive linemen soon got wise, broke the code, and ruined the surprise.

By the time Oberlin College was on the cusp of entering intercollegiate play, the scoring system had been revised several times. At one point, if no team made a touchdown or kicked a goal, the side making four fewer safeties than its opponent won the game; otherwise the safeties did not count in the scoring. By the late 1880s, the numerical guide in effect gave four points for a touchdown, two extra points for a successful kick over the crossbar after a touchdown, and two points for a safety. The kick for additional points after a touchdown, incidentally, was no simple boot. The scoring team first had to kick the ball out of the goal to one of its players, who had to make a fair catch. The team then had to kick it back over the crossbar of the goal posts from where the ball was caught. Sometimes the wind or a poor boot carried the kickout to an impossible angle.

The officiating at a game also underwent several changes. In the beginning, only a referee called a game and, because the rules were being developed even more slowly than the game itself, he exercised unusual authority that was, to say the least, arbitrary. At the Yale-Princeton game in 1876, Walter Camp made a long run and, as he was tackled, tossed the ball to a teammate who scored. Princeton disputed the touchdown, so the referee decided the argument by tossing a coin. The touchdown was allowed.[18] Six years later, a Yale man refereed a game between Princeton and Harvard, awarding the game to Harvard after a disputed call over a Harvard touchdown. For years afterward, Princeton refused to accept the decision and claimed victory.[19]

Depending on a single game official proved so unreliable that after a time judges, one from each team, were added to the officiating crew. But they proved partisan, and the game reverted to being officiated again by only the referee. Reliance on one official and the fact that there were no rules to cover every conceivable situation made for some rather bizarre games. The Yale-Princeton game in 1886 was delayed for two hours when the referee didn't show up. Finally, one was chosen from the crowd and the game began in pouring rain. When a dispute broke out over a fumble, the crowd rushed onto the field, further delaying the game. By then, it had gotten dark and the referee-for-a-day ruled that the game was no contest.[20]

As might be expected, the new system of downs, the enforcement of penalties, and settling disputes proved too complicated for one person to handle alone. By the late 1880s, a two-man system—a referee and an umpire—was again employed, and again partisanship was the result. In many intercollegiate games, each team provided an official who alternated with an opponent's in being umpire for one half of the game, then referee for the second half. Very often, both teams also had their own timekeepers.

By the 1890s, intercollegiate football was superseding baseball in popularity on campuses throughout the nation. Twenty-four thousand people alone saw the Yale-Harvard game in 1887. Games were being played as often as twice a week, usually on Wednesdays and Saturdays. The first All-American selections were made in 1889. But with the growing infatuation with the game came certain ominous developments. It took money to pay for the extraordinary expense of maintaining a football team, to cover the costs, for example, of uniforms, equipment, and travel. Gate receipts had become an all-important funding source. It was critical to have a winning team that could draw crowds. And that was leading to some questionable academic decisions at some of the country's most reputable institutions. Harvard protested that fifteen of Princeton's players were not accredited students and withdrew from the football association. Princeton responded by challenging four members of Harvard's squad. It was, ironically, John Heisman who many years later described this period in intercollegiate football as being "so full of repeaters and ringers and boiler-makers that rules were adopted requiring players to attend a fixed number of recitations weekly and debarring men who had received money at any time for their athletic services."[21]

But the rules were more honored in the breach than the observance. Oberlin, for one, ignored them—as witness the playing of Heisman himself.

3

THE FACULTY CONCEDES

And when you're up, you're up
And when you're down, you're down,
And when you're only half way up,
You're neither up nor down.
—*Anonymous, "Football Songs"*

Oberlin's initial official attitude about football was not unique for a college founded on religious principles. It tended, however, to be extreme. The problem at Oberlin was the belief initially that physical activity was not just an inappropriate indulgence, but that it might even be evil. That attitude permeated a controversy over athletics that pitted students against teachers. The faculty, which exercised unusual control over student activities, discouraged "useless sports." As one alumnus put it, "The ultra puritanical notion that all play was a wicked waste of time and mental or physical energy prevailed."[1]

On the other hand, manual labor, the school's first annual report in 1834 stated, "meets the wants of man as a compound being, and prevents the common and amazing waster of money, time, health and life."[2]

Piety, sacrifice, abstinence, dedication—all the virtues of a religious-oriented life were in the minds of Oberlin's founders—John J. Shipherd, a Presbyterian minister, and Philo P. Stewart, a former missionary to the Choctaw Indians in Mississippi. They purposely named the community and the college for John Frederick Oberlin, a self-sacrificing German pastor who in the years around the turn of the nineteenth century had served a mixed population of poor French and Germans in a valley on the borders of Alsace and Lorraine. Oberlin the town banned alcohol and tobacco, and riding a horse or in a carriage on Sundays was forbidden. Each class at Oberlin the school began with a prayer or hymn; there were compulsory chapel exercises; and attendance at Sabbath services was mandatory, as well. There was a 10:00 P.M. curfew and very strict rules about social intercourse, restrictions that were especially necessary to forestall any hint of impropriety in the nation's first coeducational institution of higher education.

Such restraints were accepted almost without question by the young men and women matriculating at Oberlin. They expected to follow a career and life guided by Christian values. But for some time there was a new force on campuses throughout the nation, one that was finally making itself felt in insulated Oberlin. Students were freeing themselves from the rigidity and the stifling effect of curricula and college life imposed by faculty. One outlet for students—which inevitably became a field of contest, thrusting them into conflicts with their professors—was athletics.

It took some time for that trend to reach Oberlin. For in the beginning, there was no time for any play. Each student, male or female, was expected to work each day after classes. At first the requirement was for four hours in the afternoon—the men taking on the heavy chores such as tilling the soil, the women tending to the kitchen, sewing, or mending clothes. As the land became cleared and the rudiments of a campus slowly evolved, the laboring hours were reduced to three a day, but that still left little time or energy for play. "The woodpile of our grandfather's day," said an alumnus of the class of '06, "served as an outlet for his animal spirits, put red blood in his veins, muscles in his back, and shekels in his jeans."[3]

The school, known at first and briefly as the Oberlin Collegiate Institute, opened the first week of December 1833 with forty-four students, fifteen of whom were young women.[4] It was the first coeducational college in the nation. By the following summer, that number more than doubled. Within two years after its founding, Oberlin took another radical step. It opened its doors to Negro applicants, the result of a revolt of abolitionist teachers and students who were welcomed to Oberlin after bolting the Lane Seminary in Cincinnati, where they had been forbidden to discuss the slavery question. Suddenly Oberlin had its own seminary and became, as well, a leading center of the abolitionist movement in Ohio. The village was a major hub on the Underground Railroad and a haven for runaway slaves second only to Canada, across nearby Lake Erie to the north. In 1858, students, professors, and townspeople rose as one to save an escaped slave who was captured by slave hunters and was being transported back to Kentucky. Their rescue became a cause célèbre throughout the nation when a number of them were arrested and jailed for violating the federal Fugitive Slave Law.

The school grew rapidly, attracting as many students from outside Ohio as from the state itself. By the summer of 1835, a mere eighteen months or so after it opened its doors, there were 38 students in the college, 35 in the seminary, and 204 in the preparatory department training for the college. Hundreds of others were being turned away because of the lack of room; there never were enough dormitories, and many undergraduates lived off-campus in the homes of townspeople.

At the beginning, Oberlin's faculty included graduates of Yale, Amherst, Williams, and Dartmouth, and in 1839 its catalogue favorably compared its curriculum with that of Yale, boasting that the two were substantially the same.[5] By 1840, Oberlin numbered five hundred students, a decade later a thousand.[6] Its Conservatory of Music, opened in 1866, quickly gained national prominence, and the traditional performance of Handel's "Messiah" at the close of the fall term drew concertgoers from across the state. Substantial brick houses and buildings had begun to replace the first crude wood cabins and edifices, but as late as 1890 the town lacked a drainage system, and the mucky swamps of mud that rainstorms caused continued to amaze visitors.

At one point early in its history, Oberlin briefly became a leading pioneer in a form of diet devised by two Eastern doctors, one of whom was a vegetarian, Sylvester Graham of graham cracker fame. The diet limited meals to a single dish and its accompaniments. No tea or coffee, highly seasoned meats, pastries, or any "unwholesome and expensive food" were permitted. It was only after the school's second president, Charles Grandison Finney, a leading evangelist of his day, decided in 1845 that diet was not a moral issue that the culinary restrictions faded away.[7]

It was reality, though, that drove the impetus for change. Even before the philosophy behind Muscular Christianity became widespread, Finney regarded the physical education of ministers as "defective." "It rendered them soft and effeminate," he said.[8] Finney was all for retaining the manual-labor system, but the scarcity of campus jobs could not be reversed, and students clamored for the chance to stretch their muscles.

The first sport to grab student attention was, of all things, cricket. In the late 1850s, as many as ten clubs made up of both students and local businessmen were competing. It had become so "alarmingly popular on Tappan Square," the *Oberlin Student Monthly* reported, that "we fear the pristine reputation of our students as 'manual' laborers, is departing."[9]

On the eve of the Civil War in 1860, students drew up a petition asking the school trustees to appropriate $200 toward a gym. They had already, with the help of townspeople, raised $350 by subscription. The trustees turned down the appeal for funds but did grant the students the land on which to build a gym, and one was completed in March of the following year, just before the outbreak of the war. The gym, however, had no regular instructor, and, as the novelty of hefting dumbbells and doing somersaults wore off, few men patronized it. The war sealed its fate. Many of the men who hadn't gone off to war got their exercise drilling with a company of Zouaves nicknamed the "Morning Glories" because they tramped about the campus before breakfast. Those who weren't in the Morning Glories joined a hand-drawn hook-and-ladder fire company that competed with rival volunteer units in races to mock blazes.[10]

Like the gym, cricket proved a fad that fell victim to the Civil War. Interest in it disappeared. But in the fall of 1865, once the war was over and male admissions ballooned again, a new sport attracted interest. Some students organized a baseball team. They named themselves the Penfield Baseball Club after a local wagonmaker who donated to the team some well-seasoned wagon tongues that were made into bats. The game's popularity spread quickly and led to the first intramural games when the Oberlin faculty bowed to student pressure and voted in the fall of 1868 to permit a "friendly" game between juniors and seniors on a Saturday afternoon.[11] However, that same fall, the professors were incensed, apparently because of the specter of play-for-pay that was raised, when students on another local team, the Resolutes, participated in a tournament in Akron, expecting to share in the gate receipts. The players were severely reprimanded.[12]

The Akron experience stiffened the faculty's resolve. Sport was sport, and not played for gain. The following year, the faculty refused to permit a game on campus with the Base Ball Club of Cleveland, and then decided that no games with outside clubs, whether on or off campus, would be permitted during term time or examination week. Moreover, concerned about the increasing cacophony that permeated the campus within sight and hearing of recitation rooms and the college chapel, the faculty restricted athletics of any kind to specific hours around the noonday meal and late afternoon. Playing at the earlier hour was especially wearing on students. "The heaviest meal of the day was served at noon," one wrote, "so that the condition of the players and the effects of their exercise upon digestion can better be imagined than described. It is a wonder that any strenuous athlete survived his college course."[13]

Despite such restrictions, the reality was that Oberlin was changing in its outlook toward physical activity. "A sound mind comes with a sound body," proclaimed James Harris Fairchild, who became the college's third president in 1866. "Every disturbance of the physical condition produces a reaction upon our highest and noblest powers. Duty to soul involves duty to the body. Again, our physical powers are among the faculties which we are to employ in the service of God and man. To neglect, or abuse, or pervert them, is to fail in the trust committed to us."[14]

There was another, subtle factor at work, as well, one that took into account the changes that other schools, prodded by their students, were undergoing. Oberlin's inflexible, unyielding abolitionist stance prior to the Civil War had created animosity even in the North. The college had earned a reputation not only for its piety, but also for its radicalism. It now wanted to change its reputation, to become mainstream, to be—as much as Oberlin could hope to be—like other educational institutions. Instead of being a fountainhead of nineteenth-century moral reform, the college began to take on the mantle of academic excellence. Visible evidence of the transformation came in the mid-1880s, when no less than six new buildings, all sponsored by alumni, were erected on the campus. They were a concrete testament to the new academic thrust. One alumnus, John R. Commons, came back to teach from Johns Hopkins in 1891 and introduced courses in institutional economics, sociology, and modern American history—the first such courses in contemporary social sciences to be taught at Oberlin.[15] Arcane rote recitation sessions gave way to a new teaching technique, the lecture. The college, which at one point had almost exclusively favored its own graduates in hiring teachers as a way to maintain its philosophy and purposes, now reached out to attract scholars trained elsewhere. The decade after 1891 saw the percentage of professors with advanced degrees double from 42 percent to 80 percent, while at the same time the percentage of faculty members who had themselves studied at Oberlin declined from 74 percent to 35 percent.[16]

The new educational thrust was reflected in the rapidly growing research sources for both students and teachers that Oberlin offered. In the past, libraries sponsored by student literary societies had boasted broader collections than the college's main library, but that was changing, too; by 1924, Oberlin's facility would be the largest college library in the nation.[17]

The success of the motives and stimulus for the transformation was demonstrated when a debate came to a head in the 1890s over whether Oberlin should turn itself into a university, with research a prime aim. One of the students who joined in the debate, Robert A. Millikan—a future Nobel laureate in physics—urged a broadening of the school's course of studies as one way to fulfill Oberlin's goals.[18] Others concerned with the school's future spoke out against rejecting Oberlin's student-oriented philosophy. The Nos eventually won out. Oberlin would not become a research institution. It would remain a teaching one, with the emphasis on a liberal arts foundation and a student's education as a "whole man."

Nevertheless, throughout this metamorphosis, Oberlin's religious heritage did not die; it merely changed focus. Coincident with the rise of industrialism and population shifts in cities, its pioneers' evangelical zeal to promote personal salvation gave way to attending to social ills—drinking and its concomitants: crime, malnutrition, poverty, prostitution. Students taking sociology and economics classes left isolated, small-town Oberlin to witness for themselves conditions in Cleveland's jail, workhouse, and hospital, as well as in philanthropic agencies.[19]

From the beginning, the persistent pressure of students for change in the college's athletic policy meant that Oberlin, if it was to recognize their desires, would have to bend some of its rigid code, something that faculties at other schools, even religious ones, realized might be beneficial when it came to sports. If nothing else, such activities drew a student body together. Guided by Fairchild, the Oberlin faculty gave in to appeals and relaxed its rules somewhat. Baseball finally took hold. Except for the time when religious exercises, such as the Thursday Lecture or Friday Prayer Meeting, were being held, students could play all they wanted on the college green. Even baseball games with outside teams were sanctioned and, as one member of the team reported, "Oberlin never lost a game during the seasons of 1880, 1881 and 1882. No less than nine men who played during this time afterward played professional ball."[20] (Two of those players were Moses Fleetwood [Fleet] Walker and his brother Weldy. A catcher, Fleet joined a Toledo ball club in 1883, the first black to play major league baseball, Jackie Robinson notwithstanding.[21])

Baseball was first played on Tappan Square, a thirteen-acre park-like field. Along its edges were several school buildings. The trees and pathways proved obstacles and fly balls were often lost in the high, unmown grass. It was the noise, however, that prompted the search for a new field. Faculty complaints finally led to the diamond being shifted across the street to behind one of the lecture halls. It was soon relocated farther north, away from any college building, in what became known as Athletic Park. The diamond was "far enough from most recitation rooms to avoid disturbing them," the *Oberlin Review* insisted. Now that playing the game no longer created a nuisance, the student weekly publication urged the faculty to rescind limits on using the field only in the afternoon and to drop its rule that the number of weekly games be restricted to only two.[22]

By 1880 it was evident that Oberlin's pre–Civil War commitment to abolitionism and manual labor had transformed into a commitment to missionary and Muscular Christianity as well as formal programming in physical education. Once sports phobic, Oberlin evolved into a leader in the physical education movement, especially for women. In 1873, a second men's gymnasium was organized by students. Interest in it was so great that a Thursday Lecture was dropped in favor of a gymnastics exhibition in the college chapel.[23] Unfortunately, like its predecessor, it, too, eventually failed when not enough students took advantage of its facilities. However, this time the faculty accepted responsibility for the program. It took control in the mid-1870s, and for a while all students, except for those few engaged in manual labor, were required to attend the gym at a fee of fifty cents.

While male students proved recalcitrant when it came to gym exercises, Oberlin's female students experienced revolutionary progress. In the mid-1880s, a women's gymnasium was opened, and in 1887 the first graduate in a specially structured, one-year physical education training course received her diploma. The course was gradually expanded, and in 1902 a woman who completed its then four-year course received the first bachelor's degree in that discipline in the nation.[24]

Meanwhile, baseball and then tennis had captured the full attention of Oberlin's men. But not football—not yet. For some time, it had a checkered career, popular briefly one moment, then forgotten altogether the next. The first instances of the game being played on campus occurred in the 1860s, but it was an unorganized roughhouse. The melee was akin to the kick-ball game traditionally played at Harvard on "Bloody Monday," an opportunity, really, for upperclassmen to raze freshmen. Football at Oberlin then "was the old-fashioned, kicking, tripping and hold game," one of its practitioners recalled. "No one dreamed of carrying the ball in those days. What was a football for if not to be kicked? When the scrimmage was most exciting shirt-sleeves would be torn off, suspenders would be burst and shins would be kicked rather more freely than the ball. The first foot-ball was an inflated bladder, without covering of any sort, and I suspect the habit of playing the game in the fall was due to the fact that more hogs were killed at that time and more bladders were available than at any other."[25]

In 1874, five years after the first recognizable game of intercollegiate football in America was played between Rutgers and Princeton, Oberlin enjoyed a "first," also. A team made up of Oberlin seniors played one composed of sophomores. It was not a truly fair game. The sophomore team outnumbered the seniors fifteen men to nine, but the latter, the *Oberlin Review* reported, "especially seem to think that Muscular Christianity is the need of the pulpit, and manifest considerable vim, ministerial of course." The game, Oberlin's first intramural match, erupted in a near-riot, though through no fault of the students. Early into the game, "some outsiders"—apparently "townies"—"intruded upon the ground, and then captured the ball, carrying it to a great distance." The students retrieved the ball, but the outsiders "continued to manifest their insolence" and refused to leave the field. At which point, the captain of the senior team grabbed hold of one of them and threw him off the field. In retaliation, the outsiders attacked the captain and a full-fledged brawl broke out, lasting until "better counsels prevailed."[26] Not surprisingly, considering how many players the sophomores fielded, they won the game, while at the end of it "several seniors lay hors du combat" with "their backs to the field and their feet to the foe."[27]

For three years after the senior-sophomore game, no recorded games of football were played on the campus, and even after that the game was played only intermittently through the rest of the decade. When football *was* played, the faculty made life difficult for its practitioners. One restriction the faculty pondered would have excluded football from the fields used for baseball games because of the damage football did to the campus grounds, "turning the park into a public mudhole."[28] Students finally were allowed, "as an experiment," to play on Wednesday and Saturday afternoons, but only if there were no more than eleven men on each side.[29]

A student athletic association was created in 1881, and under its sponsorship and faculty approval, the baseball team played two games with outside teams. But the faculty rejected a request for intercollegiate football games. Intramural football was permitted, however, and every class had a team and competed for championship of the college. The game, fortunately, was no longer the disorganized mayhem of its earlier days, but now bore some semblance to what was being played along the Atlantic coast. "A crowd of Eastern students entered the Freshman class that fall and they were responsible for starting modern foot-ball at Oberlin," explained Harlan Burket, who was captain and quarterback of his class team. Burket said "an old Michigan man" who lived in town "coached us a little." The games were played in a vacant area on what is now the main campus of the school.[30]

Student ambivalence about football prompted a pendulum-like effect in the game's popularity, which seemed to bounce back and forth with regularity from being widely played to being denounced as too brutal. By the fall of 1883, football had definitely supplanted baseball as the most popular sport on campus. "You can have your shins kicked almost any hour of the day in less than two minutes if you are willing to take an active part," the *Oberlin Review* reported.[31] But the game's popularity was short-lived. A year later, the same student weekly complained that the game was "too violent, too dangerous as regards health of body and much too brutal as regards morality and manhood." The publication predicted that football's "days are well-nigh numbered."[32]

One reason for football's seesawing popularity was the fact that intramural games could not start until November, after the fall baseball season was over. That left little time for practice sessions and a full schedule of games before the academic term ended. For another, the weather at that point in the late fall was usually unfavorable—windy, chilly, and frequently so rainy that the field turned into a quagmire. But to a great extent the chief reason for football's alternating approbation and demise was the number of injuries it caused. This was, after all, in the era when there were as yet no protective shoulder pads or shin guards or helmets.

Nevertheless, in the late 1880s, as school after school entered intercollegiate play, a persistent group of Oberlin students intensified their pressure on the faculty for permission to play other colleges. Each year they tried a different tactic. For one thing, they sought to allay fears and minimize the brutality of the sport. The dangers of playing the game, the pro-football student weekly *Oberlin Review* editorialized, "have materially decreased" as a result of the new rules and penalties for offenses that had been established. It is "doubtful," the publication declared, "whether a witness of the average college base ball games, in which various players assault each other with a sublime disregard of human flesh and blood, would award the palm of safety to base-ball over foot-ball."[33]

Another tack the students tried on the reluctant faculty was to underscore the need for exercise. Oberlin, after all, lacked a men's gymnasium. Since 1885 female students had at least a work-out room—euphemistically called the Women's Gymnasium—and the first woman to successfully pass a one-year physical education teacher's training course had graduated in 1887.[34] Without a gym for the men, though, the male students said, they had no opportunity for exercise. "The number of bald-headed, spectacled and dyspeptic people in this country is not apparently on the decrease," the *Review* said. "A horse with as many weak points as the average man would sell for—how much?" America needs "trained bodies." It had "enough of the maimed, halt and blind already."[35]

But such arguments failed to move the faculty. A game with Wooster College was proposed for Thanksgiving Day in 1887. There was logic to the students' pinpointing the holiday for the game. Thanksgiving Day games had already become enormously popular at other schools, drawing vast crowds of spectators—paying spectators. Yale and Princeton, which played their first holiday contest in 1876 in Hoboken, New Jersey, switched to New York City's Polo Grounds in 1880 and drew five thousand football fans. Within less than a decade their annual Thanksgiving game was drawing close to twenty-five thousand paying spectators, and, significantly, each team's net from the game had leaped from $238.76 in 1876 to $5,432.50 by 1889 and nearly three times that much two years later.[36] Unfortunately, those very economics were considered scurrilous by Oberlin's professorial staff. The Oberlin students who requested permission to play football on Thanksgiving Day fed right into the faculty's abhorrence of sport for gain. The students' flimsy rationale for the game, the only reason for it that they gave, was the need to raise money for the athletic association, which was in debt. Their argument did not move the faculty. Football, the professors insisted, was "too barbarous a game to be encouraged."[37]

After more years of student frustration, hope that maybe the faculty would approve an intercollegiate game surfaced in 1889. It was spurred in large measure by a sophomore, Frederick Bushnell (Jack) Ryder. Born in Oberlin, Ryder had moved with his family to New England and attended Phillips Academy in Andover, Massachusetts, where he played football. Ryder, who had just turned eighteen, was the son of a Congregational minister.[38] If his father permitted him to play, wasn't that sanction enough to convince Oberlin's pious faculty of the efficacy of the sport? Ryder spearheaded a campaign to convince the professors to permit intramural games. He succeeded, and once that was accomplished, the faculty was approached again about permitting a game with an outside team. This time, the appeal was aimed at school morale, which was critical, it was said, in motivating students to engage in some kind of activity. One or two games a year "is the only means as we believe for establishing an athletic spirit among us," the *Review* declared. "Men know that they ought to exercise but they will not do so without some present excitement to stir them to it."[39]

There had been a baseball game with Adelbert in October, which the faculty members had not only approved, but also had supported by their presence as spectators.[40] So students were confident that the faculty would agree to a football game with the same school, and again Thanksgiving Day was suggested as the time for the game. Prematurely, that fall Oberlin stores stocked and sold "large numbers" of football rules books.[41] Two literary societies donated funds to the athletic association to help shoulder the costs of fielding a team. His teammates elected Ryder captain of the "university" football team and practice workouts were held. But the students blundered the opportunity. The game they proposed was scheduled at the same hour as the traditional Thanksgiving Prayer Meeting, a conflict that, considering Oberlin's still-religious orientation, doomed the contest. The faculty again rejected the idea, considering it "undesirable" to permit a game.[42]

The students did enjoy a victory of sorts, though. All four classes fielded teams for the intramural games. Excited by the prospect, each class team immediately came up with its own uniform colors and spectator "yells." However, there was a bit of a delay in starting the games—there were not enough balls—and the weather played havoc with Athletic Park. A rather makeshift grandstand that cost $100 to erect blew down in a storm.[43] Bicycle races were called off one Saturday because the track was too wet,[44] and the intramural football games had to be played on the baseball diamond. When a sudden thaw occurred, running in a game that pitted juniors against sophomores was "out of the question" because the ball was covered "with a coating of genuine Oberlin mud."[45]

But that was the down side. There *was* plenty of cause for rejoicing. "During the entire season," the *Review* contended, "no body [*sic*] has received any injuries from the game, while on the other hand the amount of strength, and vigor, and buoyancy of spirit, received from the practice, cannot be estimated."[46]

Enthusiasm was high, but skill was not. Many of the players were ill-prepared and just didn't know how to play the game. In another intramural game, the juniors easily defeated the seniors, 24–0, chiefly because four members of the senior team had never played before and didn't understand the rudiments of blocking. Moreover, the seniors hadn't bothered to practice beforehand.[47] Scarcely a student or a ball appeared on the playing field, it was noticed, except on Wednesdays or Saturdays, when a game was scheduled. Only two or three players owned canvas jackets and even fewer had sweaters.[48] Unless football was "watched and encouraged," the *Review* said, "it will die out in a year or so."[49]

One factor in football's future at Oberlin was the uncertainty of the athletic association's finances. It was strapped for funds. The association received only five dollars a year from each college class, a total of twenty dollars to run a program that included not only football but baseball and tennis, as well. The pittance meant that each man who took a full college course at

Oberlin paid to the association a meager sum amounting to less than sixty cents, "certainly not enough to make the system a crying evil" in the eyes of the association.[50]

Hoping to defray costs and help itself out of debt, the association scheduled a lecture on campus by the well-known midwestern humorist Bob Burdette, a newspaper columnist who regularly toured the country. The talk brought in a total of $517.48,[51] of which the association netted $375.00. No other lecture in Oberlin's history had ever reaped such a profit. There was talk now of putting up a new grandstand and laying out a field specifically for football. Eleven seniors who banqueted with "the funny man" after the lecture were sanguine about the *esprit du corps* that grew out of intramural games. The *esprit* was evidenced soon afterwards when an alumnus who was a lumber dealer offered to donate the wood for the grandstand.[52] "Foot ball," all agreed, "must be made a permanency if the Association is to succeed."[53]

Meanwhile, Jack Ryder still harbored hopes of convincing the faculty to sanction an intercollegiate game. He proposed to the athletic association, and it accepted, a motion that, instead of waiting until the beginning of a new season to elect a football captain for the varsity team, the captain be elected at the close of each season. That way, there would be continuity, with the captain having a good nine or ten months to plan and schedule, God and the faculty willing, a game with another school.

By this time, Muscular Christianity had taken a firm foothold at Oberlin. The faculty was now willing, up to a point, to increase Oberlin's involvement in sports. Early in the new year, 1890, seven colleges gathered to discuss setting up what became the Ohio Inter-Collegiate Athletic Association. Its constitution provided, among other things, for an annual field day. Representatives from Wooster, Ohio State, Buchtel, and Denison had the power to accept entry into the group unconditionally. Oberlin's joining, however, depended on faculty approval.[54] That March the faculty voted to allow the student athletic association to join the newly formed organization—but with a proviso: Oberlin could only take part in baseball and tennis matches, at most three ball games and one tennis tournament each year.[55]

Nevertheless, Oberlin's joining the Ohio conference was, in the eyes of its students, "a great advance."[56] Perhaps now the faculty would allow a football game with another school. That summer, in recapitulating the 1889–90 academic year in sports, the *Oberlin Review* was optimistic. The athletic association, which had begun the year heavily in arrears, was "now less than $250 in debt" even though it had spent more than $2,000 during the year. As for football, it "has taken a hold which insures its continuance."[57]

Although each class team now sported its own colors, the college itself had been in existence for more than fifty years without having school colors. At commencements, diplomas had been tied with blue ribbon, but the choice of that color was happenchance. The school spirit that football helped to stimulate changed that. Prof. Albert Allen Wright, a geology and natural history specialist who was curator of the school's museum, traveled to Europe and visited the village of Waldersbach, where the college's namesake, John Frederick Oberlin, made his home. There he had seen two coats of arms, one belonging to Pastor Oberlin, the other to his brother, a scholar. Both sported "Cardinal red" and "Mikado yellow." Wright returned to Oberlin and urged the college to adopt the "general terms" red and gold as the college's official colors. He rose after a Thursday Lecture in February 1889 and urged the adoption of those hues. In response, every student and every teacher waved his or her handkerchief in "the Chatauqua salute." Hereafter, it was decreed, crimson and gold, as the colors were popularly known, would be "upon the diplomas, they would be displayed on Commencement day, they would deck the tennis court, they would adorn the athletic field, they would be worn on all occasions when it was appropriate to display the emblem of the college."[58]

No sooner had the faculty and the students adopted the school colors than the students, gathered on the steps of the library, took it upon themselves to also make official a college yell, "Hi-O-Hi": HI-O-HI O-HI-O / HI-HI O-HI / OBERLIN.[59] The graduating class of 1889 bragged that it was "the first one to make the campus ring" with the yell, "which was shouted that day from those steps."[60]

School morale was at its height. It was an ideal time to approach the faculty again. Jack Ryder had been reelected captain of the team, but he had decided to transfer to Williams College in the fall of 1890. Undaunted by the loss of their most successful advocate, the student athletic association cleverly replaced him with a distinguished three-man committee, hoping to impress the faculty and win its approval for an outside game with another school. Their argument was perhaps best summed up by the *Oberlin Review*'s observation that Thomas Hughes, the author of *Tom Brown's Schooldays*, "gives to foot ball the credit of having had a good share in the formation of the sturdy character of the English people." "Foot ball both exposes and develops character. It shows a man his weak points, moral as well as physical, and helps him to strengthen them to an extent which no other game approximates. . . . Coolness, quickness, suavity and endurance are surely not wholly undesirable qualities. If every college man went out from his Alma Mater endowed with these traits of character, we do not believe that we should be afflicted too frequently with the assertion that a College education is of no practical value."[61]

One member of the student committee, it was well known, was interested in pursuing a law career.[62] Another was headed for a career in the ministry.[63] The third member was David Peter Simpson, a junior from Cleveland who had played right end for his class team in 1889. Simpson was on track to being elected to Phi Beta Kappa.[64] The committee was under instructions to seek permission both for a game with Adelbert and for allowing it to be played on Thanksgiving Day, though not at an hour in conflict with the traditional prayer meeting.

Simpson's two comembers were pessimistic that the faculty would ever agree, but he had a compromise in mind. At the next meeting of the general faculty, he presented the two requests as the association had instructed. But with past history regarding a Thanksgiving Day game in mind, Simpson then wisely took it upon himself to suggest that the faculty grant permission for a game but refuse the idea of playing it on the holiday altogether, suggesting they opt instead for a different day. "After considerable discussion," he said, "this was the course finally taken." The faculty granted that an "experimental game" against Adelbert would be allowed to be played at Oberlin on Wednesday, November 5, 1890. As the Rev. Lyman Bronson Hall, a professor of Latin, put it, "the time was right for starting the game."[65]

The varsity immediately set about practicing, training indoors when the weather was forbidding.[66] Its average weight, 167 pounds, was respectable—not too light, but far from dominating.[67] The team that was to represent Oberlin was a notable example of the caliber of athletes the college could field. Though the varsity numbered only eleven starters and four substitutes, two halfbacks who were listed as possible starters would each play a prominent part in athletics at Oberlin. The oldest of the three, twenty-one-year-old Charles Winfred (Fred) Savage, would one day teach physical education at Oberlin and be its director of athletics. The other, twenty-year-old Wallace Fahnestock (Grove) Grosvenor, was already a stellar baseball player. The team's fullback, Howard (Howie) Krum Regal, a future journalist who worked part time for the *Oberlin News*,[68] would also make a name for himself on the athletic field as a high jumper and ten-second sprinter. The scholar on the team was also the oldest team member, twenty-four-year-old Lynds Jones; a budding ornithologist, he would spend fifty-eight years on Oberlin's faculty. (See appendix A for team rosters.)

The night before the game, Savage, who was one of the aspiring halfbacks, was informed that he'd been chosen to start against Adelbert. Savage was excited: he had won a place in the lineup. But the next day, a heavy snowstorm typical of the Lake Erie snowbelt turned swiftly into a blizzard. Six inches of snow soon covered the playing field. The game had to be cancelled. For Savage, as well as for the rest of the team, it was a "bitter disappointment."[69]

There is a photograph of the varsity team of 1890, the team that, sad to say, never played a game. The dream of its members to play Oberlin's first intercollegiate football game never became reality. But the die had been cast. For better or worse, Oberlin's entry into the football world was assured.

Oberlin's undefeated, untied, untried—and frustrated—team of 1890, whose only game was canceled because of a blizzard. Second from left in the back row is Lynds Jones, who went on to serve fifty-eight years on Oberlin's faculty. Wallace F. (Grove) Grosvenor, who would captain the 1891 eleven, is second from the left in the bottom row. Next to him, holding the football, is Henry W. Sperry, captain of the 1890 team. Also in the bottom row, the first on the right, is Charles Winfred (Fred) Savage, who became the school's director of athletics in 1906.

4

GAME TIME

The crowd turned out to see the play
And wear the thoughts of flunks away.
The students gather till the stand
Is filled with gents and ladies grand. . . .
Adelbert seeks o'er Oberlin
A glorious victory to win.

—*Anonymous*

I f age is an indicator of maturation, then Oberlin's students seemed more adult than most college students at the time. As in earlier days, many of the school's students came from low-income families and worked several years to save up money for tuition before they matriculated. The oldest male member of the graduating class in the summer of 1891 was a venerable twenty-eight.[1]

So it was not unusual that a sophomore who was all of twenty-two years old was hoping to make the team as the new academic year began in the fall of 1891. He was Charles Henry Borican, who had played left halfback on the freshman squad in 1890.[2] What was unusual was that Borican, who was from Bridgeton in southern New Jersey, was black. For in the years after the Civil War, Oberlin, town and college, no longer welcomed blacks with open arms. Once renowned as a sanctuary for runaway slaves, Oberlin had become caught up in what was a nationwide phenomenon, the conservative backlash of the Reconstruction era. Open, widespread discrimination had become normal throughout the North. Oberlin's experience mirrored the trend, perhaps even more so than in most other communities, because immediately after the war a huge migration of former slaves swelled the town's black population by 70 percent. The town felt inundated by the newcomers. They were disdained because, as a leading college official declared, they retained "in a great measure the ignorance and peculiar habits" of slavery. In other words, they were illiterate, ill-bred, and unhygienic. Even though Oberlin had won a reputation as the first college to admit black students more than a half century earlier, in fact blacks never made up more than about 5 percent of the student population at any time. By the 1880s, the atmosphere on campus had become overtly inimical, reflective of the national repugnance toward blacks that was, to be sure, symptomatic of the lack of sympathy and understanding that existed about the slave experience. An Oberlin professor in 1882 objected to the plans of one black student to room with a white friend. The following year, white female students in one of the dorms refused to dine with their black counterparts. The situation became so onerous that a local hero who had commanded black troops during the Civil War chided white students for the way they treated their black classmates.[3]

Borican—who, by the way, never complained publicly about ill treatment in the classroom or on the playing field—was one of more than a score of students who decided to try out for the varsity. Oberlin was now a thriving school and there was no dearth of potential football material. Enrollment in the college, the seminary, the music conservatory, the preparatory school, and a drawing and painting department totaled 1,462 students in the 1891–92 academic year. Of that total, 675 were men, all eligible to play.[4] Four years of preparatory work were now required for entrance into any of the regular courses. There were thirty regular professors where five years earlier there had been barely more than half that number. The faculty now totaled seventy-three teachers in all, and, as part of the educational transformation that Oberlin was undergoing, many were no longer Oberlin's own graduates, as had been generally true for decades, but scholars trained at a wide variety of other institutions. And, concomitant with the increase in faculty, the few elective courses offered only seven years earlier had soared to an amazing 130.[5]

Four of the varsity football prospects were students in the Oberlin Theological Seminary. One was George Robin Berry, a twenty-seven-year-old native of Missouri.[6] Another was twenty-two-year-old John Henry Wise, who was born in Hawaii to a German father and Hawaiian mother.[7]

"Grove" Grosvenor was back; he was captain of the team. His teammates from the frustrated 1890 team who were trying out for the 1891 varsity included David Simpson, Lynds Jones, and Howie Regal. Fred Savage, who had been so disappointed at the cancellation of the initial game with Adelbert the previous fall, came out again, but his starting position as halfback was far from assured. He faced stiff competition from a new candidate for the varsity,

Wallace F. (Grove) Grosvenor, when he was captain of the 1891 varsity. Note the laced-up canvas jacket and the moleskin pants. Early footballers did not enjoy the protection of shoulder pads, and the wearing of headgear was considered sissified.

a mediocre student but promising halfback named Carl Sheldon (Cap) Williams, a sophomore from nearby Wellington, Ohio. There was another young man named Williams, not related, also trying out for the team, Stephen Riggs Williams. A member of the postgraduate class of '92, "Steve" had been born in North China, where his father served as a missionary.[8] Steve helped out the athletic association as "field marshal" in charge of "the supply of bases, football and baseball suits, dirty football shoes and the like."[9]

There were two relative youngsters vying for positions on the varsity. One was William Harvey Merriam, a sturdy farm boy from La Grange, a town about ten miles southwest of Oberlin. "Will" or "Billy," as he was variously known, had entered the preparatory department in 1889. He was about to celebrate his nineteenth birthday.[10] Six months younger than Merriam and the youngest candidate for the team was the aptly middle-named Carl Young Semple. A mischievous, undisciplined youth, Semple was a new enrollee in the prep department.[11] He bragged that before attending Oberlin he had been coached by a former Williams College player, "could shade eleven seconds" in the hundred-yard dash, and "knew as much about football as *anyone in Oberlin*."[12]

The team manager, Bert Miley Hogen, was an all-around athlete—he had played on both his class baseball and football teams—but he had chosen to work on the sidelines for this first year of intercollegiate ball. The faculty had granted permission for the varsity to play five outside games, one at Ann Arbor, Michigan, one in Cleveland, and three on Oberlin's home grounds— just as long as no game was scheduled on Thanksgiving Day. Hogen was already busy lining up the contests. Letters and telegrams went back and forth to Ann Arbor and Cleveland.[13] Hogen, a Clevelander himself, was hoping "to secure games only with the strongest teams possible" in the belief that "this policy would teach us the most foot ball in the shortest time," the *Oberlin Review* reported. He might have arranged "a schedule of victories" but "that would have left no incentive for next year."[14] Actually, the way things turned out, only two of the games would be played at home.

Oberlin had plenty of potential players, but no trained coach. For one thing, Oberlin's student association could not afford one. For another, it was not unusual—at a time when football was still in its infancy and few experienced coaches were available—for a team captain to double as coach. In fact, one of the prerequisites of the team captain was his knowledge of the game and ability to teach others. That is what was expected of Grosvenor. But for all his ability as a player, Grove never pretended to be a student of the game. There was bound to be a limit to how well he could guide the Oberlin team against foes already experienced in some of the game's finer points.

Fortunately for Oberlin, someone must have known Amos Alonzo Stagg or knew someone who did. Stagg, a Yale All-American and one-time divinity-school student, coached the Christians, the football team of Springfield College in Massachusetts, a training school established by the Young Men's Christian Association. Stagg reportedly helped organize the Oberlin squad and even provided it with about six plays. The plays were all the varsity learned before opening what would turn out to be a season of high hopes and dashed expectations—a learning experience, if nothing else.

The team's first gridiron foe was the University of Michigan.[15] It certainly was not going to be an easy contest. The game, at Ann Arbor on Saturday, October 24, was, in fact, revelatory. Oberlin was now the largest college in Ohio, but Michigan had an enrollment nearly twice as great[16] and had fielded a football team since the spring of 1879, when it had played Racine College in Chicago in what was described as the "first rugby-football game to be played west of the Alleghenies."[17] Michigan sported not only school colors— maize and blue—but a nickname as well, the Wolverines. Inside of one week

The first Oberlin team to play intercollegiate football, the 1891 varsity. *Top row (from left):* David P. Simpson, Lynds Jones, William J. Jacobs, Carlton Aylard, John H. Wise, George R. Berry, Louis E. Hart. *Third row:* Paul A. Gulick, George Wilder, manager Bert Hogen, Grove Grosvenor. *Second row:* William (Will) H. Merriam, Fred Savage, Carl S. Williams, Howard (Howie) K. Regal, Charles H. Borican. *Seated:* Henry Sperry, Carl Y. Semple, Stephen (Steve) R. Williams.

in 1881, it played Harvard, Yale, and Princeton. True, Michigan had lost each one of the games, but the team's performance was so creditable that it was invited to join the Eastern College League.[18] Michigan chose instead to concentrate on competition in what was then still called the West. It fielded five consecutive undefeated and untied teams between 1884 and 1888.[19] The university began an annual rivalry with Notre Dame in 1887, and three years later, after winning four games and losing only to Cornell, the athletic association run by Michigan's students decided to hire its first nonstudent coach, a trainer at the Detroit Athletic Club named Mike Murphy.[20]

It was Murphy who accompanied the Wolverines as they trotted onto the field at Ann Arbor that eventful Saturday. Oberlin's players appeared, sparkling in new, shiny white uniforms and barber-pole striped stockings of crimson and gold. Instead of their usual practice jackets, which were adorned with both an *O* and a *C* across the front, the team sported a new design, with a single large O emblazoned on the left breast of their jackets and a golden O on the front of their sweaters.[21] As the two squads faced each other in the center of the field, prepared for the start of the game, one could tell just by looking at the Michigan eleven that the Oberlin players were in for a hard struggle. Man for man, the Wolverines outweighed Oberlin's team.

Michigan won the toss and chose Horace Prettyman to referee the game[22]—a choice that would have unfortunate repercussions for Oberlin that day and in the future. Prettyman had played for the Wolverines for eight years.[23] That left Oberlin's Henry Walter Sperry to umpire. Sperry—who doubled as both captain and coach of the ill-starred 1890 team—would ordinarily have started at quarterback for Oberlin but he had been injured in practice.[24]

Michigan also won a second toss of the coin and decided to take the ball. But before the ball was put into play, Grosvenor said he had an important concession to request: that the halves be limited to thirty minutes. That way the Oberlin players could catch the last train back to Oberlin at 5:25 P.M. School officials had made it clear that the team members had to return Saturday night, so that they would be on hand for Sabbath services the next day. The request was crucial to the Oberlin players, who wanted to remain in the faculty's good graces. The Michigan team captain agreed, and the game got underway.

At first, it looked like Oberlin had a chance of winning. John Wise—who at left guard was quickly developing into a "Percheron" of a lineman able to run "with three men on his back without noticing the extra weight"[25]—opened a hole in the Wolverine defense and Grosvenor rushed through it, scoring. Regal's kick for the extra two points was good and, amazingly, Oberlin was ahead, 6–0.

The team's headiness quickly evaporated as Michigan, in possession, swiftly ran the ball downfield in a series of plays that wearied the Oberlin defenders. The Wolverines scored, but failed to make the extra points, so Oberlin was still ahead 6–4. However, once more in possession, Michigan marched down the field again until one of its backs fumbled at the Oberlin goal line. Both the back and Grosvenor fell on the ball, tugging back and forth and grappling for possession. Prettyman the referee awarded it to the

Wolverine player and then ruled that he had crossed the Oberlin goal line with it. By halftime, Michigan led 8–6.

Prettyman's rulings dispirited the Oberlin players, who were already physically exhausted. At one point, Wise on defense broke through the Michigan line and was able to snatch the ball from a Wolverine back, but Prettyman denied him possession. The Wolverines went on to rack up five touchdowns in all, plus three successful extra-points kicks. The final score was Michigan 26, Oberlin 6.[26]

It was an inauspicious debut for Oberlin, though the local weekly *Oberlin News* said that, "considering the fact that this is Oberlin's first game and that Ann Arbor has for years played strong football, the score 26 to 6 is very creditable." But both the *News* and the *Oberlin Review* were critical of the team's lack of endurance, especially in the second half of the game when Oberlin "hardly came in sight of Ann Arbor's goal." Michigan, the *News* reported, "succeeded in winding most of the Oberlin players." Michigan's "fast play" was "too much for the slight training of Oberlin."[27]

There was one positive note—one critically important to the ethics-conscious Oberlin men. "Ann Arbor tell us that we play the cleanest gentlemanly foot ball they have ever seen," the *Review* noted. It quoted the observation in the *University of Michigan Daily* that there had not been any "slugging": "Not a single blow was struck. There was but little unnecessary talking in the rush line. . . . It is always the inexperienced players that impede the progress of the game and lessen their own effectiveness as players by incessant 'jawing.'"

The *Daily* added that Oberlin "possesses material for a first-class eleven." They would make "formidable antagonists for any team in the West" if "the team should learn to play with more promptness, practice the blocking and end running, make their 'V' more compact, and teach the center to snap the ball properly."[28]

Michigan's assessment was echoed in Oberlin. The varsity's style of play "was the hammer-and-tong, every-man-for-himself kind," the *Review* commented. "There was little interference and no team work to speak of."[29]

The loss to Michigan highlighted three major problems that bedeviled the Oberlin varsity all season long. The men might have had the will and desire to play football, but there was no one with the experience and the expertise to coach them in the rudiments or finer points of the game. Moreover, not all the starters were coming out for practice every day. Lastly, those who did come out lacked a scrub team to practice against. The varsity needed an adversary if the players were going to be able to perfect their plays and learn how to stymie an opponent's offense. But it had been nearly impossible to find students who wanted to be battered about playing second-string football.

With the team's first home game scheduled only a week away, daily practice sessions were scheduled and fervent appeals to help out the varsity had some effect. For a while, a fully manned scrub team appeared regularly to work out with the varsity, for there was excitement in the air over the prospect of Oberlin's first home game. Everyone wondered how many fans would show up. Oberlin had entered its inaugural year of football at the very time the sport had developed nationally into a major social event. Forty thousand people would witness the traditional Yale-Princeton game in New York that November; every hotel in New York, where the game was played, was booked to capacity, their lobbies decked with college banners. The country's premier team, Yale, had entered the new season with a string of thirty-five games in which it did not yield a single point while amassing 1,271.[30]

Newspapers led by the Hearst chain jumped on this new rage and helped fuel football's popularity by their ample coverage. The impact of the daily press was profound. Once relegated in newspapers to a so-called leisure-news section of society events, college athletics were now being highlighted as a permanent feature on a "sporting page," and soon football coverage alone merited full-page coverage and sometimes accounts of several pages in many newspapers. Through newspapers alone, an extracurricular physical exercise was slowly but inexorably being transformed into a national spectacle.[31] Sportswriting, however, was in its infancy, unsophisticated, indiscriminating in details and usually partisan. A typical example was the *Review*'s account of the opening moments of the Oberlin-Michigan game: "The U. of M. right-end was sent around the end, but Grosvenor tackled him for 2 yards gain. Dygert [a Michigan back] bucked the line but as he struck the line, the ball, for some unknown reason, got away and leaped over both lines and Grosvenor clasped it lovingly and was downed after a little gain. Oberlin got 5 yards on a foul by Pierson, holding Jones by the ankle. Oberlin now tried to get around the ends but could not gain 5 yards. On third down Regal made a splendid punt and ball again belonged to U. of M., in their half of the field. Again Capt. Van Inwagen tried to buck the Oberlin line, varied by runs around the ends, but the ball soon went to Oberlin after a U. of M. loss of 2 yards apiece on 3 downs."

Such prose was uninspiring, but the space that was allotted to the story of the game, nearly two pages, reflected the enormous interest of the *Review*'s readers. Like newspapers around the country, both the *Review* and the weekly *Oberlin News* were devoting columns to sports coverage, and not only the varsity's doings. Both publications covered intramural games, as well.

No better evidence of the excitement football engendered occurred than at Oberlin's Athletic Park on Saturday, October 31. The weather lent further auspiciousness to the day. Clouds and the "ominous feeling of dampness" gave way to sunshine in the early afternoon as swarms of fans began to gather.[32] A stiff southwesterly wind swept across the field, causing everybody to grab hold of their hats.[33] The team from Adelbert—a college that over time metamorphosed into Western Reserve University and ultimately Case Western—arrived from Cleveland aboard a special train. Its two cars also carried nearly one hundred fifty supporters, including a number of ladies decked out with "pleasing effect" in Adelbert's colors, cherry red and white. The same could not, however, be said of the team they were rooting for. The Adelbert players were wearing last year's "war-stained rags." They had hoped to be in new uniforms, but the pants and jackets hadn't arrived in time for the game.

By game time, the Oberlin grandstand was filled and its entire sideline crowded three or four persons deep with men waving canes and umbrellas adorned with crimson and yellow ribbons. They shouted the "Hi-O-Hi" yell "in scriptural measures" in response to "the fantastic yell raised now and then" by the Adelbert fans across from them on the opposite sideline. Inexplicably, many of Oberlin's players were without their crimson-and-gold stockings and had donned ones of "various shades" as well as caps "of all the more nefarious colors of the rain-bow."[34] Many spectators may not have noticed the odd assortment of hats because the wind kicked up clouds of dust so thick that sometimes the players were obscured. One thing was clear, however: Oberlin's line was "a little meatier."[35]

Most teams at the time opened the game with a mass-momentum play called a *V* rush. Adelbert braced to stop Oberlin's, but was tricked. Instead, Howie Regal ran around left end for twenty-five yards and Grove Grosvenor followed with a similar run for twenty more yards. But in the back-and-forth struggle that followed, it wasn't until nearly twenty minutes into the game that Grosvenor was able to score. By halftime Oberlin was ahead, 8–6.

With the wind at their backs for the second half of the game, Oberlin was expected to play a kicking game. But Regal, its leading kicker, kept fumbling the ball every time it was passed to him, and the idea eventually was abandoned. Oberlin returned to a running game until, finally, Carl Williams scurried over the goal line with it. In the lead, 12–6, Oberlin thought it had scored again when its quarterback, Steve Williams, rushed through the center of the Adelbert line for a touchdown. But the umpire would not allow it, claiming that the ball had not "touched three men"—that is, the ball should have gone from the center to Williams the quarterback, who should have passed it to a third player before it was legal for Williams to handle it again. Anyway, the touchdown had no bearing on the outcome of the game.

Oberlin's first victory set off a tumultuous celebration. As soon as the game was over, nearly five hundred Oberlin students rushed onto the field, surrounded the winning team, and hoisted some of the players onto their shoulders, all the while yelling "as though their lungs were a pair of patent automatic bellows." Regular, daily practice had paid off. "The eleven will be on the grounds every day during the coming week," the *Review* prophesized.

The *Cleveland Leader and Herald,* however, evinced sour grapes. The ground was "too hard" for "the Adelberts, who had been accustomed to play on the soft field of the Cleveland Athletic Club and they showed considerable hesitancy about falling on the ball in the headlong fashion so popular among good players."[36]

The soft field mentioned in the newspaper report was scheduled to be the site of Oberlin's next game on the following Saturday, November 7, against a team sponsored by the Cleveland Athletic Club itself. It was a game that Oberlin should never have played, and one wonders why its manager, Bert Hogen, scheduled it. Hubris perhaps? The CAC squad was made up of rough, tough, husky footballers, young muscular laborers in the main who were not affiliated with any school.

Flush with their first victory, a small group of Oberlin students joined Hogen and the team on a train to Cleveland that afternoon. By the time they arrived, their throats were "already sore with hoarseness" from cheering. While the "horn-blowers" headed off to the CAC field, Hogen and the varsity stepped into a horse-drawn carriage and were taken to the Hotel de Hollenden, where the players changed into their uniforms.

The moment the Oberlin players stepped onto the gridiron, it was evident that they were clearly mismatched. The CAC team averaged 188 pounds, 28 pounds more than the Oberlin team. Their captain, Billy Rhodes, had spent four years playing and coaching for Yale.[37]

While the game was not a runaway, Oberlin never really had a chance. CAC scored its first touchdown eight minutes into the game, a second one five minutes later, and a third before halftime. The CAC team made three more touchdowns in the second half. The final score was 28–0. All the touchdowns were made by line rushes against Oberlin's weaker defense. The *Oberlin Review* insisted afterward that the team was defeated "by physical strength and not by superior skill."

Oberlin was determined to avenge the loss, but injuries during practice to Grosvenor, Jones, and Simpson as well as to Sperry cast doubt on its ability to field a coordinated team at its next game, a home contest the following Saturday, November 14, against the oldest school in the state, the Case School of Applied Science. About a hundred spectators from the Cleveland college were on hand, wearing the brown and white of their school, when the game began that afternoon at Athletic Park.[38]

The revised starting team included several new men. Teenager Carl Semple was making his debut at quarterback; another teenager, Will Merriam, was at right end; and Charles Borican, the sole black on the squad, started at right tackle.

The game began slowly. From the very beginning, Oberlin's offense bogged down and players on both teams fumbled the ball several times. At one point, Oberlin got within three yards of Case's goal but lost the ball. The first half ended without a point being scored.

A chill had set in, and as the teams rested at halftime, the spectators left the grandstand, and in order to get their blood circulating, started tramping around the track that surrounded the field, making it look "like a circular panorama." The "decidedly bracing" air apparently had its effect on the Oberlin team when it returned for the second half. The players seemed to wake up, and for most of it they were able to keep the ball in Case's territory. More than twenty minutes into the second half, Borican carried the ball to within two yards of the goal line and Steve Williams took it over for the first touchdown of the game. Regal's kick for the extra points went wide, so the score stood at 4–0. Williams soon scored again[39] and this time Regal's kick was successful. The score was 10–0, and Oberlin was on the verge of scoring once more when time ran out.

The victory pushed the loss to the Cleveland Athletic Club to the back of everyone's mind. In fact, it is totally, and blessedly, forgotten. There is no mention of the 28–0 defeat in the Record Book maintained by the Oberlin Department of Physical Education and Athletics, and thus none in the media guide that it publishes. After all, the CAC was not a college team. From Oberlin's standpoint, the game did not count or bear mentioning.

The "four horsemen" of the 1891 squad after a mud-splattered scrimmage—Carl Semple, Carl Williams, Howie Regal, and Fred Savage. Williams transferred to the University of Pennsylvania, where his playing got him elected an All-American.

The victory over Case, however, was something else. "Oberlin," the *Review* said, "went to bed that night, with a broad spirit of benevolence for all mankind."

There was one game left on the schedule, a return match with the team that was to become one of Oberlin's chief rivals, Adelbert. This one brought Oberlin back to the CAC field in Cleveland on Saturday, November 21. The

"Adelberts" had every intention of matching the enthusiasm that Oberlin had shown three weeks earlier in its opening home game. Two hundred of them were "out in force," and "yards and yards of crimson and white ribbon" were strung through the buttonholes of coats or knotted on walking sticks. Because of a steady, pelting rain, "sundry unmelodious tin horns were surreptitiously carried under the ample folds of mackintoshes and heavy winter overcoats." Adelbert students taunted the handful of Oberlin fans who showed up—actually only nine from "the city of churches and learning" made the trip to Cleveland—with a couplet that ran: "Lickety whoop, lickety whoop, / Oberlin is in the soup." Another Adelbert cheer gloated over the fact that it had already defeated both Ohio State and Denison: "O.S.U., O.S.U. / Dennison, and Oberlin too."[40]

At first, when the Oberlin team left for Cleveland early in the afternoon, the rain had ceased and prospects appeared good for a dry game. But by the time the team reached Union Depot in Cleveland, it had started raining again and was coming down "in torrents." When the team arrived at the CAC grounds, the field was a swamp.

The game started late, so both team captains agreed to play only thirty-minute halves. Adelbert scored within six minutes of the game's beginning, on its first possession. In response, Oberlin quickly drove down the field. Grosvenor tried a buck into the line, but he dropped the ball. It rolled under the players and came out behind them. "Theolog" George Berry, who was playing left tackle, spotted the ball and, without anyone noticing him, picked it up and ran to Adelbert's goal with a clear field. As neither team made the extra points after its touchdown, that tied the score at 4–4, and gave the Oberlin players some measure of confidence. However, that quickly faded when, just before the first half ended, an Adelbert back broke away on a sixty-five-yard run. Regal scampered after him but could not catch him. Adelbert had four more points and the lead, 8–4.

Once more, the Oberlin players, too wearied to maintain a strong defense in the second half, faded. Adelbert quickly scored two more touchdowns. The struggling Oberlin players managed to flounder their way to a few more points when Grosvenor ran the ball in from eight yards out. That reduced Adelbert's lead to 18–8.

Adelbert now purposely tried to play out the clock by holding onto the ball. In the process, penalties cost it twenty yards, forcing Adelbert back to its own five-yard line. The referee then announced there were only five seconds left to play and the instant the ball was centered he blew his whistle, ending the game. But it was dark by then, "long after sensible chickens had gone to roost and when the electric lights were twinkling upon the needle-like poles in the city."[41] The referee hadn't seen, so the Oberlin players insisted, that the ball had been fumbled and John Wise had picked it up and carried it across the Adelbert goal line. The Oberlin players protested, but to no avail. The touchdown would not have changed the game's outcome; it just would have made it a closer contest. Adelbert won 18–8.

All in all, it was a sloppy game. Both teams floundered "about in a sea of pasty mud."[42] More hurtful than the loss, however, was the *Cleveland Leader and Herald*'s evaluation of the game. The Oberlin team, it said, did not seem to play as they played against the CAC, which had rolled over them. "They are great fighters," it went on, "but a fast game by their opponents appears to disconcert them. Much sympathy and regret was express[ed] by those of the spectators who were not students that Oberlin should twice have come to Cleveland and neither time had opportunity to serenade citizens of this metropolis with their classic 'prohibition yell.'"[43]

Pity, though, was the last sentiment the Oberlin players wanted. Bert Hogen wanted to arrange a third game with Adelbert, but the school would not play anywhere except in Cleveland, which, the *Oberlin Review* declared, "was manifestly unfair."[44] Meanwhile, while Hogen was carrying on negotiations with Adelbert, the team continued to practice, but with little spirit—and no visible student support. The second loss to Adelbert had taken the steam out of Oberlin's enthusiasm. "Does the foot ball spirit slumber, have we lost heart already, are we afraid of the weather, or what is the matter?" cried the *Review*. "For several days the 'Varsity [*sic*] has gone to the grounds and found nothing to line up against but the goal posts."[45] The student publication wondered if maybe it was a question of conflict with class hours that was hampering participation. "Hitherto, Oberlin, if not in spirit, has as a matter of fact, been hostile to athletics," it said. But now its president "was recently heard to remark that athletics had become an important feature in college work, and should receive almost equal attention with the work of the regular curriculum." Wasn't it time, then, to consider putting aside the last hour in the afternoon for practice and also to excuse the varsity players from chapel exercises?[46]

Oberlin's first season of football had resulted in two wins and two losses—three losses if the CAC game is counted. A promising debut? Reflecting on the season's victories and defeats, the overriding factor, it was realized, was not the conflict between classroom hours and football practice sessions, or the weather that played havoc with the playing field, or the injuries that compelled starters to miss games. "The serious question" that now presented itself, the *Oberlin Review* acknowledged, was whether Oberlin was going to play "the same or better foot ball next year?" The answer seemed clear. "We have learned a great deal this year but we cannot learn as much more next year without a coach. We must have a man here next fall who has played on one of the great eastern teams. He must be on hand when school opens to perfect 'tackling and falling on the ball' and to lay out a definite plan of play toward the perfection of which all his and the captain's efforts shall be bent."[47]

5

THE COACH

A coach should be masterful and commanding, even dictatorial.
He has not the time to say please or mister.
He must be severe, arbitrary, and little short of a czar.
—*John Heisman*

When John Heisman arrived in Oberlin in the fall of 1892, he may have been "dejected" and so desperate to coach a football team that he would accept a job without any evidence that he would ever get a salary. But he had quickly learned the intricacies of the game as a player and obviously had a strong concept about what it takes to be a coach and was eager to try out his theories of playing the game.

What brought him to Oberlin, though, is unclear. Details about how Heisman was drawn there are sketchy and contradictory. His name apparently came up when, on behalf of the student athletic association, Bert Hogen, the manager of the varsity, began the search for a coach. Walter Camp of Yale, one uncorroborated story has it, recommended him. Another says that two of Oberlin's players, Henry Sperry and Carl Williams, pleaded for Heisman's being hired on a three-month contract.[1]

Yet another story says that although Heisman offered to coach the team, there was some doubt about the advisability of hiring him. He was, all things considered, totally inexperienced at mentoring a football squad. But, so this story goes, Heisman volunteered to show what he could do without any contract.[2]

Was the example set by Camp, who played for Yale for seven years, a factor in having Heisman enroll as a postgrad? After four years of undergraduate school, Camp continued to play football for Yale while he attended medical school there.[3] But, then, who at Oberlin finagled Heisman's enrollment as a postgraduate student in the school's almost-miniscule art department? Who let him get away with skipping classes?

Evidently there was a trade-off involved. Heisman was searching for a way to start a career in football. The association did not have the financial wherewithal to offer him a wage, but there was always the possibility that enough money would be raised by gate receipts at the games, or by a guest lecture or two. Amos Alonzo Stagg, an avid espouser of evangelical athleticism and a fervent promoter of football, had spoken on "The Modern Athlete," a lantern-slide lecture on Christianity and sports, to an association-sponsored event earlier in the year. However, unlike the humorist Bob Burdette's successful appearance in Oberlin two years earlier, Stagg's talk brought in only $155.40, less than half what Burdette's had.[4]

Heisman, it appears, was obviously willing to settle for the uncertainty of an income in order to gain the experience of coaching. And he was even willing to play in a pinch, too.

Football was to be a lifelong obsession for the young man who walked onto the Oberlin playing field that afternoon in early October 1892. He was born Johann Wilhelm Heisman in Cleveland on October 23, 1869, coincidentally just two weeks before the first football game between Rutgers and Princeton. He was the middle of three sons born to Michael Heisman, a German cooper, and his wife, Sarah. Looking to make his fortune, the father moved the family to the oilfields of northwestern Pennsylvania in the late 1870s, opening a barrel shop that in time employed fifteen artisans in Titusville, the site of the first great oil discovery.[5]

Young Johann—now Americanized into John—was both a good student and an accomplished athlete. He was captain of the baseball team at Titusville High and a champion gymnast. And, despite the fact that he was slight for a football player,[6] he went out for the team, playing guard on the school's varsity teams of 1884, 1885, and 1886[7]—much to his father's annoyance. The elder Heisman absolutely refused to watch his son play. "I have never known a man more stubbornly opposed to the game," Heisman recalled. "It was brutal. It was a waste of time. It should be prohibited."[8]

The game the high school team played was soccer in style. It may have been, Heisman later admitted, "a bit crude." As he put it, "With the exception of a couple of prohibitions such as running with the ball and murder, we had few rules."[9] The rules that, through Walter Camp's instigation, Eastern colleges and high schools were playing were, Heisman explained, "still very much a mystery to us of the inland schools." At Titusville, he said, "We were having the times of our lives assaulting a round, black rubber ball up and down expansive fields."[10] So it came as a revelation to young Heisman when he happened to purchase a ten-cent rules book and discovered that the version of the game American colleges played allowed ball-carrying. "Then and there the old game lost its savor," he declared. "From that moment nothing of football which did not permit running with the ball appealed to me."[11]

Fascinated with the theater in general and Shakespeare in particular, Heisman was salutatorian of his class at Titusville. His oration at graduation ceremonies was entitled "The Dramatist a Sermonizer."[12] But his infatuation lay elsewhere. "I was football mad," he readily conceded. At the age of seventeen, he left home and traveled to Providence, Rhode Island, where he planned to take a two-year course in law at Brown University, which had innovated an elective system of broad studies. Inexperienced in the intricacies of switching rail lines, Heisman missed several trains and found himself at one point in Albany, New York, with nothing but time on his hands until his next connection. So he "rambled." "I am quite sure that destiny guided me, because presently I found myself at the edge of a large field whereon a crowd of lusty lads were playing football. Instead of the round black ball I knew they were struggling with an oval one, leather-covered. And they had uniforms—unpadded shorts—and short-waisted canvas jackets. And they had signals. But best of all THEY RAN WITH THE BALL. I missed another train."

Fate had Heisman arriving at the Brown campus the next day as a game of football between freshmen and some "town boys" was in progress. "Luck" tapped him when one of the freshmen had to quit. Asked whether he wanted to play, Heisman—still in the brand-new custom-made black suit he had worn from Titusville—"leaped into the fray." The freshman team had signals—"words, phrases and sentences"—but no one bothered to explain them to him. It would not have mattered, anyway, he said, because only the backs carried the ball and "mere linesmen could not possibly have any use for them." The theory was that it was better to keep linemen in suspense so that they would work harder against their opponents. Although he weighed only 144 pounds, Heisman was playing tackle: "All that I had to do was buck, charge, trample and otherwise assault my opponent tackle with a view to clearing that part of the field in order that the ball carrier might not meet with resistance there if perchance he elected to run through my territory."

At one point, Heisman snatched the ball from an opponent and ran "like a mad thing" with it for thirty yards before he was "fetched to earth with a crash that loosened a number of teeth." He was delirious: "I had one thoroughly black eye, and a freely bleeding nose. That suit, that gallant effort of Titusville's best tailor, was an unqualified ruin. But I was happy. *I had run with the ball.*"

Imagine, then, Heisman's disappointment the very next day when he learned that Brown's team had performed so poorly during several preceding seasons that the university had abandoned intercollegiate play. His extracurricular passion had to take second seat to his academic studies. He wound up playing left tackle for a sometime team of "town lads," and the next year, when he was up to 158 pounds, he played left guard for another pickup team.

From a football standpoint, Heisman readily acknowledged he had picked Brown "badly." But that certainly was not the case when he transferred in the fall of 1889 to the University of Pennsylvania to further study law "and play football as much as possible." The school had relocated from Philadelphia proper to the west bank of the Schuylkill River about seventeen years earlier and was now in the midst of a flurry of expansion. It was also aware of the publicity value of having a strong football team. Its team, in fact, was on the verge of becoming a major Ivy League power. It had played and defeated Rutgers, 13–10, in 1887 in Madison Square Garden in New York, the first indoor football game of its kind.[13]

Heisman went out for the scrub team, reporting on the field with moleskin pants and a canvas jacket that he had made himself—unpadded, of course. Padding, he knew, was "scorned." For no other reason than to keep cool, he also abjured stockings.[14] And, like many other college players, he'd grown a moustache.

Early in his career, as a second-string player, Heisman substituted for the Penn center in a game. In earlier years, before the introduction of the scrimmage line, a center used his foot to put the ball into play. Doing so left his hands free to fight off his opposite number. But, too often, footing the ball caused it to spin erratically off course. Or, if the center was distracted by the sparring, the opposing center might surreptitiously try to nudge the ball toward his own men. In one instance, an opponent center grabbed hold of the loose end of the lace on the football so that when the ball was footed it flipped back to him.[15]

The scrimmage line together with a neutral zone obviated the need to foot the ball. But tricks were still played. Centers now used one hand to flip the ball end over end under their legs to the quarterback. To alert the center that he was ready to start, a quarterback used one of a variety of touch signals. Penn's quarterback liked to scratch the center's leg. Which is what Heisman expected him to do when he subbed as center. He was so intent on getting the ball back to the quarterback without mishap that he didn't notice that the hand of his long-armed opposite number across the scrimmage line had circled his leg and scratched him. Heisman reacted immediately, flipping the

The versatile center-cum-end John W. Heisman strikes a dramatic pose during his playing days at the University of Pennsylvania, where he earned a law degree. The size of the pigskin made it difficult for runners and kickers to control the ball. Heisman would later coach—and play—for Oberlin.

ball backwards. Not expecting it, the quarterback missed the pass and the team suffered a five-yard loss. Heisman's solution: have the quarterback use the word "hike" to put the ball into motion so that everyone was clear when the play started.

Despite his misplay, Heisman quickly worked himself into being Penn's starter at center. It was a cause for rather nervous celebration. Heisman was well under the usual weight for a guard or center, which was 200 pounds. In fact, the two Penn guards who bracketed him tipped the scales at 212 and 243, respectively. "I was forever more very apprehensive," he said, "lest they fall on me than that injury would come from the opposition."[16]

Actually, it was a football that proved Heisman's undoing. Playing against Penn State, Heisman faced a "behemoth" opposite him who was "considerably wider than he was high." Hoping to block a punt, Heisman at the snap of the ball leapfrogged onto the crouching center's back and, as soon as he landed in the Penn State backfield, he leaped high, his arms flailing the air to block the punt. The ball left the kicker's foot just as Heisman reached the top of his leap. It went through his outstretched hands and smashed right into his nose. Half-blinded, Heisman tried to recover the ball. He saw the kicker dive to the ground, so he dived, too, and "clutched something hard and round." But it was the kicker's head that Heisman had hold of, not the ball. A teammate of Heisman's fortunately fell on it inside the Penn State goal.[17] The teammate was credited with a touchdown, and Heisman was forever after left with "a flat, pulpy nose."[18]

Heisman was a versatile player. In his last year at Penn, he was one of ten players trying out for left end. Just before a game with Lehigh, the coach came to him and told him he believed Heisman was the best man for the position, "but nobody else seems to think so." Nevertheless, the coach said he was sending him in against Lehigh. "Son, you and I stand or fall on what you do today. Get in there, boy. Play football." The coach's faith was rewarded. "I think that I'd have a fought a battery of buzz-saws barehanded after that," said Heisman, who, at the same time, learned a lesson about instilling confidence.[19]

He was also soaking up the fundamentals of football tactics and strategy and figuring out ways to improve the game. Take, for example, what experience taught him playing against the legendary Yale tackle, six-foot-four, 200-pound-plus William (Pudge) Heffelfinger, a perennial All-American. Some of the "wild-goose" formations being employed—offshoots in the main of mass-momentum plays—were "ponderous" and "deadly."[20] The star of Yale's big line, who led such attacks, Heffelfinger was a veritable human tank. A *New York Sun* reporter recounted seeing Yale's somewhat puny quarterback, Larry ("Little") Bliss, grab onto a ring handle attached to Heffelfinger's belt. Pudge then plowed ahead with Bliss clinging to the leather strap, his slight form concealed from tacklers by the huge lineman's hulk. "You couldn't stop Heff short of 5 yards," the reporter said. "If Bliss was tackled Heffelfinger dragged him ahead by main force."[21]

Heisman was one of those opponents who tried to get in Heffelfinger's way. "The black and blue bruises his shoulders left upon me and the dents I had from his hips and knees have gone long since," Heisman later recalled, "but the memory of them will be with me always."[22] The memory was fresh when he reached Oberlin, where Heisman innovated in the employment of both guards as blockers. If it was safe for Heffelfinger "to come out and lead the interference," Heisman reasoned, "it would be safe to train both guards to do it."[23]

Heisman won letters for varsity football for all three years he played for Penn—1889, 1890, and 1891. During those years, the school compiled a record of twenty-nine wins and eleven losses.[24] But the youthful enthusiast came away physically disabled. Far more serious than the injury to his nose was the one to his eyes. It occurred during a Penn-Princeton game in Madison Square Garden in 1891. While playing, Heisman somehow came into contact with the galvanized lighting system. His vision blurred and he had recurrent trouble focusing. Ordered by a doctor to rest his eyes, Heisman required the help of a reader in order to study for his law degree.[25] He was also warned not to even consider practicing his profession for two years.

So instead of joining a law firm in Cleveland as he had hoped, upon graduation Heisman was forced to look for some other means to earn a living.[26] He tried selling kitchen utensils door to door, but customers were few and far between, and Heisman subsisted for weeks on end on a quart of milk and bananas. He then tried growing tomatoes, but virtually every farmer around Cleveland was already raising the crop and his tomatoes died on the vine for lack of harvesters.[27]

It was then, in the fall of 1892, that the "jealous mistress" of his life[28] prompted Heisman to seek a coaching job at Adelbert. He had, he believed, learned a valuable lesson as an undersized player: "You see, the big fellow nearly always banks on his big bones and ponderous thews: he has learned that it pays to do so; while the little man has learned, since he crawled out of his crib, that he does well to call on his gray matter and outfigure a bigger and stronger opponent; and it is this continual stropping of that gray matter that gives to the brain of the small man of parts its razor edge."[29]

Brain over brawn. Heisman was ready to put his philosophy into play.

6

THE TEAM

On a properly organized team every man must conform
absolutely to a very rigorous system of training.
—*John Heisman*

On the eve of a new football season, the first with a coach, Oberlin College was not making any concessions for the varsity players. Transformation or not, Oberlin still dedicated itself to the education not only of the intellect but also the heart. "There is a fundamental difference between a secular college and a Christian college," Oberlin's president at the time, William Gay Ballantine, wrote in his annual report:

It is sometimes said that at a Christian college religious exercises are compulsory; rather it should be said that in secular colleges Christian men are under an unnatural compulsion of silence. What is more spontaneous than for a Christian professor, who daily prays for his students in his closet, to pray with them in the recitation room? In a Christian college the Christian life finds free expression; it sings itself continually in the sublime hymns of the Church; it pours itself out in prayer. . . . Those students who do not themselves enter the ministry, but are trained in such an atmosphere, are qualified to do the work of Christian laymen and lay women as none others can be.

This is Oberlin's claim. It is a strong one.[1]

There was a great deal for Ballantine to point to with pride that fall. For one thing, the school was flourishing. Enrollment stood at 1,492 students. There was a new hall to house forty young female students and to accommodate as many of their male counterparts at its dining tables; called Lord

Cottage, the hall was a three-story edifice with twin gables. There was also a new wing added to Warner Hall, which was devoted to music education. It contained thirty-five rooms, most of them practice rooms with new pianos.[2] The tennis grounds—twenty-nine courts covering four acres—now comprised the largest college tennis facility in the country. Unfortunately, however, the baseball diamond, which was still "an unavoidable part of the football field," was "baked almost as hard as stone by the sun and wind." The goal posts, however, were scheduled to be moved northward some distance.[3]

Ballantine also boasted about the "admirable system of sewers" that ran under Oberlin's streets. The sewers, a "fine supply of pure water, well paved streets," and electric lights now graced the village, a "remarkable" achievement, he said, for "a place of 4,000 inhabitants, of whom very few can be called wealthy, and where there is no manufacturing."[4]

"There is another thought," Oberlin's president remarked: "The very plan of Oberlin involves the doing of the highest work. . . . Much of the work now offered here in elective courses to undergraduates is of the grade of post-graduate work in the best universities."[5]

Although Oberlin had lost several faculty members—one of them, Greek scholar William G. Frost, had bowed to repeated offers and finally accepted the presidency of Berea College in Kentucky—the departees were replaced by professors who had studied at Johns Hopkins, Harvard, Syracuse University, and Grinnell.[6]

Theologian John Wise could confirm not only Oberlin's religious thrust, but also its rigorous academic standards. A lineman on the 1891 team, he was hopeful of winning back his position, but, he wrote some friends, there were a lot of demands on a student's time: "In the morning I have to get up at 6:30 and get ready for breakfast. Our boarding house is not very far from my room. We have breakfast at 7, then morning prayers right after. At 7:45 I get to my room again and study my morning lessons. At 9 I have my class in grammar[;] at 10 I have my Algebra. At 11 I go back to my room and study my afternoon lesson. At 12:15 we have dinner[;] at 12:45 I get back to my room but most of the time I take a 15 minute walk and so generally get to my room at 1 then study my afternoon lesson again: at 2:30 I go to my gymnation [sic] class[;] at 3:30 I go to my Physical Geog. class: at 4:30 I take a little walk and at 5 go to chapel: at 5:30 we have supper[;] at 6 I get back to my room and begin my next days lesson."

Such was Wise's Monday "programme." "On Tuesdays my class in gymn [sic] comes at 3 and Geog. at 4. Wednesdays the same. On Thursdays classes come in as on Tuesday. We have a lecture every Thursday afternoon at 4:30. In the evening I go to our Y.M.C.A. meeting. Fridays classes come in as on Thursday. At 4:30 we have a class prayer meeting. Saturday we have our morning classes and a holiday in the afternoon. I go in the woods most every Sat. afternoon. We have supper at 5:30 and play games with the Young Ladies after supper. We often play up to the last minute which is 7:30 then all the ladies must be in their rooms. Of course we go to our rooms too and sometimes study and sometimes write letters."

Wise's Sabbath schedule was, as you might expect, a different story: "At 7 Sunday morning I get up and at 7:30 we have our breakfast. At 8 we have our prayer meeting and we all have to say something. At 8:30 we get through then go to our rooms and get ready for our bible class. At 9 we go to the our bible class and at 10:30 we go to church. At 12 we get through and at 12:15 we have dinner[.] After dinner we sing for about 30 minutes then go to our rooms and have the afternoon to ourselves Unless at 3 I sometimes go to a prayer meeting. At 5 we have supper and at 6:15 we go to our Y.M.C.A. meeting. At 7:30 we go to church."

And then there were the rules: "Every boy must be in their room at 10:05 and not to go out till morning. Of course we don't have teachers with us every time but we are trusted to do the right [thing] always. Every boy must be at church in the morning and evening. Always send in a report every Monday morning. All the failures must be excused[;] if not for three times that boy is expelled from school. No smoking, chewing [tobacco] or drinking. Cannot go out of town unless excused by the teacher. Always be present in your classes. Always have a good lesson[,] if not make it up on Monday."[7]

One youthful student who found it difficult to follow the rules was Carl Young Semple, who had played quarterback in the final two games of the 1891 season and was a good prospect for the 1892 team. Semple joined four "city" boys in pilfering a chicken from a local coop. The youths took it outside of town and were in the process of roasting it when some farmers spotted them and decided to scare the boys. They charged into the group with clubs yelling, "kill them, kill them." In the fight that ensued, one of the farmers was badly hurt. Afterward, Semple returned to the scene of the fracas to recover a coat, but the farmers had found it first. Semple asked a friend in the theology seminary to intercede on his behalf for its return, but before he could, the Associated Press got hold of the story and Semple's name was on the front page of newspapers throughout Ohio.

Semple confessed his part in the incident to an administration official, who decided to be lenient and allow him to remain in school. But that same night Semple joined his compatriots again and went to a bar in Lorain, a few miles north of Oberlin on Lake Erie. He was caught and admonished once more. The next afternoon he visited his friends, who were playing poker, and was reported to be a participant in the game. Semple insisted he had only shown up to collect money to pay the doctor's bill of the injured farmer. But his conscience was finally getting the better of him. In the past, he said, he would file a "fixed" Monday report with the school principal "just like most everyone else did." Instead, Semple tried sticking to the rules for two weeks "and saw I could not take it." He quit Oberlin. "At that time," he said, "murder was about the only thing that was barred at Kenyon, so I transferred there."[8]

Seven less impulsive fellow members of the 1891 varsity with whom Semple had played were back and trying out for the team. Among them were Wise, fellow theolog George Berry, Lynds Jones, Will Merriam, and the popular Fred Savage. Louis Edward Hart, who had been on the squad in 1891, was back, too; the twenty-one-year-old senior, a mile runner in field events, was a strapping farmboy who modestly claimed that his only "proficiency" was "pitching hay."[9] Carl Williams returned, too; he had just been elected the team's captain, replacing Henry Sperry, who hadn't been able to return to school because of some private business.[10] The veterans turned out for practice "in form and ready to play the game of their lives," reported the *Oberlin Review*.

At the outset, the school's schedule of classes proved "almost as fatal to football as if the faculty had designed to aid the fond but nervous mothers who send their sons to college, by cutting off that 'horrible game.'" In past years, potential football players "had to scheme a little to get one or two classes transposed," the *Review* said, but now the number of changes necessary for "even one hour" of practice appeared almost insurmountable. "It has already disheartened some who might have made good players." Some potential footballers, the student publication continued, have a class at 3:00 P.M., others had to attend classes all afternoon. "Last year President Ballantine told us that we might play football while we won. Durable bricks without straw are much easier to make than a winning football team without practice."[11]

As a result of class conflicts, only about a dozen prospective football players showed up at the start of the fall term,[12] and appeals went out again for volunteers for the scrub team. A week or so later, on a Saturday after morning classes, at least forty sturdy students took the field for the varsity's first regular practice game. Bert Hogen and "Cap" Williams[13] watched from the sidelines, trying to assess each player's ability.[14] The team's greatest needs were a fullback and a center. Both the Saturday practice game and another scrimmage the following Monday were considered "well played," but no one was assured of a starting spot. The truth was, although the team manager and the varsity captain came up with a starting roster, there were questions galore. The *Review* reporter covering athletics, Steve Williams, who had played on the varsity in 1891, criticized the fact that the athletic association allowed a student to play both on the varsity team and on his class team. Williams for one thought that it was "clear to all that a man can't play his best for both college and class." Besides which, once class teams began their own practice sessions, the varsity's attempt at a scrimmage proved fruitless because not enough scrub players showed up. Williams also noted that "some objections have been made that the team has been picked too soon to give new men a chance."[15]

On September 29, the concerned officers of the athletic association appointed a committee to canvas the college, the theological seminary, the academy, and the conservatory with a view to raising a subscription to hire a football coach.[16] It was this move that led to the hiring of John Heisman.

Twenty-two years old, about to be twenty-three, Heisman was younger than eight members of the squad that turned out at his first practice session early in October 1892. One, a senior named Josiah Cattell Teeters, was one of the oldest Oberlin students ever to play the game. "Joe" Teeters was a veteran of the Purdue University team, the champions of Indiana in 1891.[17] He was an ancient twenty-nine.[18]

Age—his own or that of men senior to him—never entered Heisman's mind. He was the embodiment of a time dominated by authority figures, and he simply made it clear from the start who was boss. He exuded confidence. If any player had any doubt about Heisman's age, he did not express it. "You have to know what you're talking about and, even more important, your men must know too. And," Heisman added, "you have to know to whom you're talking."[19] He began coaching at Oberlin "hopeful," he said, "of making it clear to my men that offense means *charging* and *blocking* and that defense means *charging* and *fighting*."[20] "My men"? Referring to the students in that fashion was Heisman's way of defining roles: He was the teacher, they were the pupils. The distance between Heisman and the players was clear. As far as can be determined, he never made a friend of a man he coached. The players learned to respect his ability, but they never grew close to him or liked him.

Moreover, Heisman was not only the personification of a typical nineteenth-century authority figure, but also a snobbish type, given to affecting Dickensian prose. An amateur thespian, he also liked to quote Shakespeare. Sportswriters tried nicknames—Jack, Johnny—but they didn't stick to the man. He was too rigid, too uptight, too cold. He didn't invite jokes or joking.

Instead, Heisman was all work. The veterans of the 1891 team who were back were a known quantity. Heisman could at least get some idea of how good they were by talking to Hogen and Williams. But the newcomers were another matter. Besides patriarch "Joe" Teeters, they included Miles Eugene Marsh, who was himself twenty-six years old and, at 180 pounds, the heaviest man in the senior class.[21] His weight was a distinct advantage, but how agile was he? There were two brothers from western Ohio, Louis and Clayton Fauver, trying out for the team. The older, Lou, was a twenty-four-year-old freshman.[22] Clate, who was four years younger, was still in the preparatory department,[23] which had been renamed the Academy. Was either varsity material?

The Academy was proving the greatest feeder for the 1892 team,[24] becoming, as Phillips Exeter and Andover were, respectively to Yale and Harvard, a prime training ground and recruiting source for the varsity.[25] Besides Clate Fauver, five other "Cads" showed up on the practice field.

Heisman must have looked at the gaggle of players he faced that first day and thought them a disparate group. Steve Williams's assessments in the *Oberlin Review* give some idea of the material Heisman was expected to forge into a team. Lynds Jones might play tackle, but that "depends on how much he desires to play." Fred Savage "gets hurt too easily, and in running [he] circles back too far in trying to pass the opposing ends." A "Cad," Ellsworth Burnett Westcott, was the best bet for center, but was "rather slow as yet." Carl Williams would probably play quarterback instead of halfback—"he has a sure eye for the ball, is a splendid tackler, never 'cusses' his men"—but that would leave a vacancy at halfback "that can scarcely be filled." If Carl Williams was looking "rather anxious now he is not thinking about the rush line but the positions back of the line."[26] Lou Hart, a possibility at fullback, was praised for "superb" punting, but his "goal kicks are only fair."[27]

Heisman had a ritual he followed his entire coaching career. On the first day of practice, he would gather the players around him in a circle and hold out a football. "What is this?" he then asked in his crisp, high-pitched voice. Without waiting for a response, he answered his own question in the formal, stilted way he liked to talk: "A prolate spheroid—that is, an elongated sphere—

in which the outer leather is drawn tightly over a somewhat small rubber tubing." Heisman would then pause before continuing: "Better to have died as a small boy than to fumble this football."[28]

Heisman's admonition never failed to impress the youths he trained. David Simpson, who was present that fateful October day Heisman showed up on the Oberlin gridiron, said, "I shall always remember how that afternoon he revealed to us a knowledge of the game that resulted in his engagement as pioneer coach in Northern Ohio, and how we trounced [Adelbert] that season."[29]

The new coach may have been a bit taken aback by what he considered the "relatively scarce" number of "good men." The football candidates, he said, lacked "needed giants." He knew he would need time to judge the potentialities of the players. "The true test of a player's value to a team is revealed in the practice scrimmage," he believed. "There's where the coach picks his men. This is where he selected the 150-pounder with the baby face and rejects the 200-pound husky whose fighting qualities are all on the surface."[30]

Actually Oberlin's team averaged close to 180 pounds,[31] but without a huge Pudge Heffelfinger type to lead the blocking, Heisman decided that his "first job" as coach "was to find two speedy guards." He had six possibilities to choose from—John Wise and Joe Teeters, who were considered early shoo-ins for the positions, both the Fauver brothers, the veteran George Berry, and newcomer John W. White, a "Cad" who weighed 173 pounds.[32] Each got a chance to show his mettle.

The guards were crucial for the offense Heisman was molding. Their role as "interferers," blocking for ball carriers, was to be the backbone of the running game he planned. But it was the tackles who were all important on both offense and defense. On offense, Heisman came up with a variation on the double pass that had the center snap the ball to a tackle, who then handed off or lateraled to a halfback. On defense, he told them in his exaggerated form of speech, the tackles were to confront a ball carrier by thrusting their "projections into their cavities, grasping them about the knees and depriving them of their propulsion. They must come to earth, locomotion being denied them."[33]

Heisman had to contend with not only an unschooled team, but he must have been dismayed, as well, at the signals the team employed on offense. Fred Savage carried a crude, typed copy of them:

Vowels a, e, i, o, u, y,————————Right half back.
Consonants, b. c, d, f, g, h, j, etc.——Left half back.

Vowel followed by any number under 100 [such] as "a45"—right half-back takes the ball and goes straight ahead on his own side through the tackle.

If this signal be followed by any letters whatsoever, the right half back cuts across to the left, as, "a 53 lmn[.]"

———

Consonants followed by any number under 100 as, "b 62" left half back takes the ball and goes straight ahead. If followed by letters as "b 62 adg" cut across.

———

Vowel followed by any number between 100 and 200, as ["]e 139" full back goes between center and right guard.—If followed by any letter as "e 172 abc" He goes around the right end.

On signal "m128" (m 128) full back between center and left guard. On "P 128 def" —he goes around the left end.

———

Right guard number is "1" third figure mentioned as, "6, 5, *1*, 4, 9. Left guard is "2" third figure mentioned—["]7, 3, *2*, 4, 9." Right tackle is "3"— 4, 8, *3*, 6, 0,—Left tackle "4"— 5, 9, *4*, 1, 8,—

Any number between 100 & 200 not preceded but followed by any letters, as, 187 efg,—full back kicks the ball.

The word "OBERLIN" after a signal has been given means that the signal is to be changed, and the right signal is given after the word—"Oberlin."[34]

Confusing? Heisman must have been aghast. His solution was to set up a series of plays in advance, which not only averted confusion but got the team off to a flying start, running its opponents ragged with a nonstop offense. Once in possession of the ball, he had the quarterback call a single number that set into motion the next six plays that were to be run off. The idea, a forerunner of a game plan, was to get a jump on the other team.[35]

Modern football was in the throes of being invented, refined, devised, and revised, and Heisman was already one of its able innovators. Like other great coaches of the day—in particular Amos Alonzo Stagg at Chicago and George Woodruff at Penn—Heisman not only created new ways to play the game but also was not averse to copying and improving on the ideas promulgated by counterparts at other colleges.

As the game of football evolved over the years, every coach adopted or adapted an offensive play or a defensive ploy if he couldn't come up with one of his own. In his first year as a coach, at Springfield College in 1890, Stagg had utilized his ends as runners, using them like halfbacks. Heisman readily copied the "theory."[36] Off the field, one of the first things he did was to set up a training table in a boarding house. It was similar to the one Walter Camp had established ten years earlier at Yale. The dinner meals Camp devised offered Yale players a choice of beefsteak or mutton washed down with milk, ale, or sherry.[37] Heisman's diet was similar, though it had to abide by the Oberlin ban on alcohol. His specifically avoided fried foods and pork but added potatoes and vegetables to the fare.[38] Such hearty fare was a far cry from the spartan diet first espoused at Oberlin more than half a century earlier. Fred Savage said legends grew in particular about one big lineman, a theology student—Savage didn't give his name but it had to be either John Wise or George Berry. He "used to break training by consuming an 8-pound basket of Concord grapes every night before going to bed." As a squad, Savage said, "the non-theological boys at least, we trained honestly."[39]

Savage credited Heisman with developing "real team play." The lightest man on the squad—he weighed only 140—Savage believed the only reason he made the varsity was because he was fast. "After they found out that I was pretty good, those big men on the team sort of took care of me, and kept me from being hurt."[40]

The one thing the veterans had learned for themselves from their 1891 experience was the need for endurance. "We saw that condition counted," Savage said. The players were determined not to be outlasted.[41] Vance McCormick, captain of Yale's powerful varsity that year, put it best: "Football is a test of endurance and there is only one way to train yourself to endure hardships, and that is by hard work in actual scrimmage to harden yourself for the supreme test. If a man is not physically able to play through the season and stand this test of endurance, then it is too dangerous for that man to engage in football as a sport and he should not be permitted to play."[42]

Heisman did not have much time to train the Oberlin squad before the opening game of the 1892 season scheduled for Saturday, October 15, at Oberlin. But in the few days that he had, he made an immediate impact on the team. Oberlin, the *Review* declared, was entering "a new era" of football "and all interested in the game, who had watched the severe practice to which our team has been subjected under Mr. Heisman's efficient coaching, prophesied a striking contrast with last year's style of playing."[43] The "eleven," it said, "has this year a developed system of play," thanks to Heisman "and his indefatigable assistants," manager Bert Hogen and quarterback Carl Williams. "The team is not in an invincible condition yet, but it has developed wonderfully in the past week."[44]

His time with the squad was so limited that Heisman decided not to make any substantial changes in the lineup that Hogen and Williams had come up with. The front seven were the same, but he did make a slight change in the backfield, deciding to go with Lou Hart at fullback and switching Fred Savage from that spot to left half.[45] In the future, the roster would prove more flexible as Heisman got to know the players. Only three men would play every minute of every one of the eight games on Oberlin's schedule—and only Hart would remain at the same position for the entire season.

For the opener, Carl Williams, as expected, was at quarterback. Two Academy students had made the starting lineup. One, Louisianian Thomas Winder Johnson,[46] was at right half, alongside Savage. The other, Ellsworth Westcott, centered the line, surrounded by Joe Teeters and John Wise at guard and Lynds Jones and George Berry at tackle. The ends were Will Merriam and Max Frank Millikan. The latter was a twenty-two-year-old junior, the son of parents who were both Oberlin graduates[47] and one of three brothers and three sisters who also attended the college.[48]

The Oberlin eleven's first opponent was Ohio State University.

7

HEISMAN BALL

End runs mean hard running for all. Therefore don't call for two end runs in succession. Give the boys a chance to catch their wind.
—John Heisman

Oberlin's student weekly credited Ohio State University with having a team that was "now in prime condition." The OSU squad, it said, had fielded a team the previous year that was already "one of the strongest foot ball elevens in the state."[1] The *Review*'s assessment was hyperbole—and not at all accurate.

On the surface, the university's involvement with football was strikingly similar to Oberlin's. OSU's president was worried about the frequent accidents that occurred in the game, as well as "another evil"—its "interference" with schoolwork. But he could not buck the craze for football that was sweeping the country. Student petitions at commencement time in 1890 finally won his grudging approval and the school played its first game that May against Ohio Wesleyan, winning 20–14.[2]

Despite its initial victory, OSU's football record was unspectacular. When its football season resumed several months later in the fall, it lost to Wooster, Denison, and Kenyon, scoring only ten points in the process; the Wooster game was a breathtaking 64–0 defeat. OSU began the 1891 season with a 50–6 loss to Adelbert and a 26–0 loss to Kenyon. It subsequently defeated Denison by a meager 8–4 score, then Buchtel 6–0, to end the year with a 2–2 record.[3] So how the *Review* could describe Ohio State in a superlative phrase is mystifying.

At the time, OSU's athletic facilities were rudimentary. The school, founded as the Ohio Agricultural and Mechanical College, had an enrollment that

A meaningful postcard from the 1890s: Oberlin rolling over Ohio State.

had burgeoned from seventeen students in 1873[4] to a total of 770 in the fall of 1892[5]—a huge increase in twenty years by any standard, though its student body was still half the size of Oberlin's. Until then, the school had no gym, not even a "proper" field upon which to play baseball or football. Student requests for a fenced-in field and grandstand were refused until, finally recognizing the Muscular Christianity view that "health is the student's best capital," its Board of Trustees agreed to turn a ball ground near a dormitory into an enclosed athletic field replete with a baseball diamond, football gridiron, and quarter-mile cinder track.[6]

As the OSU team took the field at Athletic Park for Oberlin's first game of the 1892 season, there was a familiar, friendly face accompanying the Ohio players. Jack Ryder, who had been so influential in winning football's acceptance at Oberlin before he transferred to Williams College, was OSU's coach, its first paid one at that.[7] There was also a new look to the field itself. A system of posts and ropes cordoned it off, to keep spectators from spilling onto the gridiron during play, an occurrence that had happened too frequently in the past.

Within less than three minutes after the game began, Oberlin's quarterback, Carl Williams, "crawled out of a tangle of legs and arms" for a touchdown.[8] Lou Hart's goal made the score 6-0.

OSU countered with a "circus" play that Ryder was credited with importing from his days at Williams. Six of the players made a small V at the extreme right of the line, protecting a halfback positioned in back of them. The quarterback lateraled the ball to the half, who then followed his blockers smack into the Oberlin line.[9] The OSU players tried the play seven times. It got them a six-yard gain twice, but they lost as much as twenty-five yards every other time they tried it against Oberlin's heavier line, which quickly adjusted to the play.

Heisman's maneuver of having his two guards pull out of the line to lead the blocking quickly proved effective when it resulted in a touchdown. Thomas Johnson was "literally carried himself by Teeters, with a street-car load on his back. Nearly the whole opposing team were treated to a free ride."[10] Five minutes after Johnson scored, the two guards—Teeters and Wise—led the way again as Lynds Jones went over for Oberlin's third touchdown. After that, each time Oberlin had the ball, it scored. One of the touchdowns was made by none other than Teeters himself. The first half ended with Oberlin ahead 28–0.

Between halves, the two teams agreed to limit the rest of the game to thirty minutes when play resumed. In the second half, OSU's players were visibly shaken, wasting time catching their breath "instead of putting the ball in play." Oberlin's front seven stopped OSU's offense on every play; before he came out of the game with an injury, Westcott, for one, "bothered" his counterpart at center "a great deal in passing the ball." And when Oberlin had the ball, they were unstoppable. At one point, Johnson bucked behind a block by Teeters "who went through the line like a stock train on a downgrade."

In all, Oberlin scored seven touchdowns before a student timekeeper inadvertently stopped the game two minutes before the agreed-upon time. ("The calculation of the intricacies of the stop watch," said the *Oberlin Review*, "was too much for a student who had systematically avoided calculus in college.")

The final tally—Oberlin 40, Ohio State 0—was a resounding success for the team and its new coach-player. Unheralded, Heisman, it turned out, had played in half the game. Neither the *Oberlin Review* account of the game nor the story in the *Oberlin News* a day later made any mention of his participation, although it is unlikely that either publication's sports reporter would not have recognized him. It wasn't until a month later that the *Review* disclosed Heisman's involvement. Why the secrecy? There may have been concern about Heisman's bogus status as a postgraduate student. Or he may not have been enrolled yet as a postgrad student and was ineligible.

Heisman's appearance as a player notwithstanding, his impact as coach was unmistakable. "A new phase of the foot ball question has been developed," the *Review* declared. "Our team showed plainly the result of training. Their work was far more systematic, more scientific, than last year."

Heisman himself was more than satisfied that his "experiment" of having Teeters and Wise lead the runners had paid off. "When those two 'big' guards of mine, followed by the entire backfield, assaulted the Ohio State flanks little remained to do except to count the score," he said. "That's what came of studying Heffelfinger."[11]

Sweet revenge was on everyone's mind at the second contest of the season, another home game, this one against Adelbert, which had defeated Oberlin in the season's finale the previous year and then refused to play a rematch. The game, played on Columbus Day, Friday, October 21, turned out to be the roughest one the Oberlin eleven had ever played, and charges of brutality on the part of both teams reverberated for weeks to come.

This time there was no coverup regarding Heisman, who at one point made a touchdown that was disallowed. Both he and Andrew Kell subbed at right end during the game.

The Adelbert game drew a large crowd despite the fact that that same afternoon Ohio's governor, William McKinley, was paying a visit to Oberlin for a Republican rally. Hundreds of students were at the local rail depot when the governor arrived at 1:30 in the afternoon. A procession followed, led by riders upon horses adorned with red, white, and blue bunting and streamers. McKinley dined at the home of a former colleague of his in the Ohio House of Representatives, Professor James Monroe. He then went to First Congregational Church, which was filled to overflowing, to talk on a favorite plank of the Republican party, tariff protection.[12]

Meanwhile, at the football field, there was a surprise visitor. Evidently because of the congestion around the depot caused by McKinley's visit, the Adelbert team was late in arriving. Its rooters along the sideline, however, were already creating a din when, of all people, Heisman's father, Michael, appeared. The son had caught the father "in a weak moment" the night before. They had argued about football, so the last thing he expected was for his father to show up "prepared to see what all the nonsense was about." Michael Heisman had never seen his son practice much less play at Titusville, Brown, or Penn. But he had decided, the younger Heisman said, "that inasmuch as I had rejected the practice of law and had dedicated my life to the game, there must be something to football. Anyway he'd see." He came to the game with Heisman's younger brother, Michael Jr.[13]

Heisman was overseeing his men as they ran through their offensive plays. He corrected the way a lineman blocked, showed a runner how to dodge tacklers, pointed out to the kicker the best way to take advantage of the wind. His father was visibly impressed:

He watched my Oberlin team speed through signal practice. His eyes popped a bit when he saw the ball soar in towering punts. Presently he came to me.

"The crowd seems to be for the other fellows. Do you think you'll win?"

"Yes," I replied casually, "I think so."

"You think so," he repeated. "Pretty sure of it? Your team's small. The crowd doesn't think much of your chances."

"What's the matter with you?" I demanded. "You're not a football fan, are you? What do you care who wins?"

"Oh, nothing," he said. "But I don't like this partiality. I'd like to see the big fellows licked."

The elder Heisman walked away. A few minutes later, brother Michael Jr. appeared:

"Say," he said, "if you ain't pretty sure you're going to take this game you'd better let me head Dad off."

"Dad? What's he doing now?"

"Oh, nothing except walking up and down in front of Western Reserve's cheering section waving hundred-dollar bills and daring them to back their team," sighed my brother.[14]

When the game finally got underway, it looked like Heisman's boast would backfire.[15] The first time it had possession of the ball, Oberlin was forced to kick. The ball, however, landed near the Adelbert goal, where its fullback fumbled it. John Wise, who had run from his position at left guard all the way downfield, dived for the ball but couldn't get a handle on it. As the ball rolled over the goal line, Will Merriam, who had followed Wise into Adelbert territory, fell on it for a touchdown.

The team was using the hurry-up offense devised by Heisman, and at one point drew a penalty when they lined up and were prepared to snap the ball before the Adelbert men were ready. The umpire, an Adelbert player-turned-official named Stage, thought the Oberlin team "ought to be *gentlemanly* enough to wait until Adelbert was ready." The truth, an observer said, was that Oberlin's game was "too fast," forcing Adelbert to stall and call time "on every pretext." But such delays failed to stop the Oberlin offense. Before the half was thirty minutes old, Oberlin scored two more times, both on runs by Savage.

Behind, 18–0, Adelbert finally managed a successful drive with bucking and double passes that led to its first score. But when Oberlin got the ball back, Savage bucked over the line from the five-yard line, turning a somersault as he landed because he wanted to make sure he had cleared the goal line. The score was now Oberlin 24, Adelbert 4.

As the second half opened, the Adelbert umpire Stage decided his team desperately needed support. So he doffed his officiating status as referee and went in to play at left end for Adelbert.

Stage apparently had not practiced much. His first run ended in a loss and his second a fumble. He never had another chance because when Oberlin had the ball and he was on defense, Joe Teeters rammed into him. Stage fell to the ground in pain. He had sprained his ankle. The Adelbert team was incensed, charging Teeters with "assault."

The incident inflamed both sides. Stage insisted that Teeters had not done anything illegal, but that did nothing to quell the animosities. Players on both sides repeatedly and intentionally fouled. Oberlin's Miles Eugene Marsh, who had started at center, had particular trouble with his opposite number on the Adelbert line. The man, Mathias, was nudging the ball a yard forward between downs when the umpire wasn't looking and then telling the umpire to make the Oberlin linemen stay on their side of the scrimmage line. When Marsh in turn complained, Mathias grew abusive and struck out at the Oberlin center with his fist. Marsh, a senior[16] who had a reputation for being the cleanest player on the team, then got so mad that he struck back and was charged with a foul and penalized. The abusive language and fouls were so intense that the players and spectators lost sight of the game itself.

Just before the first half ended, Merriam injured his shoulder and Heisman sent in "Cad" Andrew Bertram Kell[17] to take his place at right end. However, Heisman was evidently not satisfied with the youth's performance, for as the second half got underway, he himself stepped in for Kell. Except for one play, Heisman drew little attention. He thought he had made a safety, catching Adelbert's fullback on the five-yard line and forcing him back over the goal line. But the referee in the second half, an Adelbert man, would not allow it. Other than that, and the observation in the account in the *Oberlin Review* that he had played a "good game," Heisman was ignored.

Oberlin managed to score three more times in the second half, two on runs by Johnson and a final touchdown by Savage. That last score was made on another of Heisman's innovations, a variation on the popular wedge-style type of offense. It was, as he explained, "a smaller, secondary V which was to form when the primary wedge was destroyed." The second wedge had its premiere when Savage scurried behind it for fifty-five yards and a touchdown. "Something new," Heisman bragged, "had appeared beneath the October sun."[18]

The final score—Oberlin 38, Adelbert 8—was a vindication for the Oberlin men. As far as they were concerned, the Adelberts were sore losers. "An institution that cannot take defeat fairly without whining and getting mad is not worthy of very much respect," the *Oberlin Review* said.[19]

The violence that erupted during the game was forgotten. Not another word was said about it, probably because Oberlin, after all, had triumphed. As for Heisman's father, there is no indication how much he had won on the game.

The team got a breather the following week when the scheduled third game of the season, against Case on the Saturday following the Adelbert game, was canceled because of an injured Case player. "What is worse," the *Oberlin Review* reported, was that Adelbert cancelled a return game set for November in Cleveland, "presumably" because its team needed to practice more and were awaiting Stage's recovery from his sprained ankle. In the meantime, Oberlin fans could relish the fact that while Oberlin was beating Adelbert, Ohio State defeated Marietta 80–0 and Adelbert, later in a midweek game, trounced Buchtel 52–0.[20] Imagine how Oberlin would have stacked up against those teams!

As a result of the Case cancellation, the Oberlin varsity did not meet another opponent until Saturday, November 5, when the team traveled to Delaware, Ohio, to play Ohio Wesleyan.[21] The two-week hiatus gave Heisman the opportunity to shuffle his starters around. The switches daringly put three men into positions they had never played before.[22]

The team got off to an ominous start on the afternoon before the game. "Liberally provided with liniment and accident policies," they were more than halfway to the rail junction at Wellington, ten miles away, where they could catch a train south, when the front axle on the "big bus" hired from a local stable gave way under what the *Delaware Transcript*, in a bit of overstatement, called Oberlin's "200lb rush line." Undaunted, the players flung their satchels and helped their "cripples" onto an accompanying smaller wagon and those who were left walked the rest of the way to Wellington. By the time they reached Delaware, some twenty-odd miles north of Columbus, it was about 9:30 P.M. Fortunately, they were able to sleep late the next morning.

The game was a blowout and represented a landmark for Heisman. Lynds Jones scored before the game was two minutes old. Then, after Will Merriam recovered an Ohio Wesleyan fumble on the Oberlin 10-yard line and Jones and Fred Savage ran it all the way back to the OWU goal line, the Delaware players lined up expecting a buck. They "smiled in a sickly way" as Carl Williams rounded their line for a touchdown on a deceptive double pass Heisman had devised. Jones followed almost immediately with his second touchdown, shaking off tacklers as he raced to the goal line from the center of the field. Shortly after that, Savage, with George Berry running interference, scored. Before the half was over, both Williams and Jones each scored two more touchdowns, Williams on one that was another "fooler." The score at halftime was Oberlin 44, Ohio Wesleyan 0.

At the start of the second half, Heisman made a new round of switches that revolved around having Savage replace Williams at quarterback and putting Alabama-born Washington Irving Squire[23] in Savage's place at halfback. Joe Teeters got a chance again to carry the ball from his guard position and made twenty yards. Jones followed with thirty more, and Lou Hart scored on a buck from his fullback position. Ohio Wesleyan then came closest to scoring, running the ball all the way to Oberlin's twenty-five-yard line, where Squire, racing to tackle the OWU rusher, took a bad tumble. As Squire limped off the field, Heisman took his place.

OWU never got beyond the fifteen-yard line, and when Oberlin took over, Heisman gained more than thirty yards on two plays. He replicated that after Wise recovered a fumble, and several minutes later Heisman scored his first touchdown for Oberlin.

Shortly after, with Oberlin in possession once more, Heisman looked like he might score again. He made forty-five yards, but all of a sudden, although the half was only twenty-five minutes old, the officials halted the game. No reason was given, but it might have been an act of mercy. The final score was Oberlin 56, Ohio Wesleyan 0.

Oberlin's next two games were blowouts, too.

On Monday, November 7, two days after the resounding victory over Ohio Wesleyan, the Oberlin team traveled to Columbus to play a rematch with Ohio State.[24] A grandstand had been built on the university's new athletic field, which was now also surrounded by a fence.

The first encounter between the two teams had ended in a 40–0 win for Oberlin, but since then OSU's eleven, footballer-turned-sportswriter Steve Williams said, "have learned how to smash interference, how to block, and in a measure how to guard the runner."

"The Columbus team played as hard as they knew" but still were no match for Oberlin. Briefly put, although the OSU players "today understand the game as they never did before" and managed to get the ball "uncomfortably" near the Oberlin goal line, they never crossed it. The result was a 50–0 win for Oberlin.

Afterward, Oberlin alumni who lived in Columbus hosted a reception for the team. The gala proceedings made up somewhat for the reaction of the Ohio State students at the end of the game, when Oberlin's players exploded in a rousing cheer. "The crowd," a spectator said, "was so 'chumpy' as to hiss when the winning team yelled at the end."[25]

OSU's defeat was apparently so humiliating that it was conveniently forgotten. How else to explain that its media guide lists only the earlier 40–0 loss to Oberlin in 1892.[26]

The OSU game was another triumph for Heisman, who coached the entire game from the sidelines. He was singled out for "his full share of the praise which is his due."

Heisman missed the next game, against Kenyon College, five days later on Saturday, November 12, though why is not recorded. There is, however, one curious fact that might explain the reason for his absence. The Oberlin athletic association was paying for Heisman's incidentals: for example, $1.40 for a pair of cleated shoes, and 25 cents when they needed repairing. On the day of the Kenyon game, 15 cents was paid out for an "ear bandage" for him.[27] It is possible that Heisman may have been injured by an errant kick in practice.

Whatever the reason for his absence, Heisman had coached the team so effectively that the team had no difficulty whatsoever in beating Kenyon. Clearly, the successes he had engineered had whetted the appetite of his players for more. "Our boys played well," the Oberlin Review declared, "even without the guardian eye of St. Heisman watching over them."[28]

Kenyon was a picturesque school, modeled after Oxford University in England. It was situated on a pleasantly wooded plateau above the Kokosing River in Gambier, some forty miles northeast of Columbus.[29] Its pleasant

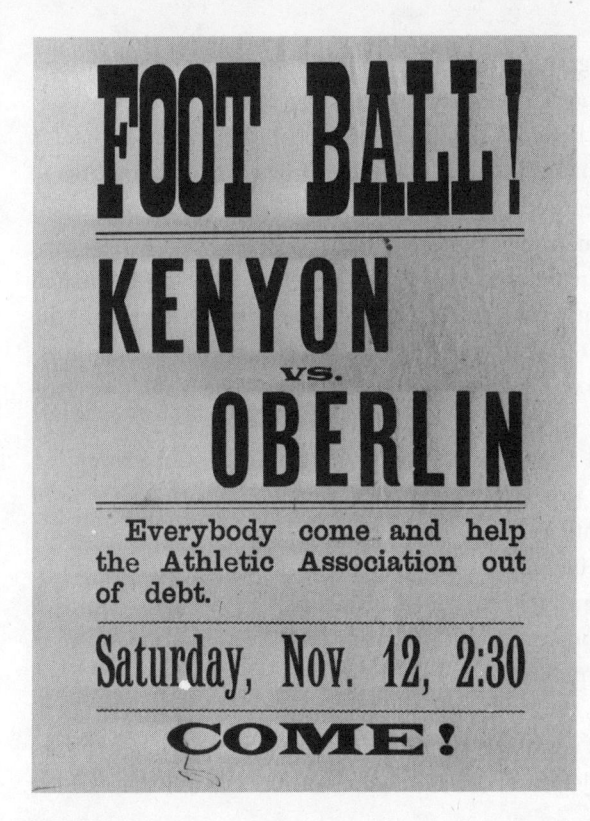

A perennial problem in the first years of Oberlin's intercollegiate sports program was the lack of money, as witness this poster for a home game with Kenyon College in 1892.

ambience, however, could not be fully appreciated. The day of the game was a gloomy one. The field was "a sea of mud" and the players "so thoroughly imbued with the ground that they seemed to be rooted" in it. Nevertheless, Oberlin had a 22–0 lead by halftime, and raised that to 38–0 by the time the game ended. Not only had every man in the backfield scored at least one touchdown, but John White, playing right guard, and George Berry, at left tackle, scored as well.

Without doubt, Oberlin had a team to be reckoned with. Only one team had scored against it in five games—Adelbert, which tallied a mere eight points. "Oberlin College is in high feather these days," crowed the *Elyria Democrat*: "She has eleven men of whom she is very proud. Who are they? Professors? No. Tutors? No. Theologs? No. Musical prodigies? No. They are the eleven men who represent her on the foot ball field. These men can command anything. They have the homage of the town. Just now a Greek root has no sort of show against an inflated pig skin, a row of Latin derivatives cannot stand a *V* wedge and a cosine and logarithm are smothered in the yells accompan[y]ing an eighty yard run around the end for a touch down."[30]

The *Oberlin Review* took a more sober attitude about the varsity's successes: "Every member of the team, every student of the institution, realizes the fact that athletics at Oberlin are in a critical position just now. We are making our reputation. The good work of our foot ball team so far this fall has added much to it, and has convinced outside institutions that Oberlin may become a considerable factor in intercollegiate athletics."[31]

The team itself defended its growing football reputation only four days after the Kenyon game when it took on Adelbert, which had finally agreed to a rematch, on Wednesday, November 16.[32] A large number of students and some members of the faculty—mostly from the Academy because college men had recitations—traveled to Cleveland by special train for the game.

There was fear that the ill will that marred the first game against Adelbert would lead to violence again. However, both teams may have been cautioned about a repetition, because no incidents occurred. From Oberlin's standpoint, the game was, instead, uninspired. Perhaps they were tired—certainly there was little time for rest between games—and injuries were taking their toll, because the Oberlin eleven played sloppily. Both Fred Savage and Lou Hart, each ordinarily a surehanded player, dropped the ball twice. So, in particular, did George Berry. Berry, taking over the left halfback spot for Lynds Jones, who was injured in the Kenyon game, was "unpracticed" and made several "expensive" fumbles. He entered the game suffering from an ear injury and finally had to leave in the second half.

Berry's departure prompted Heisman to make an almost wholesale reshuffling in the Oberlin lineup, with some men again having to switch to unaccustomed positions. The result was the poorest teamwork on offense the men had ever exhibited. Blocking was far from perfect, and runs were not so numerous or successful. But ultimately their training paid off. Oberlin's players were "like a stone wall" on defense, continually forcing Adelbert to lose the ball on downs or forcing it to kick. At one point, Adelbert tried for five points with a field goal, but John Wise and Carl Williams broke through the line and tackled its fullback before he could get the kick off.

The first half was more than half over before a touchdown was scored. By halftime, Oberlin led, 6–0. It managed to rack up ten more points in the second half, winning 16–0. In contrast to its previous games, the team made only three touchdowns in all. But it held Adelbert scoreless. And it was a victory. Oberlin was unbeatable.

The stakes were high as Oberlin's team prepared for its final game of the season, against the University of Michigan. The Wolverines expected another pushover, an even greater one than its 26–6 victory in 1891. But Oberlin was determined, if not optimistic. The game was crucial, the most important one the team ever faced. "Now is the time," the *Oberlin Review* declared: "If we win the game or make a strong fight for it, the respect of all the great institutions with which we are associated will be assured. If we are thus recognized as worthy of regard as an equal on the athletic field, we shall have far less difficulty in securing games with these leading colleges in the future than we have had in the past. We shall be able to have a number of games with such institutions each year, and that will help our athletic association at home, financially, as well as give greater standing to Oberlin in the general College world."[33]

Oberlin's standing "in the general College world" was not just a matter of concern to its students. Undoubtedly encouraged by the publicity that the football team was receiving, faculty members were flexing their muscles as well, taking "measures" to assure the school of "more satisfactory representation" in newspapers, "especially those" in eastern cities. It evidently had finally dawned on Oberlin's professors and its administrators that—as the experience at other schools was demonstrating—the football team was an asset with benefits that could accrue to the entire college. "The news as to what Oberlin is doing," they chauvinistically agreed, "ought to be sought by outsiders as much as the news of Yale or the University of Michigan."[34]

There was reason for Oberlin to be optimistic about the upcoming game. Michigan's record in the 1892 season was spotty. Its schedule was the most demanding the Wolverines had ever attempted, with a total of twelve games in all, the contest with Oberlin being its final one. The Wolverines had won six of those games, trouncing Wisconsin, DePauw, Albion, Chicago, and twice the Michigan Athletic Association. But it had also lost four games, to Minnesota, Northwestern, and twice to Cornell. A game against Purdue was forfeited in mid-play, with Purdue ahead 24–0, when four Michigan players were injured and there were no substitutes left to take their places. One of those injured was Michigan's much-heralded star halfback, freshman George H. Jewett, the first black at the university to win a football letter.[35] He was, however, expected back in the lineup for the Oberlin game.

Despite its record, Michigan entered the game cocky. The university's daily, the *Oberlin News* noted, "promised the spectators a very good practice game. Perhaps Oberlin would score, more probably not. At any rate Ann Arbor would run up a score into the seventies."[36]

What no one expected, however, was the way the game ended, and how each school, to this day, remembers it.

8

"UNBLUSHING EFFRONTERY"

*In no game and in calling is there so strong a temptation for a participant
to cheat, to take unfair advantages, to do small, petty, mean things,
to lose temper, to indulge in profanity, to quarrel, to show a nasty disposition,
and even to resort to downfighting, as in football.*
—*John Heisman*

The afternoon of Saturday, November 19, was cold and grim. Although a blizzard threatened, nearly seven hundred Michigan spectators were on the sidelines, including more than a score of fans from Toledo who had arrived aboard the private car of the manager of the Toledo and Ann Arbor Railroad.[1]

It was so cold that the Oberlin team wore canvas coats as they took the field shortly after two o'clock. Heisman himself was in uniform and planning to start. George Berry was still suffering from an ear injury, prompting Heisman to devise another shift in the backfield. Fred Savage was filling in for Berry at left half, and Thomas Johnson was taking Savage's regular spot at right half. Heisman replaced Johnson at left end.

The Wolverines were already on the field, and after both teams took some preliminary practice, they lined up, ready to play. Unlike the previous season, the Oberlin team outweighed the Michigan eleven. The Wolverines won the toss, taking the ball, while Oberlin got the west goal to defend with the wind at their backs for the first half.

It was an exciting, spirited game. The game opened with Michigan massing their men on the line as its leading runner-cum-kicker George Jewett tried going around Oberlin's left end. Heisman made a "brilliant tackle" to stop him, and after an offside play by Michigan, Oberlin took over the ball.

John White bucked for eight yards, then Joe Teeters for twelve, before a fumble gave the ball to Michigan again. At that point with a player injured, time was called. The incident that followed illustrated the disadvantage of employing a partisan referee, rather than a paid, professional one, to officiate the game.

Believing that play was halted, Oberlin's captain, Carl Williams, was actually talking to the referee, Horace Prettyman—the same veteran Wolverine footballer who had officiated at the first Oberlin-Michigan game in 1891— when, suddenly, Michigan's center snapped the ball and Jewett ran forty-five yards unopposed for a touchdown. Though he didn't even see it, Prettyman granted the score. Williams immediately objected, appealing for fair play. But Prettyman, in a rather snooty response, answered, "My deah boy, I have played moah foot ball than evah heard of. Reflect. Keep cool." The touchdown and a successful two-points-after also made by Jewett made the score 6–0 with the game less than four minutes old.

Oberlin opened its next possession with a V wedge, Savage gaining twelve yards. On the next play, Williams made a double pass, but Prettyman ruled that he had advanced the ball before lateraling it, and that put the ball back in Michigan's hands. On its first play, however, Jewett fumbled. With Oberlin back in possession, White, Teeters, Lou Hart, and Heisman each made small gains, taking the ball to Michigan's ten-yard line. Then, on a fake, Williams ran around end for Oberlin's first score. Hart kicked the goal. The game was now tied 6–6.

It was apparent that Oberlin's line was outplaying Michigan's. It opened up huge holes in the Michigan defense on bucks, and four or five linemen easily pulled from their positions to guard backs on end runs. On defense, Oberlin's men were tackling low, bringing down a runner on the spot, while the Wolverine tacklers were tackling high and being dragged several yards before they downed a ball carrier.

Back in possession, Michigan was forced to punt. At least six times Oberlin made gains, but each time Prettyman called the ball back on the ground that its center, Ellsworth Westcott, had not snapped it back properly. Thomas Johnson's sprint around left end for ten yards was finally allowed, and Heisman followed it with five yards on his own. Westcott himself then scored on an impromptu trick. He was prepared to hike the ball but realizing that his quarterback wasn't positioned to receive it, Westcott paused, tucking the ball between his legs as the Oberlin backs started in motion. Westcott then grasped the ball tightly in both hands and ran with it across the goal line. But Prettyman called him back for running out of bounds, although Westcott appeared to be a good three feet from the sideline.

(Standing nearby, Heisman registered Westcott's spontaneous response and later turned it into his favorite trick play. In the version he came up with, when the backs started in motion in one direction, the center would pause with the ball, then pass it to an end who sprinted the other way. Heisman used the trick successfully for ten years, until a change in rules outlawed it by demanding that the center put the ball into play at once.[2])

Again, as Michigan took possession, Oberlin's defense held. Jewett made eight yards on a run, but his teammates could not follow through with a first down. The ball exchanged hands twice until Oberlin drove to the Michigan twenty-yard line. From there Fred Savage ran the ball in, and Hart's goal was good. Oberlin now had the lead, 12–6.

Michigan was able to retaliate quickly. Jewett scored his second touchdown on a run from twenty yards out, but his kick failed, so the Wolverines were still behind 12–10.

Just as swiftly, Oberlin scored. Savage, John Wise, Clate Fauver, and Hart took the ball down to the Michigan goal line, where Wise rushed over for four points. Hart's kick added two more points. The score was now 18–10 in Oberlin's favor.[3]

Michigan was being outgeneraled and outfought. The Wolverines, under pressure, reacted violently, and the game suddenly degenerated into an ugly clash with any sense of fair play abandoned. Michigan's left tackle, a man named Pierson who was "famous" as a "slugger," punched Savage in the face, and then, "not satisfied" with doing that, struck the umpire, Oberlin's Orin Ensworth, in the face, too. Pierson was thrown out of the game.

A few minutes later, Michigan's Jewett advanced the ball to within a foot of the goal line, and Prettyman, without any hesitation, ruled he had scored a touchdown. Oberlin protested. Ignoring the complaint, Prettyman told Jewett to proceed with a kick after touchdown, which he successfully completed this time. The score was now Oberlin 18, Michigan 16.

Teeters had sprained his knee in the last scrimmage, so Clate Fauver moved over to right tackle and Lou Fauver took his brother's position at left tackle. Oberlin was able to advance the ball twenty-four yards, but Prettyman called another offside play against Oberlin and turned the ball over to Michigan. The Wolverines were able to score and kick a goal. Michigan now resumed the lead, 22–18.

Undaunted by what they considered Prettyman's flagrant officiating, the Oberlin players again went on the offensive. Savage made twenty-five yards around left end, and Hart bucked three times, gaining as many yards himself. The ball was now on Michigan's one-yard line with a minute left in the first half when the Wolverines' manager delayed the game by talking to the

Ann Arbor captain, thus allowing the clock to run out and preventing Oberlin from scoring.

The second half began after a fifteen-minute intermission and an agreement by both captains to stop the game at 4:50 so that the Oberlin players could catch the last train back to Oberlin and be on hand for Sabbath services the next morning—the same arrangement they had made in their 1891 contest.

Turnovers by both sides started the second half, and twice Prettyman penalized Oberlin for offside plays and returned the ball to Michigan. Each time, however, the Wolverines were unable to make a first down.

Oberlin was back in possession on its own five-yard line when Williams passed the ball to Savage. Will Merriam blocked off Michigan's left end and Savage set off downfield around him.[4] Galloping, Savage dodged a host of Michigan players, zigzagging through the field, until Jewett caught up with him and pulled him down at the Michigan's five-yard line after a run of ninety yards. It was, even Michigan fans conceded, "the phenomenal play of the day."[5] But again, Prettyman twice penalized Oberlin, once for intentional delay of the game, then for being offside. That put the ball back on Michigan's fifteen-yard line.

Keenly aware that time was running out, Carl Williams clearly had no intention of Oberlin's scoring fast and then letting Michigan get the ball back again. He leisurely gave out the signal for the next play, sending Heisman on a five-yard gain. As the teams faced off again, with now about two minutes left to play, Williams then quickly worked a double pass to Johnson who set off on a dash around right end and across the Michigan goal.

The score was tied, 22–22. The time was 4:49. The half was only twenty minutes old, but there was only one minute remaining in the agreed-upon deadline. Hart punted out to Fauver, who made a fair catch. That took thirty seconds. The Michigan timekeeper, a fellow named Spangler, told the Oberlin timekeeper that he did not think there was enough time for Oberlin to try for the extra points—"only 15 seconds left to kick a goal," he shouted.[6] But the Oberlin team lined up quickly and, cool as a cucumber, Hart put the ball over the crossbar for the extra points. Oberlin had recaptured the lead, 24–22, with only a few seconds left to play.

Both schools are still arguing about what happened next.

While the teams were going to the center of the field to resume play, the Oberlin timekeeper said time had run out—it was 4:50—and Ensworth, acting as referee in the second half, called the game. Oberlin had won.

Not so, Michigan thought. Spangler said that four minutes were left because that much time had been taken out for delays of the game. In response, the Oberlin players pointed out that both teams had agreed to stop the game at 4:50. The game was over. There was a train to catch. They had won.

As the rejoicing Oberlin players trotted off the field, the Wolverines lined up and, without a single soul to oppose them, snapped the ball. Jewett walked the pigskin over the Oberlin goal line for Michigan's fifth touchdown. Michigan, their players insisted, had won, 26–24. "Oberlin compromised herself by leaving the field before time was up," claimed the *University of Michigan Daily*, which expressed "great regret" at the way the game ended: "Referee Ensworth, an Oberlin substitute, lost all tab of time, and called the game at 14 minutes to 5, while the captain of each team had agreed to play until 10 minutes of that hour. Time-keeper Spangler also varifies [*sic*] this. Captain Williams called his men off the field and they immediately got into the bus and were driven to their hotel. All expostulations with the Oberlin captain and manager were of no avail."[7]

The Michigan paper said that Oberlin's players ran off the field "so quickly that it almost seemed pre-arranged." The *Detroit Tribune* took the same tack, saying "the losers" left the field "two minutes before time was called." Michigan won "by forfeit."[8]

On the other hand, Oberlin was just as confident that it had won the game fairly. Michigan's claims were "unblushing effrontery."[9] Prettyman, the *Oberlin Review* said, "was their best man by far. Three touch downs and more ground gained for Michigan than any other man on the team is his record." It continued:

He called time before Michigan made their first touch down, and if he will notice, at that time Capt. Williams was *off side* speaking to him, and therefore instead of Jewett making that brilliant 45 yard run you read about there was in any case only a five yard gain for offside playing. So Prettyman instead of Jewett must be credited with the first Ann Arbor touch down.

When Westcott fooled the whole team and Mr. Prettyman with the boundary trick the only hole that he could crawl out of was to say that Westcott had run out of bounds after he touched the ball in. Why even Mr. Prettyman would know enough not to do that if he had a clear field, we think. Touch down number two for Mr. Prettyman. And when Capt. Williams made a touch down from a double pass it must have taken a truly heroic effort to shut his eyes to the double pass, and call a foul. But it was so. Score the third touch down for Prettyman. No individual player can win a game but Prettyman came near doing it.

"The fact is that the whole Michigan team, counting the referee, was out played," the *Review* declared. Jewett, it said, carried "a hypothetical ball over a hypothetical goal line" and then "magnanimously" refused to kick a goal. "Here is the only instance where Ann Arbor failed to take all she could get— probably Prettyman had left the field or those two points would never have been wasted."[10]

To this day, Michigan counts the game against Oberlin as a 26–24 victory.[11] And to this day, Oberlin counts the game an Oberlin victory, 24–22,[12] and cause for celebration. Indeed, that Saturday night, when news of the victory over Michigan reached the town by telegraph, "the exuberance" of "youthful spirits" went—by Oberlin standards—overboard. Students raided every pile of boxes and barrels outside of every building and soon a "monstrous bonfire" lit up the campus and attracted a cheering crowd of onlookers that included both students and professors. There were speeches, and then, when the fire burned low, a band led the spirited throng in a march to call out other faculty members, including the school's president, from their homes. The excited celebrants gave three cheers for every member of the starting team, for the team's substitutes, for Hogen its manager, for Heisman, and even for Prettyman. After all, Oberlin had won.

The 1892 season was, the *Oberlin Review* proclaimed, the college's "red letter year."[13] The varsity had scored 262 points to its opponents' 30. It was undefeated in all seven of the games it played. Heady stuff indeed! Oberlin College's varsity had, in little more than a month, gained a national reputation. The school's name was bruited about from coast to coast. The football team had achieved for Oberlin what every college was hoping its team could inspire: recognition, prestige, envy—gilt by association.

The celebration in Oberlin went on unabated. Ladies furnishings in Edward Brothers' store window on West College Street gave way to crimson and gold bunting on which the scores of the varsity's triumphs were arranged, with the tally of the Michigan victory in the center. A local insurance agent gave an oyster supper to the team members.[14] Fred Savage, who—alone with Lou Hart and Thomas Johnson—had played every minute of every game, went home to Churchville, New York, to be regaled at a "Conundrum Tea" in the Congregational Church. It included appetizers such as "Bottled Tears" (horseradish) and "A State of difficulty" (pickle) and such staples as "Bostons

The undefeated Oberlin eleven—the 1892 varsity coached by John Heisman, who also played in several of its contests. *Back row (from left):* Louis Hart, Louis (Lou) B. Fauver, Will Merriam, Bert Hogen, John H. White, George Berry, Orin W. Ensworth. *Second row:* John Heisman, Lynds Jones, Josiah (Joe) C. Teeters, Miles E. Marsh, Clayton (Clate) K. Fauver, John Wise, Thomas W. Johnson. *Bottom row:* Washington Irving Squire, Fred Savage, Carl Williams, Ellsworth B. Westcott, Max F. Millikan, Harry Zimmerman, Andrew B. Kell. The woolen cap that Berry is wearing was the only kind of "helmet" that was acceptable.

Ideal Dish" (beans), "The Unruly Member" (tongue), "What falls from a Woodman's Axe" (potato chips), and "Murphy in a Stew" (potatoes). Desserts ranged from "The result of a squeeze" (jelly) to a "Musical Cake" (doughnut) with "Impertinence" (sauce).[15]

Savage was back in Oberlin when the faculty of the Conservatory, assisted by the college Glee Club, gave a benefit concert in Oberlin's Second Church to raise money for the next football season. The choir railing was draped in crimson and gold, and from the center of the bunting a football tied with ribbons of the same colors was suspended. In the midst of the performance, the football team "in full 'battle array'" leaped onto the platform to act as a chorus while Savage, who regularly performed as the bass singer in a vocal quartet, recounted in rhyme the victories.[16]

There was also a special get-together in the evening of the Wednesday after the Michigan game. Oberlin's mayor, a book-and-wallpaper-store proprietor named A. G. Comings, had the entire team to his home for a party. Refreshments were served, the Glee Club sang several songs, then John W. Mott, president of the student athletic association, called on Heisman to speak.

The hero of the season, John Heisman talked for a few minutes, "plainly and seriously, on the future of our athletics," an eyewitness said, and after brief words by the mayor and a faculty member, Bert Hogen took over the proceedings. The football manager talked about the work that Heisman had done with the team, and then, in a gesture meant to repay him in some fashion for the glory he had brought Oberlin, Hogen concluded by presenting Heisman "with the purse which the students and the Glee Club had raised as a slight testimonial of their appreciation of the work which he had done with the team." The party concluded with everyone giving three hurrahs for Heisman and shouting out the cheers of Oberlin and the coach's alma mater, the University of Pennsylvania.[17]

There is no indication how much money the students had raised by passing the hat, but it obviously was not enough. At the height of Oberlin's euphoria, Heisman was leaving for more lucrative employment. He'd evidently been approached and offered $750 to become the director of athletics, and the school's first football coach, at Buchtel College in Akron, some forty miles southeast of Oberlin. He had not decided what to do yet, but his commitment to Oberlin was over—for the moment at least.

9

THE WINNING SPIRIT

Make melody for thrilling anecdote.
(Of battered noses and of broken bones.)
In tuneful strains relate the valiant deeds
(The skillful punting and the dashing bucks,) ...
The furious onslaught of eleven foes,
(Reserve went down, Columbus bit the dust—) ...
—Paul Leaton Corbin, Class of '03

ootball had put Oberlin College on the map in a way no other event since the Civil War period had. Everyone—teachers and students alike—now had something to crow about.

In the spring, when the Columbian Exposition opened in Chicago to enormous crowds, the school took a booth in the grandiose Industrial Building. Handsomely furnished with a bright canopy of crimson and gold, the Oberlin booth was near those of Harvard, Yale, Princeton, and the University of Michigan. On its wall, enlarged views of the school's former and present buildings were displayed. A huge revolving globe showed the many places over the world from which Oberlin drew its students, and a series of statistical diagrams illustrated the growth of the college and enumerated the various occupations of its alumni. The booth, it was reported, attracted "many casual visitors and has probably done much to spread the general reputation of the college."[1]

For students, the national attention stimulated feelings not only of pride but also, in one case at least, snobbishness. Members of the class of '94 tried to take on the airs of an Ivy League school. In an attempt to emulate the senior class at a number of other schools—among them, Harvard, Yale,

Princeton, and Dartmouth—the Oberlin seniors voted to wear caps and gowns around the campus.[2] Their desire was not to arouse "town and gown" discrimination, the *Oberlin Review* explained, but rather to establish a custom that would "add to the picturesqueness and dignity of college life."[3] A similar proposal spawned at Northwestern supposedly prompted students there to advertise for books on the "Etiquette of the Mortarboard and Gown" because "they are troubled as to how the cap should be lifted and what is the proper mode of crossing a muddy street."[4] But Oberlin's president, William Ballantine, saw no humor in the idea and promptly squashed it. He objected that, among other things, the wearing of cap and gown would tend to pit the students of other classes against the seniors.[5]

One thing is clear. The team's success fed into student agitation for more of the kind of freedoms that students at other, less pious schools across the country were demanding and getting. Oberlin's students were becoming more vociferous, seeking more concessions—and sometimes getting them. They were able to convince the school to eliminate the heavy noon meal, for one. A successful trial was made at several boarding houses to make the six o'clock dinner the major repast of the day. As a result, the *Review* said, "lunch at noon left none of the disagreeable after-feeling of a hearty meal, while the dinner, coming when most needed and best enjoyed, was not necessarily interfered with by immediate study."[6]

The students also succeeded in having the school agree to an extension of the 10 P.M. curfew, which the *Review* had decried as a "superfluous restriction." No student, it insisted, had any desire to make late hours "far into the night" a custom "as it has in some institutions." That evil "seems to arise out of other evils, card playing, drinking, etc., which the ten o'clock rule in itself is powerless to affect." No sooner did the faculty agree to extend the curfew by half an hour than the students demanded a further "series of extensions of a half hour each."[7]

Make no mistake, though. Oberlin was still a serious-minded community. A nationwide prohibition movement became an organizational reality when the Anti-Saloon League of Ohio was organized in Oberlin's First Church just before classes began in September 1893. Within a year, the Oberlin Temperance Alliance had a hand in the formation of more than 240 local leagues throughout Ohio. Nationwide, the league became an unrivaled public pressure group, one of the most influential, if not the most influential, lobbies in America.

But while the fame associated with Oberlin's victories on the gridiron brought welcome attention to the school and boosted morale on the campus, ambivalence over the benefits and disadvantages of football still stirred strong reactions. In mid-November 1892, while the football season was in swing, two of the college's literary societies held debates on the subject, to a mixed response. One debate was on the question of whether school athletics "are detrimental to the best interests of the college." The negative, in support of football, won it. The other debate was on whether "foot ball as a college sport should be discouraged." The affirmative, against the sport—led, oddly enough, by the varsity's manager, Bert Hogen, and one of its star running backs, Lynds Jones—won that one.[8]

Another thing is clear. The faculty might still question the extent of Oberlin's commitment to football, but it was no longer an obstacle. A yearbook spoof entitled the "Faculty Foot-Ball Team," dreamed up by the class of '95, poked fun at the professors without, obviously, alienating them. The satire could not have been written, or appreciated, just a few years earlier. The captain of the faculty team was, of course, the college president, William Ballantine, who played left halfback. The other halfback was the college librarian. The director of the Conservatory was the fullback. A math professor played center, while another math teacher was left tackle. The quarterback was a professor of metaphysics. His backup was an associate professor of English. Another English teacher played right end on the fictional squad:

Ballantine does most of the bucking and double-pass work, as Root is too fast for such plays. At full back, Rice is a fair runner and as a kicker is unsurpassed in the West. He takes great interest in the team but insists on using classical signals. In fact, the only difficulty in the team has been over the signals. Every man wanted to use a different set. Anderegg devised a set of signals from Trig. Roe wanted to use some simple expressions from Schroeder's "Logik," such as unter-begriff-halten, saying that the Juniors would never understand them, and Rice insisted on the use of scales prepared by his advanced harmony class, but Ballantine refused them both, saying he was neither a Dutchman nor a singer. Magoun produced a set of signals by a mixture of Sanskrit and Irish stories, but the team couldn't learn the Sanskrit and didn't see any sense in the stories. Thomas and Cressy put together their favorite quotations from Shakespeare, and the team tried them. Ballantine, in despair, tried to use his new canons but Anderegg said if they didn't agree with Mill, they were N.G. . . . A few of the best [signals] used were: "Close now," meant off kick; a buck, was "hin mack a muck"; a double-pass, "cos A 1.41592 sine 0"; right end run, "ha rju anta"; a left end run, "Die Logik der Beziehungen."[9]

As for participation in physical exercises in general, the school's experience with football was obviously proving beneficial to the student body as a whole. After a year in office, Oberlin's director of athletics, Dr. Fred E. Leonard—"sponge carrier" on the imaginary faculty team—reported that "interest in athletics has been increasing with as yet few signs of those excesses and irregularities which have caused uneasiness among educators in the East." Both varsity and class football games in the fall of 1892 had furnished sixty male students with from one to two hours of "vigorous open-air exercise each day," he said. What accidents had occurred "were trivial in nature, and were the cause of only one case of absence from classes." And, in answer to the question of whether football undermined studies, Leonard proudly declared that six of the sixteen men on the varsity squad "reached a standing of over 90 per cent in their studies for the same term, and ten exceeded 80 per cent."[10]

For all the glory that the 1892 football team had brought Oberlin, the student athletic association was still strapped for funds. Expenses mounted rapidly, especially for football. Each ball cost $5, an inflator $1 more. Board at the training table came to $6.05. The sums seem minor, but they and the outlay for sundry items such as liniment, ankle supports, shin guards, and bills from doctors who treated injured players added up quickly. Uniforms for the team cost a total of nearly ninety dollars. In addition, the team's travel expenses and game guarantees ate up hundreds of dollars. The association paid $75 for Ohio State's team to travel to and from Columbus for the first Oberlin-OSU game in 1892. The game brought in $148.62, but the cash loss from it and the Ohio Wesleyan game came to $60.58. The cash loss from the Michigan game alone was $81.50. The association had to offer Adelbert a $75 guarantee for the first Oberlin-Adelbert contest. The game brought in $220, but the second match between the two teams, in Cleveland, cost $61.75 in rail and hotel expenses. The Kenyon game brought in $86.46, but Kenyon got $71.85 of that as reimbursement for travel costs and its share of the gate receipts.[11]

The only recourse the athletic association had was to raise the admission to home games in 1893 from twenty-five to thirty-five cents, which, considering a prolonged industrial depression that year and Oberlin's own financial condition that fall, was a steep increase.[12] The school might brag that it was "unquestionably the first college in Ohio," but like other institutions in the state it was experiencing the repercussions of a nationwide recession. Panic over the depletion of government gold reserves precipitated a sudden, dramatic crash on the New York Stock Exchange in June 1893. Before the year ended, almost five hundred banks and more than fifteen thousand commercial institutions had failed. In the wake of the panic, Oberlin saw total enrollment for the new 1893–94 academic year down by ninety-five students, a nearly 7 percent drop from the previous year. The hope was that the construction of "electric roads"—a trolley line—between Oberlin and the shores of Lake Erie about a dozen miles to the north would prove a boon to the college's summer school, which the faculty was already contemplating ways to enlarge.[13]

The other hope was in the football team. Oberlin, under Heisman, had drawn national attention. Locally, its successes had apparently quieted the opposition to the sport. How long would that last? Was the team's performance in 1892 a fluke? Could it repeat its spectacular victorious season?

Seven members of the football varsity had graduated the previous June, and an eighth, captain and quarterback Carl Williams, had transferred to the University of Pennsylvania on the recommendation of John Heisman.[14] One of the graduates, Joe Teeters, was still in Oberlin in the autumn of 1893, studying as a postgraduate and could have played, but he confined his extracurricular activities to coaching the varsity's scrub team.[15]

Gone, too, was the team's manager, Bert Hogen, another recent graduate. Taking his place was Charles (Charley) Clark Brackin, a senior with only limited experience in playing football: his only connection with the game was as quarterback on his class team three years earlier.[16]

There was another newcomer on the playing field, a new football coach. He was E. B. (Jake) Camp, who was hired during the latter part of August.[17] Unlike Brackin, Camp was well grounded in the game: he had played left halfback for seven years, the first four with Lafayette College, the rest with the University of Pennsylvania, where he had known Heisman. During the last Penn-Princeton game, Camp had scored the touchdown that gave Penn its first win ever over Princeton.[18] It is possible, in fact, that Heisman—already committed to Buchtel—recommended him to Brackin and the student athletic association.

The details of Camp's contract are unrecorded. He was, as it turned out, not signed for the entire season. The reason evidently was the athletic association's precarious financial situation. Camp, who was living in Chicago, was due to arrive at Oberlin on Monday, October 2, when the "real work and training" was to begin.[19]

The largest contingent in the team's brief history turned out for the varsity to greet Camp—in all, thirty prospects. There were eight veterans from the 1892 team who showed up on the practice field. Clate Fauver, the team's reliable left tackle, was back. His teammates from 1892 included his brother

Lou, Orin Ensworth, Thomas Johnson, Andrew Kell, John White, and Will Merriam. The last, Merriam, had been elected captain of the team at the end of the previous season, but he felt unqualified for the job and had just resigned. Clate Fauver was chosen to replace him.[20]

In addition, Lynds Jones, who had spent the summer as a "charioteer" pushing deck chairs at the Chicago fair, was back; though he had graduated from the college, he was a seminarian now and eligible to play.[21]

There were three other familiar names. Charles Borican, a sub on the 1891 varsity, had played with his class team in 1892 and had returned to try for a starting spot on the varsity. Steve Williams, who had played in three of the games in 1891 "during which," he said, "I hung on by my eyelids,"[22] was back after sitting out the 1892 season. He was hoping to win the quarterback spot now that Carl Williams—no relation—was gone. Howie Regal, the 1891 team's fullback and mainstay kicker, was trying out for his old position.

Regal, who "hustled mail" during summer recess, had just returned from Chicago, where he participated in a championship meet held in conjunction with the world's fair. He took second place in the broad jump.[23] Another Oberlin student at the Chicago meet, a new candidate for the team, was the swift Ernest Howard Boothman. "Boothie" or "Boosie" or "Boozie," as he was variously known,[24] made it to the finals in the 75-yard dash and took third place in the 150-yard dash.[25] He was one of fourteen new candidates hoping to make the varsity. Five of the prospects were from the Academy—two who had graduated and were now freshmen in the college, and three who were still in the preparatory school.

Jake Camp had only five days to prepare for what was going to be a difficult schedule. A week before his arrival, the Oberlin faculty voted to permit the varsity to play ten games, seven of them out of town. The away games included three contests on a projected western trip that would pit Oberlin against Northwestern, Chicago, and Illinois.[26]

One school, though, Oberlin had no intention of playing: Michigan. The previous year's controversial game was won, the *Oberlin Review* declared, "in the face of slugging players, dishonest refereeing and tricky stopwatches." Michigan had snidely suggested a return match "for Oberlin's benefit." Charley Brackin offered two dates to the university but the Wolverines suddenly withdrew their offer "for no reason whatsoever." As far as Oberlin was concerned, that was just as well. "Owing to previous experience," the *Review* said, "we side with the majority of colleges and prefer not to play on Ann Arbor grounds. As Cornell declined to meet U. of M. on home grounds, for obvious reasons, there is a perfectly safe precedent established." Oberlin would

The versatile Clayton (Clate) King Fauver played both line and back-field positions, was captain of the 1893 and 1894 varsities, was a member also of the 1895 squad, and in 1896 became the team's coach.

be "delighted" to play Michigan "on any neutral field with neutral umpires, on any dates not already reserved."[27]

During the summer, some work had been done to soften the football field, which had been the cause "of many hard bruises" in the past. There was now more opportunity to practice falling on the ball "in which the team was extremely weak last year." Practice actually started two weeks before Camp's arrival, but without a coach to oversee the training, teamwork fell by the wayside and almost everyone was criticized for being in poor playing condition. Even Clate Fauver, before he was elected captain, was censured for being "slow in following the ball."

On the eve of Oberlin's first game of the season, a home game against Kenyon on Saturday, October 7, Jake Camp had still not picked a starting lineup. He has been "doing good work with the team, paying particular attention to the interference," the *Oberlin News* reported. But, it said, "there is no place in the team that belongs to any one man."[28] The *Oberlin Review*'s new sports reporter, one-time footballer Washington Irving Squire, predicted that the Kenyon game was not going to be a "walk over, as our team is too new to be expected to play a steady game, though they can play a long one."[29]

The question on everybody's mind was whether the team could play up to the standards set by John Heisman the previous year.

10

CAMP TIME

Old boy! here's my hand.
All hail the high kicker!
—Anonymous, "Hi-O-Hi"

The pressure was enormous. The Oberlin football team had experienced the glory of victory. But all the publicity the men had attracted had its downside, too. Winning was now all the more important. The players were under pressure to repeat the undefeated 1892 season, to do even better, as if that were possible. The pressure was both internal and external, for it wasn't only the varsity men who felt "they must play up to last year's record," the *Oberlin Review* said. "Surrounding colleges assume from last year's record that we have the strongest team in Ohio, and expect our team to equal, even to surpass last year's standards." If Oberlin were to play football at all—"and who would see it abolished?"—she had to maintain a certain standard of play.[1]

Under a burden like that, Jake Camp was understandably nervous. As the team took to the field for the opening game of the 1893 season against Kenyon, a large, eager, noisy hometown crowd was on hand at Athletic Park. What miracle could he wrought after only four days of practice?[2]

The starting team that Camp sent out was, overall, lightweight for a college eleven. It averaged only 158 pounds.[3] By comparison, that fall Harvard's team averaged 173; its linemen alone averaged 182 pounds each.[4] Moreover, Camp decided to start an untested freshman, Frank C. Ballard, at quarterback.

There was little to make the game—a seesawing, much-ado-about-nothing affair—interesting. On top of that, a number of injuries made it worrisome. Another Oberlin newcomer, a brilliant, scholarly sophomore named Robert Henry Cowley, had to come out in the second half with a shoulder so strained

The 1893 team on the scrimmage line. The center was McMurray, the guards White and Spindler, the tackles Fitch and Clate Fauver, and the ends Merriam and Stewart. In the backfield are Mott at quarter, halfbacks Boothman and Lee, and fullback Regal. McMurray has his hand on the ball, prepared to snap it back to Mott in the way Heisman devised at Buchtel that year. Note the way both White and Spindler line up close to McMurray and place a protective hand on his shoulder.

that he was out for the rest of the season. Ballard was disabled trying to stop one of Kenyon's charges, so scrawny John Mott, a 138-pound English-born senior and one-time president of the athletic association, took over at quarterback. Veteran Will Merriam suddenly left the game, too, though the reason for his doing so was not explained.

Kenyon's longest gain was twenty-five yards, while Oberlin's "only brilliant play" of the game, Washington Irving Squire reported in the *Oberlin Review*, occurred in the first half when Howie Regal burst through the line. With three of his teammates running interference, Regal ran through the Kenyon backfield for a touchdown. Regal also kicked the goal. Oberlin—Regal all alone, for that matter—won the game, 6–0. A not inspiring beginning.

There were immediate recriminations. The team had won, but it had not lived up to expectations. Where was the teamwork, the *elan*, the aggressiveness of the previous season? The *Oberlin News* called the game "a victory which is almost as bad as a defeat." After last year, it said, "we had cherished the hope that a new era in foot ball had dawned upon us." Instead, the game had demonstrated "our weak points. Alas, that they were so many."[5] Squire enumerated some of them in the *Review:* center Orin Ensworth was "poor"; Newell Coe Stewart, a "Cad" with then-undetected eye trouble who subbed for Merriam, tackled too high, many times failing to down the ball carrier; Ballard has "an unlimited amount of 'nerve'" but his weight "handicaps him greatly."

Fortunately for the team, and Camp, the team had two weeks before its next two encounters, a southern trip that would set Oberlin against Ohio State in Columbus on Saturday, October 21, followed two days later by a return match with Kenyon in nearby Gambier.

At first, after an initial touchdown by Oberlin seven minutes into the game, it looked like the *Ohio State Journal'*s observation was true: The Oberlin team, it said, "had been an enigma to the University boys, but that they would solve it that afternoon."[6] Oberlin's teamwork suddenly broke down. OSU's coach, Jack Ryder,[7] had his men open with the "old wild west, run-down-at-the-heel *V*," a ponderous, almost trite mass-momentum play it had employed so ineffectually in 1892. But this time, the play "seemed to rattle" the Oberlin eleven and a "tragedy of errors" ensued. When Oberlin had the ball again, fumble followed fumble until, in a "dismal fluke" lateral between Boothie Boothman and Coe Stewart—he of troubled eyesight—the ball tumbled across the Oberlin goal line, where an OSU player fell on it. A successful two-pointer made the score Ohio State 6, Oberlin 4.

The crowd on the sideline began to chant, "Oberlin can't play ball, Oberlin can't play ball." But the team rallied, and after a series of short, hard rushes by both backs and linemen, Solomon S. Lee—a sophomore transfer student who had played halfback for Olivet College—plunged across the OSU goal.[8] Regal's kick was successful, bringing the score to Oberlin 10, Ohio State 6. Oberlin quickly scored again when Mott recovered a fumble. The team worked the ball downfield until Clate Fauver took it over for the team's third touchdown.[9] That made the score Oberlin 16, OSU 6.

Both sides exchanged touchdowns, with Boothman this time scoring for Oberlin. At halftime, the score was Oberlin 20, OSU 10.

The Ohio State crowd by this time had stopped chanting. Many were now taking out their frustration by hissing. A big band with "a dozen instruments" had filled the sky above the stadium with stirring, resounding sounds, tearing "the welkin into shreds" with a victory march each time Ohio State had scored. But now it, too, was silent. "The instruments began dropping out one by one, like cats returning from a night serenade," Squire reported in the *Oberlin Review,* "until at last only the bass drum was left to bay at the moon."

Oberlin was in full command in the second half. It stymied Ohio State bucks three times, only six inches from its own goal line. Then, after the ball exchanged hands and OSU lost it again, Boothman rounded an end and dashed fifty-five yards for his second touchdown. After another exchange, Boothman broke loose again and scored another. And when Oberlin had the ball again, Lee scored his second touchdown.

Oberlin now held a firm 34–10 lead. It scored once more in what was the highlight of the game. Ohio State got within thirty yards of Oberlin's goal but was blocked again and forced to kick. Regal caught the ball on the five-yard line and, dodging and swerving to avoid tacklers, ran the entire length of the field to register Oberlin's eighth touchdown.

After the narrow Kenyon win, the final score—Oberlin 38, Ohio State 10—prompted a sigh of relief. "The interfering of our team has improved 100 per cent," Squire wrote. The *Ohio State Journal* contended that Oberlin had resorted to "every dirty trick known to evil-minded players," as witness the frequent hissing "for their evidently malicious attacks." The *Oberlin Review* responded to that charge by quoting the OSU student paper, the *Lantern:*

> To charge the Oberlin foot ball team with brutal and indecent playing is to slanderously misrepresent a company of gentlemen, who do great honor to their college. Our men have met them upon several occasions, both when they were our guests and we theirs, and without exception they have conducted themselves with a becoming spirit of courtesy, dignity and generous good breeding. As to their foot ball playing, the worst that can be said of them is that they play so terrifically, so desperately, so splendidly, in short—that often, perhaps, they play a little rougher than the average team of less skill and fame. Their manner of playing, in fact, is the kind which Mr. Ryder is trying to instill into our men and which is having its good effect. The truth is, you can't find a University man who has ever lined up against Oberlin who will say that their playing was brutal. The game last Saturday, for example, was in every way a model one. Unlike so many games which disgrace the sport, there was not in it one blow struck or one word of wrangle or dispute or profanity uttered.[10]

Boothman. Merriam. Mott. Stewart. Bracken. Streator. White. Spindler. Fauver. McMurray. Shields. Cole. Lee. Regal.

'VARSITY FOOT BALL TEAM--1893.

The 1893 varsity, which lost only one game. *Back row (from left):* John W. Mott, manager Charles (Charley) C. Brackin, James (Jim) H. McMurray. *Second row:* Will Merriam, Newell Coe Stewart, Victor T. (Ole) Streator, Clate Fauver, Percy (Perce) C. Cole. *Front row:* Ernest H. (Boothie) Boothman, Elmer B. Fitch, John White, Frank Nicholas (Spin) Spindler, Clyde H. Shields, Solomon S. Lee, Howie Regal. E. B. (Jake) Camp of Yale was hired to coach the team, but left after the first four games. John Heisman returned to handle Oberlin's first "western" trip, guiding the team to victories over the Universities of Chicago and Illinois.

Fired up by the victory over OSU, the team approached its next game confidently. The fact that Kenyon's varsity was a heavier squad did not seem to bother any of the players.[11] What did worry them, though, was the fact that a number of Kenyon footballers had attended the OSU game and, the Oberlinites believed, deciphered their signals.[12]

It looked like their fears were justified when the game began. For twenty minutes, the ball passed back and forth as the two teams struggled without either making any real headway. Oberlin's offense seemed stymied. Finally, however, Boothman leaped over a man trying to tackle him and bolted thirty-five yards for a touchdown. Regal kicked the goal, giving Oberlin a 6–0 lead. The score remained that close throughout the rest of the half as, again, "both sides fought as if possessed."

As with Ohio State, Oberlin took command in the second half. It now didn't seem to matter whether Kenyon knew the signals or not. Boothman sprinted for two more touchdowns, one on a twenty-yard run. Then Clyde Shields—a twenty-year-old freshman[13] and one of Oberlin's brightest prospects, who was starting his first game at halfback—scored two touchdowns. His second score came with only thirty seconds left in the game. Kenyon was able to answer the onslaught with only two touchdowns. The final score was Oberlin 30, Kenyon 8.

"Mr. Camp has done marvels with the boys," Squire wrote.[14]

As if to prove Squire's assessment, Oberlin went on to swamp Adelbert five days later at its fourth game of the season, at home, on Saturday, October 28.

Except for a five-yard run for a touchdown, Adelbert was never able to score again, no matter how close it got to Oberlin's goal line. By that time, anyway, the score was 16–0 in Oberlin's favor. Its nemesis from the 1891 game, the referee-cum-player named Stage, subbed at right end for Adelbert, but the only time he got the ball he was caught in the backfield by Will Merriam for a 12-yard loss.

In all, the rookie halfback Clyde Shields, making his second start, scored three touchdowns for Oberlin. "No one would guess from Shields play that he is a Freshman," Squire commented in the *Review*. Boothman, who only played part of the game, scored twice. John White and Howie Regal each got touchdowns, too. The final score was Oberlin 40, Adelbert 0.

Despite the victory, the ever-critical Squire was unimpressed. The team's tackling was "high and far from sure." Boothman, Regal, and Mott "tried to embrace their man instead of tackling," and when they did stop a runner he was always able to fall forward and gain ground.

But there was high praise from a different quarter. The much-respected Bert Hogen, erstwhile varsity manager and now a YMCA state secretary, chanced to be in Oberlin and caught the game. He saw, he said, "how our boys are playing better ball than they did last year."[15]

Jake Camp left Oberlin after the Adelbert victory. With the barest of training time, he had fashioned four straight victories in fewer than four weeks.

Oberlin was still undefeated. Counting its 1892 triumphs, it had a string of eleven wins.

Camp left with $250 in his pocket. He may have left because the athletic association could not guarantee any further salary. It had paid Camp in dribs and drabs—$50 on October 7, $25 on October 18, $125 two days later, a final $50 on October 28, the day of the Adelbert game.[16] By then, knowing the association was, as always, borrowing from Peter to pay Paul, Camp might have decided to seek his future elsewhere.

What was Oberlin to do? Northwestern had bowed out of playing Oberlin, but the team still faced games against two new western rivals, the University of Chicago and the University of Illinois.

Obviously someone—manager Charley Brackin most likely—sent a letter or a wire to Akron asking John Heisman to take over the responsibility of coaching the team for the brief but important western trip. There was only a week to go before the games. The one with Chicago was scheduled for Saturday, November 4, the other with Illinois two days later, on Monday, November 6.

How was the team going to adjust to the change in coaches? True, Heisman was more experienced than Jake Camp, but could he just step in on barely a moment's notice and guide Oberlin to another victory?

11

WESTWARD HO!

They may sing of the "Tiger" of Princeton,
Harvard's sons to the Crimson be true,
And Yale on the wings of the breezes,
May wave her fair banner of blue,
But over the western prairies
Our banner is proudly unrolled,
And dear to our hearts shall be ever,
The name of the Crimson and Gold.
—Alma M. Penrose, Class of '01

Ll autumn of 1893, Heisman was working miracles with the Buchtel varsity. The college—which later became the University of Akron—first fielded a football team in 1891. Its record was dispiriting. Its only victory, in 1892, had come before a crowd of twenty-four people. Up until then, the school did little to support the team. Members had to pay for their own uniforms and travel. So few students wanted to play that Heisman found himself pleading at a chapel convocation for anyone 150 pounds or heavier to come out for the team. Heisman's plea was not totally successful, because he sometimes had to fill in as quarterback or at whatever position was unmanned.

Undaunted by the lack of enthusiasm, Heisman continued to create, experiment, change the game. Despite all the drawbacks he faced, he guided Buchtel to a wondrous 5–2 record in 1893.[1] In doing so, Heisman invented what he called "the direct snap-up." His inspiration was Buchtel's starting quarterback, a gangly six-foot, four-inch youth who had trouble bending all the way down to the ground to pick up the ball. Too often, before he could scoop it up, the onrushing defense smothered him.[2] "I hit upon the idea,"

Heisman said, "of having the center rush snap or toss the ball directly up to the quarter, instead of rolling it back on the ground on its lacing, or snapping it end over end, as was the method employed throughout the East."[3] Before long, as word of the innovation spread through college football circles, every team was following suit.

It was also at Buchtel that Heisman originated the use of a scoreboard to indicate the down and yards to be played.[4] Until then, spectators were often confused as to the goings-on, and even game officials sometimes lost track of what down was being played and how many yards remained for a first down. The game continued to be difficult to follow, however, especially in rain or snow when mud covered the players. Scorecards were available, but they were useless in telling one player from another because they still did not wear numbers or names on their jerseys.

The spirit Heisman instilled in his Buchtel players and his win-at-all-costs approach was, however, running into problems with Buchtel's faculty. They protested the kind of devotion he asked of his players. Football was taking up too much of their students' time.

To everyone's relief in Oberlin, Heisman managed to arrange his schedule to travel the forty-some miles to the town to supervise the training for Oberlin's games against Chicago and Illinois. He must have arrived shortly after Jake Camp's departure because from the way the football eleven performed on the practice field it was evident he had a hand in improving on Camp's legacy. By the time the players boarded a sleeper for the rail trip to Chicago on Friday, November 3, Heisman, the *Oberlin Review* said, had instilled in the varsity "the 'idea' of foot ball."[5]

The team had left the Oberlin depot to the echoes of "some very expressive" cheering from a "multitude" of students. But its arrival in Chicago the next morning was less than auspicious. Most of the morning was spent in searching for a hotel "in the peculiarly compact mixture of Chicago fog and coal smoke."

Heisman was going with the same starting lineup Camp had employed for the Adelbert game, with one exception. Solomon Lee was starting at right half instead of Clyde Shields. Perhaps Heisman didn't trust the freshman sensation.

Chicago's playing field was well-groomed and marked off, the "nicest" in fact that Oberlin had ever played on, though the university, which opened in 1892 and was even newer to football than Oberlin was, did not have a grandstand to go along with it, and there were no ropes to hold excited spectators back from the sidelines. More ominous, though, was the impression the Oberlin men got when they faced off against the squad that Amos Alonzo Stagg was now coaching.

Chicago's team was a sign of the future, for as the university's director of athletics, Stagg openly recruited players for his team. John D. Rockefeller, who had sponsored the Baptist school, set up a trust fund that Stagg was able to use to lure prospective footballers,[6] though Stagg himself, like Heisman and a number of other former footballers who had become player-coaches, found he had to play as well as coach because his men were "so very green."[7] Unlike Heisman and the others, however, Stagg's position at Chicago was unique and unprecedented. Although he had only two years of coaching experience at Springfield College, he was nevertheless appointed to a tenured faculty position and had a clear mandate from Chicago's president, a former professor of his from Yale, biblical scholar William Rainey Harper. Harper believed that athletics was "an important part of college and University life." As for football, "We may grant," he said, "that limbs are broken and lives lost; but we must remember that there is no form of life's activity which is not attended with risk."[8] Harper wanted to put the fledgling university on the educational map, and it was clear to him that one road to that destination crossed the football field. As one trustee said that fall after Chicago defeated Michigan 10–6, "We will have a college here soon if this keeps up."[9] Stagg, the one-time seminarian who believed wholeheartedly in the credo that linked manhood and Christianity, came to epitomize the successful professional college coach, the first of a new breed of football mentors who were responsible for turning the student-athlete into the athlete-student. As one historian has observed, Chicago's coach was so instrumental in building the university's image—and his influence within the institution was so great—that the school might properly be called "Stagg's university."[10]

As the two teams lined up to play that first Saturday in November, an observer said that the Oberlin line "looked like pigmies beside the Chicago six-footers." For one, Oberlin tackle Elmer Brown Fitch Jr.—who was five feet, ten inches, but weighed only 147 pounds—"was pitted against a corker."[11]

Moreover, Stagg, an innovator himself, was trying a new defensive strategy. He had each of his halfbacks move up into the line between an end and a tackle. They were assigned to breaking up the blocking on mass-momentum plays.[12] But, fortunately for Oberlin, the maneuver didn't work. On its opening drive, Oberlin took the ball all the way to the Chicago five-yard line, though there Oberlin lost it on downs. Its own defense held, and Chicago was forced to kick. Clate Fauver blocked the punt and fell on the ball. Solomon Lee tried a run around left end. Then Chicago "bit" on a double pass between Lee and Boothie Boothman, with the latter racing around right end for a touchdown. Howie Regal's kick made it Oberlin 6, Chicago 0, six minutes into the game.

The game, a tough, mauling affair, swung back and forth. It was Lee's turn to score on a double pass when Oberlin got the ball again, but Chicago quickly retaliated. Oberlin still led, 12–6, but the Chicago drive seemed momentarily to rattle the team. Oberlin fumbled. Fortunately, Chicago was eventually forced to punt, and Lee, Boothman, Elmer Fitch, and Regal moved the ball to Chicago's ten-yard line. Boothman took it over from there for his second score, making it Oberlin 16, Chicago 6.

After Chicago lost the ball on downs, Boothman hustled down to its twenty-yard line. The timekeeper announced there were only five seconds left in the half, so Regal tried a drop kick. It sailed squarely between the uprights for five points. Almost with a sigh, the "ardor" of the Chicago fans suddenly "dampened." The half ended with Oberlin ahead 21–6.

Minutes into the second half, Chicago drove to within six yards of Oberlin's goal, but John Mott broke through center and tackled its ball carrier four yards back of the line. However, he was called offside by the referee, Ben Nyce. Nyce was a one-time Oberlin student who had left Oberlin to go to Princeton.[13] The umpire was another Oberlin man, Wallace Grosvenor, captain of the 1891 varsity, who was studying medicine in Chicago. "Grove" was studiously fair in his rulings. But Nyce, evidently afraid of appearing partial under the circumstances, was bending over backwards. He favored Chicago on every dispute, at one point making Regal kick a points-after goal twice because a Chicago man was offside. Nyce wouldn't change his call against Mott, so Chicago retained the ball and eventually made a touchdown.

With the score now 21–12, it was Oberlin's turn to retaliate. It quickly marched down the field on alternate runs by Lee and Boothman, with the latter making his third touchdown. As soon as Oberlin had the ball again, the team scored once more. It was Oberlin 33, Chicago 12 as the game ended.

There were celebrations on the field and more than three hundred miles away in Oberlin. On the field, one of the Chicago players presented Boothman with the team's mascot, a mongrel dog. During the presentation, however, other members of the Chicago team sneaked it back.

When news of the victory reached Oberlin, the school cheer, the "Hi-O-Hi," rang out through the town. There was a victory bonfire—which was becoming traditional—and speeches by several students and professors. Some overeager students took to ringing the town's firebell, which caused a bit of pandemonium when volunteer firemen raced to their engines in response.[14]

Oberlin's eleven was flush over their triumph. They had outplayed a much heavier team, but they had paid a steep price. The men were so beat up by the rugged game that they could barely move. Heisman watched as his players limped from the field, "reduced to crutches, canes, splints and yards of plaster."[15] The battered team left Chicago that night, bound for Champaign, Illinois, 120 miles south.[16] Their next game was only two days off.

The Illinois team, newspaper reports said, was lightweight, but the reports were untrue.[17] Illinois clearly had the advantage as the two teams lined up on Monday afternoon before a large crowd. Oberlin's starters were the same as in the Chicago game, except that this time Heisman had returned Clyde Shields to the backfield in place of Solomon Lee. Oberlin's manager, Charley Brackin, found himself volunteered to serve as the school's representative on the officiating team, which made him decidedly uncomfortable.

Oberlin got off to a quick start, scoring on its first two possessions and taking an early 10–0 lead on the strength of the two touchdowns and one successful points-after. When Illinois had the ball back, its fullback bucked over the goal line but lost the ball just as he crossed it, and John Mott recovered. But Brackin, who like Ben Nyce two days before was bending over backwards to appear impartial, allowed the touchdown. The same situation occurred several minutes later, this time when Regal recovered a fumble over the goal line. Again Brackin gave Illinois a touchdown, a decision that, he afterwards admitted, was a mistake. The score was now Illinois 12, Oberlin 10.

Unfazed by their own manager's ineptitude, Oberlin went on to score four successive touchdowns. Clate Fauver took it over on an eighteen-yard buck. Boothie Boothman circled around end on one of his fifty-yard sprints. Shields carried it over on an explosive buck. And Howie Regal rammed through the center, dodged two Illinois backs and ran sixty yards for a touchdown. The score at halftime was Oberlin 30, Illinois 12.

According to the reporter covering the game, it was "best not to dwell on the second half." Brackin continued to make questionable decisions, and, as an autumn afternoon gloom set in, a game of "hide and seek" ensued. Illinois scored twice and Oberlin once, but, the reporter said, it was "too dark long before time was called to see who had the ball." The final score was Oberlin 34, Illinois 24.

The *Chicago Tribune* was effusive in its praise of the visiting varsity: "Oberlin, far down in Ohio, has sent forth a magnificent eleven, and Chicago and

Champaign have already been met and vanquished. The backs of Oberlin are of the winning sort, and the team interference is the best this side of the Alleghanies [sic]." The *Tribune* said that Oberlin could give Purdue or Minnesota "a hard tussle," and suggested that a series of games between the three schools "would bring out the best football in the West and would be worth a long journey to see."[18]

There was jubilation again in Oberlin—though "more suppressed" than after the Chicago win—when news of the Illinois triumph reached the town on Monday night. The school, and the town, were saving their rejoicing for a gala greeting being planned for the varsity's return on Tuesday. What no one realized, of course, was how bruised and battered the victors were again after the Illinois game.

"We staggered off the field," Heisman said, "the very groggy victors." That night, he said, he had a doctor lance "the cauliflowered ears of three of my warriors. Eight other members of my team were under the hands of surgeons although none of them was seriously injured—that is, seriously for those days."

Homeward bound, the team took coaches to Toledo, most of the players sleeping "heavily, nervously." Charley Brackin, though, was in extreme pain with stomach cramps. At midnight, they reached Toledo, where they had to change trains for one back to Oberlin. They were a sorry sight, Heisman said, as they disembarked:

> We dragged through the station gates at Toledo, some with arms in slings, some on crutches. I don't think there was one of them that did not have his head bandaged and his face court-plastered. And to lend an even deeper hue of gloom to the picture the team's manager was carried off the train on a stretcher. His injuries had, however, been acquired indoors. He had so lost control of himself that he had eaten himself into a painful attack of acute indigestion. There was a considerable crowd at the station for midnight, but they had not gathered to cheer us.
>
> A mob closed in upon us clucking and murmuring solicitude and pity.
>
> "Good heavens," cried a woman standing near one of my total wrecks, "look at this one. He must have been underneath."
>
> "I was, madam," he groaned. "Every time, it seems."
>
> A go-getter interne [sic] from a hospital came scurrying over to me.
>
> "All right, sir, all right," he cried. "The ambulances are over this way."
>
> "See here," I said a bit peevishly, "we did get bounced around a little but you people are overdoing this. We can make it under our own steam."

And about that time newsboys arrived carrying still warm newspapers. "Heee yah, hee yah. Yextraaaa. . . . . All abouta wreck ona Clover Leaf. . . . Yaaaaaaah."[19]

The players had been taken for survivors of a train wreck.

When the wounded footballers arrived later that morning at the Oberlin depot, they were met by a fleet of carriages decorated in crimson and gold. Slowly, painfully, they dragged themselves aboard hacks and, escorted by six hundred students, were taken to Tappan Square, where another equally large crowd awaited them. Again and again the "Hi-O-Hi" rang out. "The desire of every loyal son and daughter of Oberlin is that our College be held in honor by all who hear her name, and no more practical service can be rendered than that which was accomplished at Chicago and Champaign," the *Oberlin Review* declared. "Those who witnessed the games, and thousands more through the public press, have been taught to 'say Oberlin' with a meaning that will not be lost to the future of the College."[20]

After the rally the team was feted at a dinner, and after the festivities, Heisman took his leave. In his pocket was $21.12 from the athletic association.[21] It was minor recompense for his work with the varsity, but the association, despite taking in more than it expended, was still in debt by several hundred dollars.[22] The recent western trip alone had cost $194.82.[23] More important for the team's future, though, was the association's appeal that Heisman return next fall to coach football again.

Obviously, Heisman felt welcome in Oberlin, a sharp contrast to his experience in Buchtel, where the faculty was demanding that his contract be terminated. If Oberlin could pay a salary, he would be back.

Oberlin still had three games left on its schedule. One was a game against Western University of Pennsylvania, another a return match with Adelbert. But neither took place. The WU game, set for November 18, was cancelled for reasons not made public. The Adelbert rematch, scheduled for November 28 in Cleveland, had to be called off because of a snowstorm that left eight inches of snow on the playing field.

It was just as well. The team was spent. It would have been beneficial if the final game Oberlin played, against Case, had been canceled as well. For one thing, Oberlin's exam period cut into many of the players' practice time.[24] For another, the team went into the Case game without a coach and still reeling from the battering the players took on the trip into Illinois.[25] The number of substitutions during the game were an indication that the

Another look at the 1893 starting team plus substitutes. *Back row (from left):* Kell, Robert (Bob) H. Cowley, Regal, manager Brackin, Spindler, John W. Price, Arthur G. Thatcher. *Second row:* Merriam, Ensworth, White, Clate Fauver, Fitch, Streator, Jones, Stewart. *Front row:* Lee, Cole, Boothman, Frederick C. Ballard, Mott, McMurray, Shields.

men were still hurting. Among others, Clate Fauver, ordinarily a lineman, had to shift into the backfield.

Case took an early lead and never relinquished it. The score was 22–8 by halftime, with Clyde Shields and Boothman scoring Oberlin's two touchdowns. But the ever-reliable Regal failed to kick both goals, and Oberlin never scored again.

It was embarrassing. The crowd, the largest ever assembled in Oberlin for a home game, was visibly disappointed. "After the first fifteen minutes," Washington Irving Squire reported in the *Oberlin Review,* "the college yell became a thing of history, and our boys might as well have been playing in Zululand, as far as support was concerned."

The final score was Case 22, Oberlin 8. It was a bitter end to what had been an otherwise successful season. Even though the Oberlin eleven had racked up 189 points to its opponents' 80, Case crowed that, with the possible exception of the University of Minnesota, it had the best football team in the West. Case had played better than Oberlin, its student publication *Integral* said, but it acknowledged that "to win from a team which has a large number of its best players disabled is an altogether different thing than to defeat such a team as Oberlin boasted before its Western trip."[26]

Oberlin's only solace came afterwards in the accolades of the sports editor of the popular *Outing* magazine and his counterpart on *Harper's Weekly*. The latter was Caspar W. Whitney, who, with Walter Camp, had originated the annual All-America selections. Both men placed the Oberlin varsity in the same ranking as the teams of Minnesota and Purdue.[27]

Dr. Fred Leonard called the members of the varsity in for checkups once the season ended and declared, amazingly, after examining all the players, that no one had sustained a serious injury.[28] Nevertheless, the beat-up appearance of the players on their return from Illinois fueled the continuing debate not only about the brutality of the sport, but about its long-range impact on the school, as well. Despite the fact that football had become a fixture at Oberlin, its president, William Ballantine, echoed the ambivalence toward it.

Ballantine was sanguine about the "many benefits arising from the general interest in physical culture." Among them, he said in his annual report, are "the indirect moral value of an innocent and healthful outlet for youthful prowess, and one which conduces to college loyalty." He acknowledged that "time and patience will be required." But, he added, "an undiscriminating condemnation of foot-ball would be most unreasonable."

Yet, at the same time, Ballantine declared, Oberlin had to remain on the alert:

> The enormous pecuniary expense, so out of harmony with the general economy of the institution; the intense rivalry, tempting to betting; the regular assembling of large crowds of spectators to stand idle in the chill November air when they would better be exercising on their own account, not to mention the presence in these crowds of low sporting characters; the interference of Saturday games with the proper observance of the Lord's Day, even when railroad travel is not involved, the players themselves being exhausted and the talk of all spectators being yesterday afternoon's game; the diminution of many weeks of interest in nobler matters—these evils force us to ask whether we need to pay so high a price for the *corpus sanum*.

Ballantine's cautionary remarks about what he called the "evils" of the game were in line with the school's religious legacy. But what was astonishing was

Ballantine's statement that "the evils which have attracted public criticism in the East have not appeared in this region in forms so serious."[29] Didn't he read his own student publication? Was he ignoring what a lot of other people knew?

Desperate for players, Oberlin had resorted to using a ringer in the Case game. At the start of the second half, Louisianian Thomas Johnson, a "Cad" who had played on the 1892 varsity, went in for the ocular-impaired Coe Stewart at left end. But Johnson had left Oberlin the previous spring and gone on to the University of Pennsylvania. He was playing for the Penn team along with a teammate from 1892 who was making quite a name for himself there, quarterback Carl Williams. Case's captain objected when Johnson first trotted onto the field, but to no avail.

Johnson's playing pricked the conscience of at least one Oberlin student, Fred Green. A senior, Green questioned Oberlin's renowned pious record. He found the "intensely religious atmosphere of Oberlin" to be "commonplace rather than as anything unusual." Green, who was the son of a minister, may have been hypercritical about that point, or failed to recognize the transformation Oberlin was undergoing. But he was also a proponent of the school's athletic program,[30] and he felt personally chagrined about Johnson's playing. He also called into question John Heisman's participation in the 1892 season. "While every man on the grounds breathed a sigh of relief when these two crack players took their place in the line," he wrote in the *Oberlin Review,* "yet almost every student felt really shamed of it." Green said that "neither of these men had a particle of right to play, except by the most flimsy technicality." Oberlin, he insisted, "can not afford to do a 'shady' action simply because other colleges do, while we can well afford to set a high standard of college honor."[31] Green's point was well taken. If Oberlin was going to be self-righteous about the game, it had to set the proper example. The scent of victory had overwhelmed moral choice—and that was dangerous indeed for a school founded on strong moral principles.

Still, these issues were set aside for the time being as the school grappled with the lesson of its second successful season—and its final loss to Case. "The last few weeks' experience in foot ball has taught the absolute necessity of having a coach here next year throughout the entire foot ball season," an editorial in the *Review* declared. "Undoubtedly, if the Oberlin eleven had been able to have their coach here during the week preceding the defeat by Case, that defeat would never have happened." Success, the *Review* continued, "depends largely upon the presence during the entire season of a competent coach."[32]

"With the departure of Mr. Camp, if we except the few days when his place was filled by Mr. Heisman, a disintegration was plainly evident in team work. A good, live coach, to be on hand during the entire season, *must* be provided for next fall, and the Athletic Association must give the manager of next year's team the assurance that sufficient money will be forthcoming."[33]

PROS AND CONS

*At most schools and colleges a boy is not permitted to play
if he begins to fall down in his classroom work.
Behold the game has made the boy a student.*
—John Heisman

The divisive battle over football never seemed to abate, no matter how popular the sport was becoming. There was still widespread, often vehement opposition to football that was reflected in Oberlin, in other schools in Ohio, and throughout the nation.

During the Christmas–New Year vacation in January 1894—after the 1893 football season was over—representatives of Ohio's college association held a special meeting devoted to football. The game was roundly denounced, though no mention is made that any Oberlin participant voiced a negative comment. A specially appointed committee reported back with two recommendations: One deprecated the accidents connected with football and demanded a reform; the other was a sweeping condemnation of all intercollegiate contests, including baseball and tennis. Both resolutions drew strong support in particular from professors from two small colleges, Hiram and Baldwin, both of which had poorly trained teams. The *Oberlin Review* was quick to rush to football's defense. "If men will play who are not fit to play, it is no fault of the game if they get hurt."[1] It pointed out that new rules had been adopted "in the face of sweeping and often most lamentably ignorant criticism of the game."[2]

One of the new regulations, recommended by Walter Camp and adopted by the Intercollegiate Football Rules Committee, provided a penalty for piling on a ball carrier who was already downed. Its purpose was obvious. Another rule required that at the start of each half and after every goal, the ball must be kicked at least ten yards toward the opposing side. This rule was intended to eliminate a new and particularly savage tactic, the so-called flying wedge, in which a team ganged up in a mass-momentum formation that was responsible for numerous serious injuries in the first full season it had been employed. In an attempt to eliminate unfair play, a third rule provided for a linesman to keep time and watch for slugging or other unsportsmanlike play. As a result of the new regulations, "no mother," said the *Review,* "need fear for her son, nor her son for himself, that by playing foot ball he will become either a ruffian, a cripple or a corpse."[3]

The game's "evils" nevertheless spurred a continuing outburst of criticism. The president of Allegheny College said he viewed all athletic sports "as a kind of necessary evil with possible good which I am not clear about."[4] His counterpart at Illinois Wesleyan, however, was "fully persuaded that evil in athletics is largely in the intercollegiate games," and the head of Ohio Wesleyan went further, refusing to sanction any such games at all.[5] A meeting that fall of zealous deacons and pious section leaders of Oberlin's First Church unanimously adopted a resolution condemning intercollegiate football games. Their argument was familiar: "Foot ball and salvation do not and cannot go together."[6] Afterwards, one of those present at the meeting wrote:

> When one goes into these games, it is not certain that he will come out alive. If he does he may be bruised or maimed or scarred for life. . . . We are credibly informed that eight young, precious, hopeful, human lives in this country were sacrificed last year to this Moloch. . . .
>
> The mark of Cain is upon them [the games]. They are an "interloper." They do not properly belong to this Christian age, to a land of bibles, churches, christian colleges and schools. They are a relic of barbarism and should, were it possible, be relegated to the age of old Rome and to the gladiatorial shows and pastimes of the amphitheater. . . .
>
> Not that foot ball is played in Oberlin on the Lord's day. No! No! But things are so arranged that these big games come off Saturday afternoons, and when teams go abroad it sometimes happens, we are told, that they are unable to reach home till after the midnight hour!
>
> What possible apology or excuse for this flagrant violation of the fourth commandment. And beside, what a preparation this for the service and worship of the day? . . . The forbidding and terrible thing about it is that the minds and hearts of the people are full of these games during the sacred hours of the holy day . . . that at a table where he [a pastor] was boarding the topic morning, noon and night was the ball game played

the Saturday previous; and that, too, in spite of his efforts to change the subject. And the astounding thing of all was they were Christians.[7]

The leaders of First Church weren't the only ones condemning the sport. Writers in publications as varied as *The Nation*, the *New York Independent*, and the *Chicago Tribune* were openly critical. Caspar Whitney, the sports editor of *Harper's Weekly* who had helped to initiate the annual All-America selections, described a Harvard-Yale game as "the vehicle of pent-up venom turned loose." A spectator at that game, which, incidentally, drew $44,800 in admission fees, said it was "high time civil law stepped in and stopped such exhibitions." The *Berea (Ohio) Advertiser* ran a poem entitled "The Hero That Won":

"Comrades, help me, I am injured,
    Injured in my back and side.
'Tis so painful, I—can't—bear—it,"
    Then he gave one groan and—died!

One good student full of promise
    Died for what? For glory's name . . .
"Did they win it? His side win it?
    Win the prize for which they tried?"
"Yes!—they—won—it, won the laurels,
    Which they carried home with pride."

But one life was bartered for it,—
    Sacrifi[c]ed for glory's name;
Read upon his marble headstone,
    "HERO OF THE FOOT BALL GAME"[8]

Opposition to the game was still so pervasive that a number of educators and business leaders, all supporters of football, banded together to form a committee to look into various aspects of the sport. Its purpose, it was all too clear, was to rationalize the playing of football. The committee asked Walter Camp to assemble the data. The result, a book published in 1894 entitled *Football Facts and Figures,* was a compilation more of opinion than fact, a jumble of disparate ideas and some suspect statistics intended to answer the constant criticisms being voiced across the country. Based on more than a thousand questionnaires, it was meant to be a comprehensive study, taking into account all the favorable aspects of the sport and answering all its critics, but it was very one-sided. Camp—who had singlehandedly taken upon himself the role of being the saviour of football—pulled together the responses from scholars, physicians, even former Yale All-American Pudge Heffelfinger, all of whom had been contacted for their thoughts and whatever supporting evidence they possessed.

One of the educators who responded to Camp's inquiry was Prof. Eugene Lamb Richards of Yale. He described football as "eminently an intellectual game" that was "won by the superior mental work of the winning team as embodied in the generalship of the captain and the thoughtful work of his men."[9] It was also, he said, beneficial physically, bringing "into activity almost every muscle of the body."[10] Richards said that there was "no other college sport which so brings out the best virtues in a man." The most successful teams in Yale, he added, "have contained the most moral and religious men."[11]

Naval academy surgeon Henry G. Beyer advocated football as a builder of bodily strength. He noted that twenty-five of the Annapolis players in the 1893 season showed an average increase in weight of more than seven pounds. Their lung capacity increased eleven cubic inches on average, their total strength by more than 16 percent. That last point was seconded by the experience of Heffelfinger, who wrote Camp that he had gained twenty-two pounds over the years he played for Yale, and that he was now "much better prepared to stand any hard strain or work than before entering college."[12]

A. B. Newell of the State University of Iowa dealt with the criticism that many schools permitted students to play football at the expense of their studies. He said his school, for one, had a rule that no student with a standing below a grade of 75 was permitted to play.[13]

Amos Alonzo Stagg spoke to the school morale that the game engendered. He reported that after only two years of varsity play at the University of Chicago, "football has done a great deal toward arousing college spirit where little or none existed, so we feel it has been of special value in our university life. In fact our athletics have done more to create a college spirit than all the rest of the student organizations."[14]

As for charges of brutality, Col. O. H. Ernst, superintendent of West Point, said Army's team suffered nine serious injuries in the past season but recovery was expected in all cases.[15] He then pointed out that while there were eleven football casualties during one month alone, there were at the same time three times as many accidents involving cadets who fell off horses.[16]

A physician named Loveland, with the college football association, explained that the reason for the number of broken noses was that "the nose 'gets there' before the player." But such injuries were things of the past, Loveland said, now that players were beginning to wear nose guards. The chief medical problem was the knee: "No football rules can protect" it.[17]

Everyone realized that football was not a perfect sport, endangered in good part by the recruiting, even paying, of players. Beyer of Navy, for one, prophetically warned that the "greatest danger that threatens football, by unanimous consent, seems to be the introduction of the professional element."[18]

Richards of Yale recommended that schools require all players to take physical examinations and that they appoint a director of athletics to a seat in the undergraduate faculty as a better way to control sports[19]—proposals that Oberlin had already instituted.

In summation, Camp's committee as a whole was concerned about two factors: "the amount of time devoted to 'summer practice' and 'morning practice'" by numerous college teams; and the burgeoning expenses being experienced in many schools and, to make up for them, the increasing gate receipts. "We feel," the committee concluded, "that the collegian should not use his sport for profit." Recent admission charges are "too high." They "shock the public sense and breed extravagance on the part of the youthful managers of the sports."[20]

There is no way of telling how instrumental *Football Facts and Figures* was in preserving or encouraging college football. For all the arguments for and against the game, its popularity grew. In fact, football became the most attention-getting sport on college campuses. Yet many of the issues brought up in the 1890s resonate today.

In early September 1894, before the academic year began, a tournament involving five Ohio colleges was held on the state fair grounds in Columbus. Oberlin was invited, considered the offer, and decided against sending a team, perhaps because it could not count on rounding up enough players before the start of classes. Whatever the reason, the decision was prescient because the games aroused bitter feelings, with each team accusing its opponents of using players from "Yale, Harvard, and Oberlin."

Who were the players from Oberlin? None is mentioned by name. The only known person who could be connected with the school was John Heisman. He played quarterback on the Buchtel team.

The tournament pitted Buchtel against Ohio State University.[21] It was to be a brief game, with halves of only twenty minutes' duration. But after the forty minutes of play, the score was tied 6–6 and went into a sudden-death overtime. Embarrassingly, Heisman had fumbled in the first half and was determined to make amends. He guided the team to Ohio State's four-yard line, then called time, summoned the Buchtel players around him and delivered a pep talk. When play resumed, he took the snap from center and planted it in the "breadbasket" of the Buchtel fullback. "Fortunately, he either saw it or felt it—and got it," said Heisman. "Then we all went like mad." Heisman grabbed the fullback by the back of the jersey and, with the rest of his teammates pushing and shoving, dragged him forward. "And we all went through together just like the water of a mill dam when the dam goes out." With one last yank, Heisman tore the jersey off the fullback's back, "but what did it matter since we were all across?" he added. A field goal made the score 12–6. The game has remained Buchtel's only victory over Ohio State.[22] It was also, as far as is known, the last college game that Heisman ever played.

There was no chance that Heisman would ever play again for Oberlin, because the college was one of the first schools to come to grips with the problem of eligibility. The question of what determined a bona fide student athlete was a recurring field of contention among schools that participated in intercollegiate sports. Eligibility rules varied from school to school. Could graduate students play? What about "special" students who attended classes in a nondegree program? What about nonstudents, like the seven members of Michigan's football team who had no connection whatsoever with the university?[23] At Oberlin, a newly established Committee for the Regulation of Athletic Sports composed of faculty, students, and alumni ruled that "no one" would be permitted on any team "unless he can satisfy the Committee that he is a *bona fide* member of the College." Even then, the person had to have been a student for at least one term and be "an amateur."[24]

But that didn't mean that Heisman couldn't coach Oberlin. Spiriting him away from Buchtel was evidently easy. He was already experiencing difficulties with the faculty, many of whom were determined that he be dropped as athletic director. Early in the spring of 1894, Charley Brackin, who was about to graduate, passed on the management reins of the team to a well-known figure in Oberlin, John T. Ellis. He was the son of the Rev. John M. Ellis, a professor of mental and moral philosophy who but a few years earlier had been under consideration to replace James Fairchild as president of the college. Young Ellis sought Heisman out and offered him $50 a week if he would return to coach eight weeks of the coming fall season—"or longer at same rate at option of Manager." Heisman would have to pay his own expenses.[25]

Hiring Heisman seemed to answer an issue raised by the *Oberlin Review*. "Western foot ball is still in its infancy," it said, "and it devolves upon the coming generation of students to decide whether or not Oberlin shall maintain the high place which she has assumed."[26] Obviously, the student athletic association had every intention of maintaining that "high place." School officials, who had come to terms with the sport, now proved flexible. Twice, for example, team members that fall were excused from Wednesday afternoon recitations so they could practice.[27]

And certainly, football was not detrimental to Oberlin's reputation. Enrollment was back up in the fall of 1894, though still below the 1892–93 peak year. It now stood at 1,427 students.[28] Nor had football caused any lessening of the school's standards or its strict entrance requirements. Its academic reputation was solidifying. Oberlin now compared itself with nineteen other colleges—including Yale, Princeton, Dartmouth, and Cornell—to demonstrate that its requirements in literature, American history, plane geometry, Latin, and prose composition were unique. And in other categories—rhetoric, physics, solid geometry, Greek, French, and German, to name a few—Oberlin said it required more courses of study. "The men who have gone east for post graduate work," the *Review* said, "have demonstrated the worth of Oberlin training by the scholarships and honors which they have won."[29]

The college could point with pride also at the national attention its athletes had won. Clate Fauver's "muscular form" graced a full page in the Spalding athletic-equipment company's latest football guide, and two Oberlin baseball players were commended in the influential sports magazine *Outing*. If nothing else, Oberlin's winning teams had contributed to the school's "widening influence and reputation in athletics"[30]—ergo, buttressing its academic standing nationwide. As the *University of Chicago Weekly* put it, "The best colleges are, as a rule, the leaders in athletic games."[31]

One of the baseball players singled out by *Outing* was right-hander Henry Bert Voorhees, a pitcher. A conservatory student known as Cy, Voorhees also hoped to make the football team.[32] He was one of more than a dozen prospects who showed up for practice nearly a week before school opened in September. As the days wore on, more than twenty-five "enthusiastic candidates" appeared on the field.

Practice sessions had come a long way from the hit-or-miss, unschooled training that the first Oberlin players experienced back in 1890 and 1891. Just how strenuous and demanding they could be was highlighted by an anonymous new student, a hefty youth who decided to go out for football and kept a diary of the fun, foibles, and ferocity he ran into. He was attracted to the game, he readily said, because "they have some pretty girls here"—an unwitting acknowledgment of the role football was playing in a new world of sexual relations evident not just in Oberlin but on every campus. All the young female students talked about was football, he wrote, "and it seemed to me that it was the only thing that they knew anything about." They wondered, he said, "whether *she*"—one of the coeds?—"would let Cowley play this fall":

TUESDAY.—Some one asked if "Cub-bear would captain the scrub this year, or not?" and I began to wonder what kind of a thing he was. One fellow, they called him a "Cad," said that a man named Edgerton was a "corker," if they could only get him to play. I thought he ought to play if he was as described. I learned a great deal at dinner about the different players and the team, and one told me I ought to play myself, "because," as he explained, "you have lots of beef about you." . . .

I bought a football suit, and when I put it on a little later I was surprised at the result. I made up my mind that I would go to the grounds that afternoon and try to play. I felt very funny in my padded knee-breeches. "But," I thought, "the other fellows must feel the same way." On the way to the ground I thought that everybody I met would laugh at me, I felt so strangely, and every little ways I would look down at my knees to make sure that I had on pants.

When I got out there I did not find many fellows there, but they seemed to be having a good time. I "did as the Romans did," and we all stood in a circle and threw the ball from one to the other. I think that a foot ball is a bad thing to play catch with, and that if they want to play catch they ought to use a base ball. . . . After awhile they got to kicking the ball at what they called the goal. I don't see how anybody could do that. We stayed out there a while longer, but didn't do much. I went home, and after my first experience thought that I should like to play foot ball if it was no harder than that. I am pretty sleepy now, and so will go to bed.

WEDNESDAY.— . . . When I got out there to-day they set us to work "tackling" one another. As I understand the thing, they run toward each other and one of the men grabs the other fellow by the knees and squeezes his legs. What he has to do is to stop the other fellow from running past him. One of my friends introduced me to Mr. Boothman. . . . He is a very nice young man, but he walked around with so much of a limp that I asked one of the fellows if his leg was broken. He did not tell me anything, but just laughed. There was another fellow I noticed. They called him Cy. He was yelling at the Freshman team when I saw him. . . . Cy had on red and yellow stockings. He is a long fellow naturally, and when he had on knee-breeches it made him look very long, indeed. He seemed to be making those Freshmen run a good deal, but I suppose that is part of football. . . .

THURSDAY.— . . . [I] went out to the grounds this afternoon. I am awfully sore and almost feel that I ought to give up football. I am afraid that it is too violent exercise. . . .

FRIDAY.—I went out to the Athletic grounds this afternoon, determined to do good work on the scrub team. I thought that Mr. Boothman was a good sort . . . and when I addressed him as Mr. Boothman the boys all laughed and said that they called called him "Boosie." I ran into a big fellow they called "Clate." I have a distinct recollection that I ran into him—no, he ran into me—at least that was the way I reasoned it out afterward. I distinctly remember that he hit me. I am no little fellow myself, but I thought at that moment that he was a little larger than I. Once today I tackled a fellow named Peirce. I mean I tackled at him. He fell on me and I was almost persuaded then and there that I was not cut out for a football player and that my future would be anything but brilliant. . . .

SATURDAY.—I begin to think that I can play football. I am awful sore, but then I know what they mean when they say to "buck," and then I have played in all, four days. They say that no one knows what the coach will do when he gets here, so I stand as good a show as any one else of getting on the 'Varsity. . . .

MONDAY.—I think I will stop playing football. It is too rough a game. I believe that when men get to be forty years old the ones that took care of themselves when they were young are better off than those who bruised themselves up in such rough games.

TUESDAY.—I had a cramp in one of my legs last night. I could hardly sleep, I was so sore and tired. This football is a hard life. . . . Gould knocked me in the shins this afternoon and McDonald nearly broke one of my ribs. I am dead tired and sleepy tonight and will choke off early.

WEDNESDAY.— . . . I have quit playing football. I guess I had better begin to study a little more. I think I can do more that way than as a sport.[33]

Despite the neophyte's decision to abandon the game, by the time John Heisman arrived on Saturday, September 22, the football field "was literally covered with men in uniform." Will Cleland (Bib) Clancy, an expert kicker on the sophomore class team—he could kick perfect goals with either foot—was now covering sports for the *Oberlin Review* and remarked on the "first-class trim" of the returning varsity veterans. Mainstays such as Clate Fauver, Boothie Boothman, Lynds Jones, Will Merriam, and Elmer Fitch were on hand. So, too, a number of other members of the 1892 squad: native Oberlinite Percy (Perce) Cole, sophomore James (Jim) Henry McMurray, and

Oberlin College Foot Ball Team–1894.

The 1894 team on the scrimmage line. That's Heisman in the background, supervising the practice. McMurray is at center, flanked by Streator and Bogrand as guards. The tackles are Fitch and McDonald, the ends Merriam and Cole. In the backfield, William Miller is at quarterback, the halves are Clate Fauver and Boothman, the fullback Young. Although the squad had a disappointing season—losing three and tying one of its eight games—football was now entrenched in Oberlin as a major sports activity.

Charles Victor Streator. The last, Streator, a conservatory student who tipped the scales at a hefty 178 pounds,[34] was known as Ole Streator,[35] a reference perhaps to the noted violinist Ole Bull. They were "all ready for business—a foundation good enough for any team," said Clancy.

There were a number of positions up for grabs. Over the summer, the varsity had lost eight players; some had graduated, others had left the college. One loss was tragic: Clyde Shields, the freshman halfback who made such an impression in his first year of varsity play in 1893, had drowned while bathing in Manhattan Beach near Chicago during the latter part of August, only a month before his twenty-first birthday.[36]

The new rules, Clancy said, would lead to "more a running game than ever," so not being a "200-pounder" should not discourage anyone from coming out. Notwithstanding that, "The line," Clancy said, "promises to be heavier than last year." The prospects, in fact, included eight men who weighed well over 160 pounds; one of them, Rae Shepard Dorsett, a chubby nineteen-year-old junior from Iowa, weighed 226 pounds.[37]

Four varsity candidates were former Academy players. Two, both of them theologs, were named Miller. In fact, in all, there were three fellows named

Miller eager to make the squad, all unrelated. One of the theologs, Willis Jay Miller, was, at almost twenty-nine and a half years old, the oldest player ever to go out for football at Oberlin; he was four months older than Joe Teeters was when Teeters played for Heisman's first Oberlin team in 1892.

There was one prospect whose presence was a clear example of the attraction the game now held for many youths. He was Floyd Henry Bogrand, a 199-pound lineman who entered Oberlin "to play football primarily." Bogrand had been captain of the Hiram College team in 1893. He was lured away by the reputations that Oberlin and Heisman had gained. Bogrand was actually staying at the same boarding house on North Professor Street where Heisman roomed. The team had its training table in the same house,[38] and the 1894 candidates were already taking their meals there, following a menu that Heisman had forwarded to the landlady before school opened.

"We have the best coach in the West," boasted Clancy, "we have more and better games scheduled than ever before."[39]

PLAY BY PLAY

The finest punting is of little value unless your linemen
can get down under it and nail the receiver.
—*John Heisman*

For John Heisman, the game was more than just winning. It was also an opportunity to invent, improvise, improve upon.

Before Oberlin's first game of the 1894 football season, he had an inspiration. Heisman looked at his fleet but relatively slight left halfback and a thought struck him. Boothman, a slender five feet, seven inches tall, was up to 157 pounds,[1] a gain of eleven pounds since he last played in 1893.[2] The sudden surge in weight may have been due to the influence of a freshman who was a professional trainer and was guiding Boothman's workouts; the young man had been an assistant in the Yale gym before entering Oberlin.[3] But Boothman was still underweight, considering his responsibilities in backing up the line when the opposition had the ball.

On the other hand, one of the new prospects Heisman had his eye on for fullback was a hefty 170-pounder from Cleveland, Henry Alfred Young, a freshman who had captained the Hudson Academy team in 1893.[4] Young wasn't a particularly effective field-goal kicker, but he was formidable on defense. Heisman believed he had the answer.

It was a simple enough solution, but nobody else had ever thought of it. "No one," Heisman said, "had ever heard of a man playing any different position on defense from what he played on offense: if he was a half back on offense that's what he played on defense and that ended it. . . . I became impressed with the senselessness of my left half-back, a very fast but very light man, battering himself to pieces helping to repel the heavy onslaughts while my full-back—a big, strong, husky fellow stood away back practically doing nothing for nearly all the time that opponents had the ball. So I put the little fellow at the full-back's place and rested him up whenever we lost the ball, and had my big full-back come up and help back up the line." The innovation worked "like a charm" and was soon copied by every team that season. Heisman bragged that it "spread like Mohammedanism in the eighth century— only that as it was the quarter-back who was usually the lightest man on a team; it was and is usually he who trades places with the full-back on defense."[5] So Boothman started at left half on offense, but traded places on defense with Young, who easily won the fullback spot on the starting lineup.

For the rest of the starters, Heisman had made some unusual changes. Jim McMurray, who had filled in at center for the team in the past, was in the quarterback slot. Opposite Boothman at right half was Clate Fauver, the team captain and ordinarily a tackle. Four newcomers had won starting spots on the line—a circumstance that raised questions about both Oberlin's blocking on offense and its ability to stop a rush on defense. One of the newcomers was Rae Dorsett, the chubby 226-pounder, now the center.[6] On one side of him at left guard was yet another new face, Heisman's neighbor at the North Professor boarding house, Floyd Bogrand. Bogrand rather than Young was going to be responsible for kicking the extra points after a touchdown.

Any doubt about the team's capability was squashed at the first game of the season, at Athletic Park in Oberlin, against Mount Union, a team from a small Methodist Episcopal college situated in the budding industrial town of Alliance, Ohio.[7] The contest was such a pushover that the *Oberlin Review* referred to it in a headline as "A Good Practice Game"[8]—which was not to say that Oberlin had played brilliantly or without mishap.

Heisman had, of course, introduced the center snap he invented at Buchtel to the Oberlin squad, but McMurray, who was not accustomed to the quarterback slot, had trouble taking the snap from Dorsett. He fumbled several times, until Heisman finally relieved him, sending in William Raymond Miller to take over. "Billy" Miller was a slight, 150-pound freshman who had quarterbacked the Academy team the previous fall.[9]

The game was so lopsided and Mount Union's defense was so porous, Bib Clancy wrote in the *Oberlin Review*, that it was difficult to distinguish between bucks and runs. The line plunges by Young often gained more than fifteen yards. With Boothman and Clate Fauver leading the way, there were nearly twenty runs of more than twenty-five yards, five of forty yards, and two of nearly sixty yards. In all, both men made four touchdowns apiece, while Young and Bogrand each scored once. Bogrand made nine out of eleven points-after kicks, and Young himself made a successful drop kick for five points.[10]

Mount Union got within Oberlin's twenty-five-yard line only twice, and except for three times, lost the ball on downs every other chance that it had the ball. The final score was 67–0. Still, even the *Oberlin News* said the game "served admirably to show the weak points" of the Oberlin team. Its reporter was also particularly shocked at "the use of profane and indecent language" by the referee, a Mount Union man. Maybe he was just upset at the way his team was playing. He enforced his every decision with swearing.[11]

The game was such a blowout that Oberlin fans were skeptical when Otterbein, scheduled to play Oberlin at Athletic Park the following Saturday, canceled the game. Was the Oberlin team so good that it scared off other colleges? After three losses in the past two years, Ohio State had already decided not to play Oberlin.[12] Now, Otterbein was backing out. It claimed that several of its players were injured and the trip to Oberlin did not seem advisable. When pressed to keep the date, the Otterbein team took a vote and one man refused to go. "On the face of it, it looks more as if our little score, 67–0, had made an impression upon Otterbein," the *Review* said.[13]

Alvan Woodward Sherrill, the varsity's assistant manager, tried to fill the open date with a game against Adelbert or Hiram, but neither team was available. As a result, the Oberlin varsity enjoyed a two-week hiatus before its next contest, a home game against Kenyon on Saturday, October 13. During the interval, Dr. Fred Leonard put into effect a new regulation adopted by the committee on regulating athletics and began pre-game physical exams for all the Oberlin football players. He checked for weak hearts and lungs, and so far found all the men in good condition.

After the easy win over Mount Union, the players' physical condition was the last thing, however, on anybody's mind. Of more concern was the morale of the players and the fans. Their enthusiasm might flag. Worried that both players and fans would lose heart during the interval between games, the *Review* declared that the varsity wanted "four hundred students out daily to see the practice, not as though they were watching a weird, silence-compelling ghost dance." What the *Review* was hinting at obliquely was the need for a release of pent-up excitement that the game of football, or any athletic contest, engendered—a healthy one in particular for students. One of the features of a recent Harvard-Yale game, the student weekly said, was the cheering. "All through the fall while the Varsity practiced playing, they practiced cheering. We must do likewise." Moreover, Brown University was planning to have a staff of cheerleaders present at every game, and its students had already devised eight cheers, including a "yell" given when a touchdown is made. The Oberlin varsity, the *Review* went on, "want to practice to

A typical pileup in a game in 1894. The spectators are being held back by a rope.

accompaniments; and they want them loud, sharp and clear. They want the
Hi-O-Hi yell to shatter the air twice each minute for an hour daily. They
want individual plays in the practice applauded and the player's name used
in the yells. They want a half-dozen more kinds of yells. The enthusiasm of
fifteen hundred students can't be voiced through one lone tune."[14]

Despite the Mount Union triumph, Heisman was dissatisfied with the starting lineup and shuffled some of the men around. Jim McMurray was back
at his old position as center, leaving Billy Miller in the quarterback slot.
Heisman had his two ends switch sides, but he decided to keep Clate Fauver in the backfield.[15]

From the outset it was clear that the Kenyon team was not as strong as
its predecessor, the 1893 squad. Its blocking was weak and tackling "an absolute minus." Oberlin ran up the score quickly. Two plays and three minutes into the game, Boothie Boothman raced around end to score, and the
next time Oberlin had the ball, he scored again. With Floyd Bogrand kicking successful goals, Oberlin led, 12–0. Bogrand himself made the next touchdown, bucking across the goal line, but failed in the points-after. Then Boothman ran around end, crossing the goal line near the corner, for his third
touchdown of the day.

By halftime, Oberlin had compiled twenty points and Kenyon had never
gotten out of its own territory. It made a successful stand on its ten-yard

line, but no sooner did Kenyon have the ball than one of its backs fumbled, and Ole Streator recovered. Fauver soon carried it over for a touchdown. He scored again when Oberlin next had the ball. Oberlin's final points came on a "screw wedge" that sent Billy Miller "out of a whirligig" and across the Kenyon goal. It was Oberlin 38, Kenyon 0 as the game ended. The Kenyon team limped from the field. Its captain was carried off. His hip was only slightly fractured, but he was suffering so much from the pain that a report circulated afterward that he had died.[16]

Only two games into the 1894 season, Oberlin had racked up 105 points, its opponents none. But Bib Clancy in the *Review* was cautious. The team was "just as strong, perhaps a little stronger, than last year, but thus far the team work is not up to its old form." Heisman's shakeup of the starting lineup was apparently his way of trying to rectify that situation, for as the Oberlin varsity prepared for their third game—on Saturday, October 20—he again tried a new lineup, though only two players were involved this time around. Oberlin's opponent was to be Wittenberg, a Lutheran-sponsored college in the west-central Ohio town of Springfield.

If the Oberlin eleven expected easy pickings again, they were in for a surprise. Wittenberg, which was taking Ohio State's place in the Oberlin football schedule, was no pushover. It had, in fact, beaten OSU the previous Saturday, 18–6. By game time, the day was unusually hot for late October, the grounds dusty. Despite the heat, the Oberlin team came out dressed in newly purchased sweaters. Heisman had Clate Fauver back at his old spot, right tackle, and scholarly Bob Cowley taking Clate's place in the backfield. That's how the Oberlin team started. All during the game, however, Heisman moved players around, sometimes because he had no choice when a man was injured.

Even though the teams had agreed to thirty-minute halves—and, in fact, the second half was called after twenty-two minutes—the game was as fierce a struggle as Oberlin had ever experienced. Neither team could advance the ball more than two yards at a time until Fauver finally made a five-yard buck and Boothman ran for fifteen more. Will Merriam and Henry Young then brought the ball close enough for Fauver to buck across for a touchdown. The four points were followed by two on Bogrand's kick, leaving the score Oberlin 6, Wittenberg 0 at halftime.

The second half of the game was almost a repetition of the first, except that Heisman had to switch his men around as one after another limped off the field, injured. The Wittenberg ends were particularly effective on defense, scarcely ever letting Boothman, for one, make any appreciable gain. Boothie, in fact, came up lame on an ankle and gave way in the backfield for Cy Voorhees, the conservatory student who'd never played before. Bogrand then hurt his shoulder. To replace him, Heisman sent in a bruiser, Royal Chauncey Peirce. Peirce, a six-footer, weighed 212 pounds.[17]

Voorhees had only three opportunities to carry the ball, but on one of them he plunged through right tackle, shook off a number of linemen, dodged the Wittenberg fullback and raced twenty yards across the goal line. With Bogrand out, Billy Miller kicked for the extra points. The game ended Oberlin 12, Wittenberg 0. The Oberlin players walked wearily off the field, nursing aches and pains. At least they had nine days to rest up before their next game, against another team Oberlin had never played before, Washington and Jefferson, on Monday, October 29.

The "W & J" game, the first "eastern" trip ever undertaken by the Oberlin football team, represented a new opportunity for the college to promote its name nationally. It was considered so important that a local merchant arranged to have "the principal features" of the game sent by telegram back to Oberlin so that he could post the details in his shop window. Washington and Jefferson, which was situated in Washington, Pennsylvania, about twenty miles southwest of Pittsburgh, had already made a name for itself in midland America. Its squads had played forty games in the past five years against strong teams in western Pennsylvania, eastern Ohio, and West Virginia, losing only one of them.

The Oberlin varsity's trip there began on a frolicsome note. The team set off on the 150-mile journey into Pennsylvania on the Friday morning before the game, accompanied by a number of spirited fans who sang, joked, and practiced their cheers. Their train headed north to Elyria before switching onto tracks that took it south to Tuscarawas Crossing.[18] As the train passed through Medina, near where his home was, Cy Voorhees leaned out of the window and "astonished his old neighbors with the greatest college yell in America." The team disembarked briefly at a coal-and-water stop to down sandwiches and milk before the train crossed the Ohio River into West Virginia. Saturday night was spent in Wheeling, and after what was for them a "tardy breakfast" Saturday morning, the players boarded another train for the thirty-five-mile run to Washington, passing enroute through scenic hills and valleys and the oilfield at Taylorstown.

Once the team reached the college at nine o'clock, Heisman wasted no time. He immediately ordered a signals practice, making the men run through their repertoire of offensive plays before excusing them so that they could tour the town. Meanwhile, he had decided on a new lineup, compelled in part because Floyd Bogrand was still out with a sore shoulder. The versatile Clate Fauver switched back again to left halfback, and Voorhees moved over from left half to fullback in place of Henry Young.

Until game time, the Oberlin players had enjoyed the pleasant trip. But once the game began, their mood turned grim. The game was fraught with questionable officiating decisions. Billy Miller was penalized twenty-five yards when he brought down a W & J ball carrier on what everyone else on the Oberlin eleven thought was a fair tackle. Then, when Oberlin had the ball, Will Merriam ran all the way to the goal line before he was brought down, but the umpire called the play back, no reason being given publicly. The ruling, said one spectator, Dr. O. J. Bennett, "seemed to take the life out of Oberlin for a while." Bennett, an 1888 Oberlin alumnus who practiced medicine outside Pittsburgh, believed that Oberlin would have scored if the play had been allowed.

The first half ended without a point being made by either team but with tempers short. The mood became even more grim as the second half began. Oberlin got off to a flying start with Fauver blocking for Miller as he streaked seventy-five yards for a touchdown. But the referee again called the ball back, this time explaining that he had called the ball down before Miller broke from scrimmage. "This could not have been so," Dr. Bennett insisted, "as the Oberlin boys were rushing the ball through the center, all of them in a bunch, when all of a sudden the bunch opened up and two went down the field, one with the ball, the other interfering. A touchdown was made, and nothing but barefaced robbery took it away from them."[19] (Afterwards, the manager of the hotel where the Oberlin team was staying said he knew that the official "had considerable money up on the game."[20])

The rest of the game remained scoreless, a boring tussle but one that turned ugly as the last seconds played out. Animosities, especially those of spectators that ordinarily were confined to yelling and screaming, edged closer to physical expression. "Why it was rotten," declared Dr. Bennett. "The treatment the boys received was a disgrace. They were guyed, horns blown, and drums were beaten when they had the ball, so that it was hard to hear the signals."[21] The demonstrations got so serious that W & J players had to help hold the crowd back as the Oberlin players left the field. And later, when the Oberlin men headed for the train depot, they were mobbed. Floyd Bogrand, who had umpired during part of the game, "was cursed and blackguarded in a most disgraceful manner."[22] As he was making his way to the train station he was struck in the face by a bystander.[23] "I never in my life witnessed a college game where any college men showed such unsportsmanlike treatment to their opponents," Dr. Bennett declared. "The Washington and Jeffersons are hard losers—that explains it. They cannot say that the ill treatment came from the hoodlums and town fellows, for it did not." Officially, the game ended in a 0–0 draw. The doctor thought the score should have been 12–0 in Oberlin's favor, had the Washington and Jefferson referee been fair.

The *Oberlin Review* recorded the game as 0–0, but the first 0 in its headline was an oversized one and inside the oval was the number 4. And when W & J subsequently canceled a return match scheduled for November 10 in Oberlin, the *Review* concluded that it was not surprising: "Bullies are usually cowards."[24] Why, a number of Oberlin fans were now asking, didn't the football manager arrange a game at home "with some strong western school" rather than take upon itself the eastern trip? The answer was simple, Bib Clancy responded in the *Review*. The cost of such a game would be greater than the cost of Oberlin's first three games because of the guarantee Oberlin would have to offer to a team such as Wisconsin. "How can $400 be paid to a team and only $200 be taken in just to please a few admirers of the game?" he asked.[25] As it was, the student athletic association stood to lose "a large amount of money" because it could not schedule a game of equal importance to replace the return game canceled by Washington and Jefferson.[26]

The season was one month old. Oberlin had amassed a record of three wins and one (disputed) tie, scoring 117 points in all to not one scored against it. How long could that last? Especially with the next game scheduled for Saturday, November 3, against Case in Cleveland? Case: the team that had ruined Oberlin's otherwise unblemished record in the last game of the 1893 season.

Another question fans were asking had to do with Oberlin's starting lineup—or rather lineups. They kept changing so often that the same eleven men never started more than one game in the same positions for Oberlin. Injuries couldn't be avoided, but what was Heisman trying to accomplish? If he spoke or wrote to explain his reason, it went unrecorded. One can only speculate that Heisman—still only twenty-five years old and with but two years' experience coaching—was testing out some theories. He was certainly learning on the job.

Revenge was on everyone's mind. Oberlin was excited at the prospect of another go at Case, especially because the Cleveland school was bragging that its 1893 team had beaten Oberlin 22–8. The school's newspaper *Integral* ran a full-page picture of the varsity under the heading "Champions of Ohio." Case had earned the sobriquet, the *Integral* said, by having "proven their superiority over all other teams of the State." Such braggadocio was too much for the *Oberlin Review:* "She did not go outside the State and played *only three* games, confessedly easy, near home, until she encountered Oberlin, just returned victorious from a hard and fatiguing series of games in the West. . . . [S]he certainly *did* nothing upon which she could base any claim to the State championship."[27]

Everyone in Oberlin, so it seemed, wanted to go to the game, but there were only two Lake Shore Railroad trains to Cleveland in the morning—at 6:30 and 8:47 A.M.—and none again until 4:49 in the afternoon. Catching one of the morning trains would compel students to miss Saturday morning classes.[28] The hue and cry was such, however, that the athletic association arranged for a special train to leave at 12:30. Reservations for it were quickly filled. Its six coaches bore nearly 360 students and professors.[29] On the way they rehearsed the words of a song they intended to render at the game. The tune was "Sweet Marie":

Oberlin, sure to win,
Sure to win, Oberlin
Sure to conquer Case today, Oberlin
While the conflict rages high,
And the victory is nigh,
We will shout the Hi—O—Hi, Oberlin.[30]

Heisman and the team had taken an earlier, morning train to Cleveland and proceeded upon disembarking to change into their uniforms at the Kennard House before game time.[31] That afternoon, dressed in red sweaters and striped stockings, they rushed out onto the field to the cheers of the Oberlin "four hundred"[32] and Heisman's words echoing in their ears: "Fellows, the day of days is here. In a few minutes we'll find out how well you remember the humiliating licking Case gave you last year. Yes, you had sick and injured men that awful day and you lacked practice because of exams. But it's different today, fellows. You're trained, you're fast and you're strong and you're good enough to win if you and you and you and you and every man Jack of you remember that 'In any fight for glory it's the heart that tells the story.'"[33]

Wrangling over the rules by officials delayed the kickoff by more than a half hour. One of the officials was Charles Browning, an Oberlin alumnus, class of '92. The others were men from Yale and the University of Pennsylvania. Undeterred by the interminable-seeming argument, the Oberlin fans "kept up a continual racket," singing, shouting, and cheering, Bib Clancy reported in the *Oberlin Review*.

A recovered Floyd Bogrand kicked off for Oberlin. Heisman had him back at left guard, with Ole Streator at right guard. Boothie Boothman was starting at left half instead of Clate Fauver, who moved over to right half in place of Bob Cowley. Young was back at fullback. Backed by the hundreds of cheering supporters, Oberlin's eleven was formidable. A Case back was carried off the field with a broken leg after being tackled on a buck through the line. Then, using Heisman's system, Oberlin went into a quick-start opening series of plays, engineering a 60-yard gain "almost before" Case was lined up. Bucks drove the ball to within three yards of the Case goal. Bogrand then carried the ball over for a touchdown and also kicked the extra points. Thirteen minutes into the game the score was Oberlin 6, Case 0.

As soon as Oberlin regained possession, Boothman took the ball around right end for thirty-five yards and a second Oberlin score. It was now Oberlin 12, Case 0. The closest that Case got to the Oberlin goal occurred when Ole Streator dropped a kick on the twenty-yard line. That set off a series of juggled balls by both teams until Oberlin recovered a fumble and Boothman raced around right end again for his second touchdown. Oberlin was on its way to yet another score, Fauver racing fifty-five yards around left end deep into Case territory, when the half ended with Oberlin leading 18–0. The only grumbling so far was about Browning's refereeing. He reversed decisions by the other two officials on several occasions, "doubtless by a desire to avoid all possible suspicion of unfairness."

As the Oberlin players mopped away their sweat and grime and caught their breath, Heisman waved the team together. With Oberlin ahead by three touchdowns, he said, "I took upon myself to tell my young men how good they were—how pleased and proud I was. And as if that were not enough I said that I would not ask them to do better.

"'Play as you have been playing,' I said fat-headedly, 'and everything will be beautiful.'"[34]

Heisman later bit his tongue. "Alas," he regretted. "Those words went to my players' heads."

Case came out in the second half a different team, fighting for every inch. Oberlin was a different team, too, sitting back and glorifying in its achievement. Almost immediately, a Case end rounded Oberlin's left side, dodging both Young and Boothman and, with Fauver in hot pursuit, ran eighty yards for a touchdown. A successful kick made the score Oberlin 18, Case 6.

Oberlin was able to move the ball down to the Case one-yard line, but Case made a stand and Oberlin lost possession after four downs. Rather than risk a kick and a possible scoring run-back, Case chose to down the ball back of the goal line. The touchback gave Oberlin two more points. By now, however, it was getting so dark that neither team could lateral with any accuracy. The fans on the sidelines could not see a thing. Only the voices of the game officials gave any indication of where the ball was. Under these conditions, with spectators in suspense, play went on for fifteen minutes until time was called. The final score was Oberlin 20, Case 6.

While the streets of Cleveland "echoed with a profane yell, too vulgar to repeat, with which the defeated school solaced herself,"[35] a joyous crowd returned to Oberlin on the special train.[36] "Case's last chance in which to prove herself 'Champion of Ohio' is gone," Bib Clancy wrote, "and she is again back among second rate teams where she belongs, and from whence she crawled by the merest accident last season."

"Organized cheering and singing have come to stay," the *Review* editorialized. "The enthusiastic singing and the thunderous cheering of Saturday spurred every player on to play his best, and gave the Oberlinites a chance to vent their enthusiasm in a definite and telling manner." The *Review* credited Heisman and Fauver "for the excellent work of the team." But Heisman was rueful. His words at halftime "went to my players' heads. They played that second half as though nothing of any importance depended upon what happened. Case scored one touchdown and very nearly another. I was never gladder in my life to hear the timekeeper's whistle ending the game."

Heisman never forgot the lesson. "'Play as you have been playing,' I said fat-headedly, 'and everything will be beautiful.'" That was a terrible mistake. "In three hundred games thereafter I never took it upon myself to tell my teams, between halves, how good they were. There were times when their playing dazzled me by its speed and general brilliance, but, believe me, I never told them so. All they got from me was criticism for their technical blunders, however trifling. I could and did find fault with near-perfection. But I was always sure that I was picking at flaws which my men recognized as flaws. I was always haunted by the fear that I'd lay it on too thick and injure the spirit of the more sensitive."

As Heisman readily admitted, "I, too, was young."[37]

DOWNS

Victory isn't all-important in football.
How the game is played is the thing.
—John Heisman

Brain over brawn. That had worked for Heisman and the Oberlin eleven on more than one occasion. Well-trained, aggressive, the varsity in its first years was a team to reckon with, thanks in great measure to Heisman and Jake Camp. But in football there is a limit to how well a team can compete when pitted against a bruising, larger-than-life squad that many schools—alert to the financial rewards that a winning season offered—were fielding. Football in the 1890s was flirting with becoming big business. For all their talk that academics came before athletics, Harvard and Yale, with their emphasis on intercollegiate football, had become the role models for the commercialization of the sport. The public image that a winning team inspired—the revenue it brought in, the prestige it stimulated, the alumni support it garnered—was superseding academic philosophy at many schools, just as it had at Harvard and Yale.[1]

So there was yet another lesson to be learned, one about being overmatched, especially in the face of a grueling schedule. This lesson involved John Ellis. He had resigned as the team manager, leaving his assistant, sophomore Alvan Sherrill, to take over his duties. But long before he left, Ellis had, among other things, arranged a game with Adelbert. He offered a Saturday date in October, but Adelbert wanted a Wednesday instead. Ellis, feeling that Oberlin's failure to play a return game in Cleveland the previous fall "placed us under some obligation to favor them in the matter of date this year," agreed to the Adelbert request. (Had he forgotten that eight inches of snow had forced the cancellation of the Adelbert rematch?) Back in July 1894, when Ellis was solidifying the varsity schedule, the only date available was Wednesday, November 7, four days after the Case game and three days before a Saturday contest on November 10 against Geneva College of Beaver Falls, Pennsylvania. As Ellis later explained, there was no reason to suspect how "tired out, crippled, stiff-jointed, over confident" Oberlin's players would be after the Case game—nor that Adelbert scouts stood on the sidelines at the Case game, studying Oberlin's strategy and signals, nor that Adelbert would have a much stronger team in 1894.[2]

For once there was no change in the lineup, which was a surprise in itself and amazing considering the rundown condition of the Oberlin men. The players were in a daze after the exhausting Case game only four days earlier, pooped but bloated with overconfidence after the victory, their third of the year. As game time approached, a snowstorm savaged the field, leaving it in "wretched condition," Bib Clancy reported, and "making it impossible to play a running game, upon which Oberlin depends much more than does Adelbert."

The Adelberts began by simply bucking into, and through, the Oberlin line almost every time they had the ball. Slowly but surely, they tramped down the field. "The whole team seemed to be in a trance," a dumbfounded observer said.[3] Before the first half was over, Adlebert had amassed fourteen points on three touchdowns. Oberlin's biggest gain was the twelve yards Clate Fauver was once able to make. Fauver, however, never had another chance to make yardage. He was injured on a play and limped off the field. Floyd Bogrand took over as captain.[4]

For a while, it looked as if the players under Bogrand's prodding had wakened in the second half, but soon Oberlin "relapsed in that easy-going state which characterized her play in the first half." The truth was that the hearts of the Oberlin players weren't in the game. Even John Heisman didn't know what to say or do. Adelbert was ahead 18–0 before Bogrand managed to squeeze across the goal line for Oberlin's first, and only, points. By the end of the game, Adelbert had scored another touchdown and the score, from Oberlin's standpoint, was a dismal, shocking 22–4 in Adelbert's favor.

To add insult to Oberlin's defeat, after the game Adelbert students distributed the words to their first football song. It was a parody of Oberlin's, sung to the tune of "Sweet Marie" but with "a rare combination, one part profanity with two parts rhyme."

The loss must have rankled Heisman. His men, said the *Oberlin News*, "played as though they had never learned the game." A small crowd of fans met the team at the train depot when they returned that night, but after two or three cheers "everything was quiet as death."[5]

Former manager John Ellis quickly penned a letter to the editor of the *Oberlin Review*, responding to his critics and trying to justify scheduling the Adelbert game so closely after the Case one. The game, Ellis acknowledged, was a "lamentable result" that would "doubtless" lead to his being criticized for scheduling it in the first place. But he had no choice, Ellis insisted. Allowance always had to be made for the "probable failure of some of the games to materialize." "Please bear the above-mentioned facts in mind in making your comments upon the disaster," he asked.[6]

The student weekly was sympathetic. The team management did not deserve "censure" for the defeat. Instead, the *Review* insisted, "the players cannot be too severely criticized for the manifest conceit and over-confidence with which they entered the game." But, it rationalized: "As long as Oberlin pursues her broad-minded policy of the past and goes east and west risking defeat at the hands of strong teams outside Ohio, just so long will it be possible for Ohio teams, by abstaining from playing hard games and by careful study of their own and our schedules, to win games from a partially disabled team." "Still," the *Review* concluded, referring to both the loss to Case in 1893 and now the Adelbert debacle, "it is to be hoped that the lesson of two defeats has been so thoroughly learned that no manager in the future will ever repeat the fatal blunders of the schedules of the past two years."

Luckily for Oberlin, the Geneva game three days later was called off at the last minute because of the prospects for bad weather. The cancellation was fortunate, the *Oberlin Review* noted, because "it is scarcely probable that more than a score would have braved the storm and shouted our boys to victory." The respite, though, was temporary. Oberlin was scheduled to play the University of Michigan at Ann Arbor on Saturday, November 17. And to take the place of the Geneva game, Alvan Sherrill scheduled what would be Oberlin's first game with a major eastern college team, Pennsylvania State, at Oberlin for the following Saturday, November 24.

Surprisingly, the Michigan team was as formidable as the one Oberlin had played in 1892 to a controversial 24–22 win (or 26–24 loss in Michigan's eyes)—surprisingly because in 1893 the Wolverines were so strapped for funds that for one away game the players jumped a freight train and rode in empty boxcars to avoid paying the rail fare. There was nothing left in the team's athletic treasury by midseason, and the varsity barely managed to play out its ten-game schedule on a one-hundred-dollar loan secured by four professors. After the season was over, the university senate felt compelled to create a special board responsible for hiring coaches and trainers and supervising all school athletics.[7]

On paper, the two teams looked evenly matched. Oberlin had a 4-1-1 record, Michigan 5-1-1. But the average weight of the Michigan team was a solid 170 pounds. Despite the many heavyweights that had come out for football, Oberlin's varsity averaged fifteen pounds lighter.[8] On the other hand, the teams that Michigan had faced, with two exceptions, were not highly rated ones. In fact, the University of Wisconsin was miffed by Michigan's refusal to play its varsity. Wisconsin's *Daily Cardinal* said that in athletics Michigan "has fallen out of the first class among the western universities" and that, "in order to conceal this, she is attempting to consider herself an eastern university, considering that there is more honor in being at the bottom of eastern athletics than of western."[9]

There was some truth to the Wisconsin argument. The Wolverines had played and defeated the teams of more humble schools—Albion, Olivet, Orchard Lake, and Adrian. A first game with Orchard Lake had ended in a tie. It could brag that it had beaten the University of Kansas 22-12, but Michigan's only loss was to a first-rate team, Cornell, by a 22-0 score.[10]

Oberlin's varsity, demoralized by the Adelbert defeat, left for Ann Arbor on the Friday afternoon before the game, stopping overnight in Toledo, before continuing on early Saturday morning.[11] Accompanying the team were a mere half-dozen rooters. The hostilities experienced at the last get-together of the two teams prompted the Michigan athletic association to station guards around the football field; anyone caught fighting faced expulsion from the school.[12] And this time, to eliminate charges of unfair judging—and apparently at the insistence of Oberlin—the officials chosen were all from other schools: Amos Alonzo Stagg of Chicago was the umpire, a Harvard man the referee, a University of Pennsylvania man the linesman. There was one new addition to the grounds that would, theoretically, avoid crowding along the sidelines and the possibility of encroachment by fans: Spectator stands for four hundred people had been erected.[13] Actually, some two thousand Michigan fans witnessed the game.[14]

Heisman was back to shuffling the starting lineup. Clate Fauver started at left tackle, Bob Cowley at right half, and, critically, an Academy student who had never played varsity ball before, John Francis (Rudey) Rudolph, was taking over the quarterbacking chores from Billy Miller. The game began smoothly for Oberlin. Early on, Michigan got to within twenty-five yards of the Oberlin goal line, but a punt that cleared the goal was not allowed.

Will Merriam subsequently recovered a Michigan fumble. On the next play, Boothie Boothman took the ball around right end, threw off a Michigan halfback, ducked from a lunging fullback, and scored. Floyd Bogrand's kick made the score Oberlin 6, Michigan 0.

It was a good start, and Oberlin was holding back Michigan's "heavy line of beef" when suddenly Bob Cowley, a mainstay of Oberlin's defense, dropped to the ground with a sprained ankle. Cy Voorhees replaced him, but before Oberlin could recover, Michigan took advantage of Cowley's absence and was able to score. Its kick, however, failed so the half ended with Oberlin leading 6–4.

The second half began disastrously. A lateral from Rudolph was intercepted by Michigan near the Oberlin goal line and the Wolverines quickly ran the ball in for a second touchdown, but again no points-after. The score was now Michigan 8, Oberlin 6. The stiffest playing of the game followed. Each team held fast, forcing its opponent to constantly punt. At one point, Henry Young, Boothman, and Merriam made gains taking Oberlin to Michigan's fifteen-yard line. But the usually reliable Boothman then fumbled. With Michigan in possession, its tackle raced for forty yards, throwing off Boothman twice, before scoring. This time, Michigan's kick was good. Michigan led 14–6. Even Heisman realized that "by this time the Oberlin line was shattered."[15]

With the game coming to a close and Oberlin without any hope of changing the outcome, what Bib Clancy called an amusing incident occurred. In retrospect, it appears that it was more an example of frustration and purposeful vindictiveness than something humorous. As the men lined up for the kickoff, Michigan's huge center, a man named Smith, stood up, brandishing his arms in a haughty manner. As he was doing so, Bogrand booted the ball straight at him, hitting Smith in the stomach. The ball rebounded into the hands of Oberlin's center, Jim McMurray, who ran downfield for fifteen yards before he was tackled. It was the closest Oberlin ever got to scoring again.

Ironically, to Heisman's credit, everybody thought Oberlin had played the better game. Stagg said afterwards that Oberlin had been beaten "not by superior science, but by superior weight." The *Oberlin Review* thought that "with such brilliant material Michigan should play a much better game than she does, more of a team game, a more scientific game." Heisman himself thought his players had executed a better game than Michigan. "In attempting anything of a more scientific nature than a buck, Michigan invariably failed to gain," he told a reporter for the *Elyria Chronicle-Telegram*. "They tried our revolving wedge twice, a well-conceived double pass and ten or a dozen end runs but every one of them came to grief without having gained an inch, many of them resulting in losses."[16]

At the request of the *Ann Arbor Courier*, Heisman wrote a story detailing the game's action. A realist, he was convinced that if Michigan's former captain, a halfback named Dygert, had legs "a trifle longer" or if Boothman's had been "a little shorter," Oberlin would not have scored "even a single point" and the Wolverines would not have begun "to see visions of defeat." "As it was the ex-captain handsomely missed the Oberlin sprinter on an end run that resulted in the only touch-down and goal the Ohio boys got. . . . From that time until the end of the game Michigan held them down to small gains. Boothman was watched like a thief, and despite his ten-second legs he could not get around Michigan[']s end. And their line went all to pieces. It was repeatedly bucked for long gains, while Michigan[']s line proved as invincible as a stone wall."[17]

It was a sorry loss for Oberlin. Michigan, Bib Clancy wrote, played "fully sixty per cent better than she did against Case." The most that could be said of the game was that it provoked no fighting on the field or off it, and no controversial officiating. "We were beaten fairly in a clean, well-played game," said Clancy.

Meanwhile, all during the time the game was being played in Ann Arbor, two oddly attired dogs sat in the store window of Oberlin druggist F. H. Smith. One, the pet of a local insurance agent, was togged out in regalia representing Oberlin. The other, belonging to Smith, a Michigan fan, represented Ann Arbor. The druggist claimed that his dog began a loud and continuous barking at exactly 4:30, when, he later discovered, the game actually ended. The Oberlin dog, he said, took the defeat in "a commendable manner."[18]

Oberlin's two losses in a row failed to diminish the enthusiasm of students and professors as the team prepared for the final game of the season, a home one against Penn State. It was bound to be memorable. With the exception of the University of Pennsylvania, Penn State had the strongest team in the Keystone State. It had recently played Navy to a 6–6 tie.[19] In the four years that Penn State had fielded a football team, its elevens had scored 470 points to its opponents' 52. No opponent had scored against it the year before except the University of Pennsylvania, which beat it by one touchdown, 18–12. A month earlier, Penn State had defeated Lafayette, a college considered in the same class as Oberlin, by a score of 72–0.[20]

Oberlin students translated their enthusiasm in a variety of "yells": "Rickety ax coax coax, / Rickety ax coax coax, / Hullabalu, Hullabalu, Oberlin."[21]

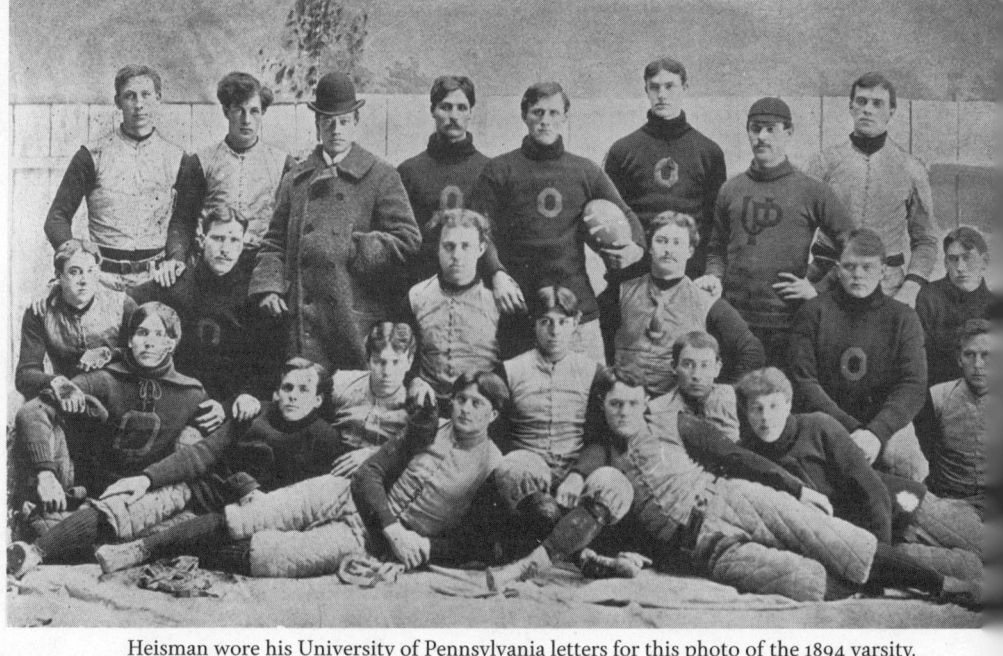

Heisman wore his University of Pennsylvania letters for this photo of the 1894 varsity. *Back row (from left):* John Behr, Perce Cole, manager Alvan W. Sherrill, Ira D. Shaw, Clate Fauver, Henry B. (Cy) Voorhees, Heisman, Royal C. Peirce. *Second row:* John F. (Rudey) Rudolph, Samuel D. (Dave) Miller, Ole Streator, Boothie Boothman, Floyd H. Bogrand, Rae S. Dorsett, Henry A. Young. *Front row:* Elmer Fitch, William (Billy) R. Miller, Charles G. (Mac) McDonald, Will Merriam, Bob Cowley, Walter Y. Durand, William H. Baer, Jim McMurray.

There was a new football song, to the tune of "If You love me, tell me with your eyes":

Rudey at the quarter, Fauver behind the line;
Young can punt forever, Boozie's runs are fine.
Ole, Jim, Mac and Bogrand,
Merriam, Fitch and Cole,
They'll make Pennsy's rusher think
They'll never reach our goal.[22]

Players like Rudey, Boozie, and Ole had won a strong dose of idolation from the school's female students. Their charisma stirred the heart of many female students. One anonymous but obviously smitten coed penned a poem:

Blessings on thee, favored lad,
   Foot ball boy with unshorn head!
With thy padded pantaloons,
   And thy bruises and thy wounds;
With thy rushes and thy springs,
   With thy bones tied up in splints,
With an 'O' upon thy sweater—
   Crimson ground and *Golden* letter;
From my heart I give thee joy,
   Wish I were a foot-ball boy![23]

In anticipation of the game, the school itself seemed to take on an added glow: "There was no spot on earth that surpassed the tranquil beauty of our campus this autumn when the evening sunlight fell upon the elms, and our stately college buildings were outlined against the western sky. . . . All that is Oberlin to her sons and daughters,—the elms of Tappan walk, the tower in Peters, the campus and the immortal trysting place, the pie-shop, will make literature that will be relished by all who love the Crimson and Gold."[24]

Despite his lack of experience, Rudey Rudolph was Heisman's choice as quarterback again. He had Clate Fauver back at right half in place of the unrecovered Bob Cowley.[25] The game was one of seesaw struggles, each team making substantial gains but then being thwarted by fine defensive stands. The ball changed hands several times, sometimes on downs, other times on fumbles, until bucks by Fauver and Henry Young brought the ball close to the Penn State goal line. Fauver carried it across for four points, and Bogrand's kick added two more.

On the next series of plays, Penn State's fullback, punt-and-points-after-touchdown specialist Charlie Atherton,[26] who was the son of the university's president, fumbled. Perce Cole, rushing from his position as left end to get the ball, was visibly held back by Penn State's two halfbacks. But none of the officials saw the foul. Atherton recovered his own fumble and ran for twenty-five yards before being tackled. Penn State followed that up with a surprise play. Atherton positioned himself way off to the side and when the ball was hiked, the quarterback lateraled to him. Atherton made fifteen yards before he was stopped. But Penn State was not able to make any further headway and lost the ball on downs. The half ended with Oberlin ahead 6–0.

The Penn State eleven returned in the second half invigorated. They quickly took the opening kickoff downfield. Atherton smashed through the Oberlin line and scored. But his attempt at the points-after kick, booted into a sudden 70-mile-an-hour gust, failed, leaving Oberlin in the lead 6–4. Both sides now knuckled down to a strong defensive game, the ball exchanging hands several times. Then, when Oberlin was stopped deep inside its own territory, Young punted and a Penn State player made a fair catch. What happened next threw the entire game into doubt.

According to the rules, Penn State was entitled to a free kick. But instead of a return punt, its team set up for a place kick. Atherton booted the ball. It sailed directly over the crossbar of the goal that Oberlin was defending. Penn State claimed five points. Oberlin protested: Atherton's kick was not a legal field kick, ergo it counted for nothing. An argument broke out. The officials were in a quandary. Two of the officials were Oberlin men—*Review* sportswriter Bib Clancy was one of them, a junior, George Frederic White, the other. Neither was sure what to do. The third official, a man from Allegheny College, was uncertain, as well. The rules book did not define a field kick. What to do? If the play were legal and the points were allowed, why would any team, as Oberlin did, dare to punt when near its own goal line? A compromise of sorts was finally worked out. White, who was serving as referee during the second half, was responsible for making the final decision. He ruled against Penn State. The points would not be allowed. But to be fair, his ruling would be appealed to football's final arbiter when it came to rules, Walter Camp.

The game ended with Oberlin ahead 6–4 and, while a telegram was sent off to Camp, the *Oberlin News* insisted that it did not matter who won: the Oberlin varsity "made a most creditable showing against a strong eastern team."[27] The *Review* called the game the "best exhibition of foot ball which has ever been witnessed on Athletic Park." The Penn State team left Oberlin, it said, "in perfect good humor even though a very critical decision about which the highest foot ball authorities differ had gone against them." Walter Camp's ruling was not long in coming. Fred White was wrong; he had made an incorrect decision. Atherton's kick *was* legitimate. It *was* worth five points. Penn State *had* won the game. The final score should have been, *was*, 9–6.

How was one to judge the 1894 season? Oberlin had scored 153 points, allowing only 49 points to its opponents, holding four of them in fact to none at all. Yet, it had lost its final three games. Some schools were measuring their success by what other schools had done, making comparisons against teams they had never met on the gridiron. What if Oberlin did so? Well, its defeat by Penn State had hinged on a questionable kick and it would have won if the referee's rule had been upheld. Consider that Penn State had defeated Lafayette 72–0, and Lafayette had beaten Lehigh 28–0, and Lehigh had lost to Cornell by a narrow 6–4 score, and Cornell had lost to the University of Pennsylvania by only 6–0, and the University of Pennsylvania had defeated Harvard 18–4. So what did that say about Oberlin's status on the national scene?[28]

Or looking at it another way, Oberlin's defeat by Michigan was not discouraging if you took into account Michigan's games against some other schools. Michigan went on to defeat Cornell in a return match before a crowd of fourteen thousand spectators, 12–4, thus becoming the first western school ever to defeat an established eastern football power.[29] It closed its season with a 6–4 win over Stagg's Chicago team.[30] The Wolverines, after all, had also trounced Case and the University of Kansas.

It was a moot question. When all was said and done, Oberlin's record was 4–3–1. It was hubris that had done the team in, the *Oberlin Review* believed. "Over-confidence must be more carefully guarded against in coming seasons both by managers in arranging dates and by teams in playing games." It urged the formation of a "midland league" that would include Michigan, Cornell, and Oberlin. The Wolverines's victory over Cornell was, the *Review* declared, "epoch making in the history of Western foot ball. It means that the West is to play in the future much the same style of a game as that in the East." Oberlin's game with Penn State "was a similar proof that Western foot ball will soon differ as little from the Eastern game as base ball in the West differs from that in the East." Oberlin's successes, the *Review* added, were "due mainly to superior coaching."[31]

Oberlin's coach left town after the Penn State game ended. Ostensibly, John Heisman was heading home to his family in Cleveland.[32] But he left behind a mystery that has never been solved.

15

END RUNS

Pass when the enemy's secondary defense is playing
close in to the line. Rush when it's lying back.
—*John Heisman*

The item on a back page in the *Oberlin News* of November 29, 1894, was a brief two lines long, and on the surface it seemed to contradict the even shorter one-line item several inches above it in the same column that said that John Heisman had returned to Cleveland after the Penn State game. The second article said that Heisman and Miss Dorothy Emerson Fairfax Brown "were married at Buffalo, N.Y., Saturday." Miss Brown "was a student in the Academy."[1]

Had Heisman returned to Cleveland—a train trip that ordinarily took little over an hour—and then gone on to Buffalo to wed Miss Brown? Some Lake Shore Railroad trains from Oberlin made a connection that continued on to Buffalo, but the trip took nearly nine hours in all and would have put Heisman in Buffalo in the early hours of Sunday morning. And if Heisman had done so, why Buffalo? Miss Brown was from Elgin, Illinois.[2]

The *Oberlin Owl* carried a similar story nearly five weeks later, but its account provided a few more details. Miss Brown was a "handsome young lady," an orphan, and "wealthy." She had boarded on South Professor Street (not far from where Heisman had roomed on North Professor Street). The couple "ran away" to marry "much to the surprise of their many friends."[3] It must have been a whirlwind courtship, and evidently clandestine. The young woman had enrolled in Oberlin Academy less than three months earlier in September,[4] when Heisman returned to coach the football team. Heisman had been engaged to marry someone else in Buchtel. Was Miss Brown aware of his betrothal in Akron? But there the story ends. No biography of Heisman even mentions Miss Brown's name. Were the news stories incorrect? If they were, a retraction would have seemed in order.

One can only imagine what might have occurred. Is it possible, likely, that, being an orphan, Miss Brown had a guardian who protested the elopement, refused his/her consent, was able to stop the marriage, or sought and won an annulment proceeding? Did the marriage ever take place? It is strange, because there are two other mentions involving Heisman in the *Oberlin News* that raise questions about Heisman's actions. Three days after the Penn State game, on Tuesday, November 27, the Oberlin varsity had its team photo taken. Heisman appears in it, so he was in town that day.[5] A week later, the same local weekly, in a brief item, noted that Heisman refereed a football game between Case and Adelbert in Cleveland on Thursday, November 29, only five days after the marriage supposedly took place.[6] According to alumni records, Miss Brown was enrolled in Oberlin Academy only for the academic year 1894–95. There is no other mention of her.[7]

Other than putting in an appearance for the 1894 team photo, Heisman, as far as it is known, never returned to Oberlin. He completed and mailed back an alumni questionnaire in 1908. By that time, his career was well established, and he was coaching some of the country's most powerful teams. He had spent five seasons at Auburn—then called the Alabama Polytechnic Institute— before going on to Clemson. He made a name for himself at both schools, so much so that in 1904, a decade after leaving Oberlin, Georgia Tech offered him a two-thousand-dollar salary and the promise of 30 percent of the net gate receipts for the football and baseball games he coached if he would move to Atlanta.[8] Heisman was at Georgia Tech in 1908 when he filled out the Oberlin questionnaire, describing himself as "Physical Director" of both the college and the Atlanta Athletic Club, president of the Atlanta Professional Baseball team, and manager of Heisman Theatrical Enterprises. He gave his wife's name as Evelyn Barksdale, and the date of their marriage as October 24, 1903, one day after his thirty-fourth birthday.[9] A widow, her name was actually Evelyn Cox, and she had a son, Carlisle Cox. She was an actress in a summer stock company with which Heisman was associated.[10] Heisman and his wife eventually divorced, and when she, a native of Atlanta, elected to remain in the city, he resigned from Georgia Tech in 1919 and took a coaching position at his alma mater, the University of Pennsylvania.

Until then, Heisman had enjoyed a remarkable career, with successive winning records with every team he coached. He had compiled a record of twelve wins, three losses, and one tie at Oberlin over the years 1892–94 (not counting the Kenyon game in 1892 that Oberlin won in his absence). His record at Buchtel was 5–2. Heisman's teams at Auburn won thirteen games, lost four, tied one. That tie, though, ought to count as a win. Auburn was beating Georgia 11–6 when the referee called the game because of darkness and declared it a 0–0 draw. Heisman appealed to the Southern Intercollegiate Athletic Association and was awarded the game, though it is still not officially recognized.[11] Subsequently, in four seasons at Clemson, his teams compiled a record nineteen wins, three losses, and two ties. At Georgia Tech from 1904 to 1919, his teams never had a losing season. In all, over the sixteen years, they won 102 games, lost only twenty-nine, and tied six times.

Heisman's string of successes continued at the University of Pennsylvania, but his personal reputation suffered. Penn teams never had a losing season and, in toto, won sixteen games to ten losses and two ties over the three years he coached them. But Heisman's mood, for some unrecorded reason, changed dramatically. Although he had a reputation as a straitlaced, uptight authoritarian figure, he had never in the past been unfriendly. At Penn, he became hostile, openly antagonizing players and others.[12] He left abruptly after Penn's last game in the fall of 1922 and took up coaching at Washington and Jefferson. He was there for one year, compiling a record of 6–1–1. There was a ninth game on W & J's schedule, but Heisman refused to let his team play it. Its opponent, Washington and Lee University, forbade interracial sports and it would have meant not letting Heisman's halfback, a black, play.[13]

Heisman's refusal was creditable, but his reputation as both a coach and a person suffered again at his last coaching position at Rice Institute. There, in four seasons, he experienced his only losing record: fourteen wins against eighteen losses and three ties. Always an advocate of a training table and special hearty diet for his players, Heisman at Rice was also able to set up an athletic dormitory where his men ate, studied, and resided together—and where he could keep an eye on their regimen.[14] But while he was there, at Rice, he was accused of favoritism, of telling quarterbacks not to give the ball to players he disliked.[15]

By then, Heisman had remarried. His second wife was Edith Maora Cole, a native of Rhinelander, Wisconsin.[16] The two had met back in 1893, when he coached the Buchtel team and she was a student at the college. The two had planned to marry, but Miss Cole developed tuberculosis, and they decided not to go ahead with the wedding. She eventually recovered and thirty years later Heisman, then divorced and alone, resumed his relationship with her, and the two were finally wed.

In spite of the way Heisman the individual became identified as an irascible, unfeeling person, no one ever questioned his place in the pantheon of great football coaches. He was the prime sponsor in getting the forward pass legalized in 1906; doing so opened up football to a revolutionary offensive strategy, though it was several years before the new rule reached its full potential. Heisman was also instrumental in the rule that divided the game into quarters.

All through his coaching years, he was innovative, devising innumerable plays and defense strategies. He was also devious and sometimes stretched or violated the rules when it suited him. A favorite play of his at Auburn for many years, until it was outlawed, was the hidden ball trick: The quarterback stuffed the pigskin inside his jersey after faking a handoff to a back. Heisman also devised a special long count to draw opponents offside and, against a rule at the time banning coaching from the sidelines, signaled in semaphore fashion special orders to his quarterback.[17] At Clemson, he fired a gun from the sidelines to start a play. Undeterred by another rule against replacing the football except at the end of the half, Heisman had a substitute run onto a wet field with a dry ball hidden under a raincoat.[18] In a ruse against Georgia Tech, he had his Clemson scrub team arrive in Atlanta and spend the day ostensibly carousing in the city so that a complacent and lulled Georgia Tech team was easily defeated the next day, 44–5, when the Clemson varsity arrived to play.[19] (In fairness, it should be added that a long count, signals from the sideline, and the use of a dry ball all eventually became legal.)

At Georgia Tech, Heisman was an early proponent of the screen pass, invented the system of having guards drop back to protect the passer, and developed the so-called Heisman shift, a countermarching maneuver to keep the defense offguard until the moment the ball was snapped. His "spinner" play was the result of a misunderstanding of signals between one of his quarterbacks and the center. The miscue occurred at a time when the rule against a quarterback's keeping the ball on the snap was no longer in effect. Without warning, Heisman's center hiked the ball to the quarterback, who stood holding it without anyone to give it to, then plunged ahead. As Heisman watched in wonder, the quarterback "plowed through the line all by himself for a 12-yard gain."[20] Heisman immediately added the deception to his play book; he had the quarterback fake handoffs to a succession of backs who, one after another, dove into the line, confusing opponents as to who had the ball. He subsequently added a wrinkle to the ruse by having leather patches in the shape of footballs sewn onto the front of their jerseys so that the backs all looked as if they were carrying the ball. On another occasion, after helmets came into fashion, he had the headgear painted tan so that they looked like footballs in color, then had a player cradle one in his arms to mimic the pigskin while another ran in the opposite direction with the real thing.[21]

Heisman was never a shrinking violet. He was miffed when sportswriters refused to call his undefeated 1915 Georgia Tech team the national champions because Vanderbilt had scored more points that season. Heisman was angry because he could have left his first stringers in many games and run up the score, but he often purposely replaced his starting lineup after the first quarter once a lead was established. To prove that high scores were not a true measure of a team's capabilities, the next fall in its first game his Georgia Tech team scored a 61–0 win over Mercer. Later that season, in a benevolently shortened game against Cumberland College, he further underlined his point when his men scored every time they had the ball, gaining 528 yards alone rushing, 220 on punts, and 220 on kickoff returns. Without one pass being thrown, Georgia Tech defeated Cumberland 222–0.[22] The next year, Georgia Tech won the national championship, winning all nine of its games and scoring 491 points to its opponents' seventeen.[23]

In all, before he retired in 1927, Heisman had coached for thirty-six years, longer than any other coach except Amos Alonzo Stagg. But unlike Stagg, who, once there, never left Chicago, Heisman was an itinerant journeyman who is identified with eight different schools. His teams won a total of 189 games—if the two Oberlin games on the western trip in 1893 against Chicago and Illinois are counted, which they ordinarily aren't, and the Auburn-Georgia tie is credited, too. Against that can be counted seventy-one losses and eight ties.[24]

Heisman was a founder of the American Football Coaches Association and was its president in 1923 and 1924.[25] He moved to New York, and in 1930 he joined the newly opened Downtown Athletic Club as its physical director. He was initially against the proposal that the club award a trophy each year to the most outstanding college player, saying that football was strictly a team game. But he relented and became a supporter of the award. The first DAC trophy, presented after the 1935 season to the best player east of the Mississippi, went to a quarterback whose team, the University of Chicago Maroons, had only a so-so record of eleven wins, eleven losses, and two ties during the three years he played for them. He was Jay Berwanger, an all-around athlete who ran, passed, punted, kicked, played defense, and returned punts and kicks.[26] Upon Heisman's death early the next fall from bronchial pneumonia—less than three weeks before his sixty-seventh birthday—the award was made nationwide and renamed in his honor the John W. Heisman Memorial Trophy.

Heisman was elected to the National College Football Hall of Fame in 1954, three years after it was established. An Ohio Historical Marker designates the site of his birthplace on Bridge Avenue in Cleveland. The local football field in Titusville, Pennsylvania, is named in his honor. An eight-foot bronze statue of him stands just north of the football stadium at Georgia Tech, bracketed by two gray marble plaques. One chronicles Heisman's coaching record, the other bears two quotes of his:

A team that won't be beat can't be beat.
In the lexicon of football there is no such word as fail.[27]

OVER TIME

Ah, trembling harp, you have a worthy theme;
(Eleven worthies, noble "canvas-backs.")
To sound the glories of the football team.
(It teems with heroes and with crackerjacks.)
—*Paul Leaton Corbin, Class of '03*

T he careers of the students who played for Oberlin proved, on the surface at least, the contention of proponents of football in the nineteenth century that the game built character. Of the sixty-eight Oberlinites who were on the college's initial football teams, three were elected to Phi Beta Kappa at Oberlin, and eight went on to do graduate work at institutions such as Harvard, the University of Pennsylvania, and Cornell. The teams in the years from 1890 through 1894 included six theologs; they and three other team members became ministers. Three of the ministers worked abroad as missionaries. Ten other team members became doctors, one a dentist. Thirteen were educators, during either all or part of their careers. Seven were lawyers. Of the fifteen who entered the business world, three were bank presidents, a fourth a bank vice president. Two were journalists, and two were state legislators. Seven varsity members worked for or were active in the YMCA for all or part of their lives. Three served during the Spanish-American War, five in World War I. A doctor who served in the Spanish-American War also served, at the age of seventy-one, in World War II. For a time, five of the players actually coached football, and one became a football umpire. Two played in professional baseball. (See appendix B.)

Moreover, when, shortly after the 1894 football season ended, an anonymous letter writer in the *Oberlin News* raised the question once again whether football and salvation were consonant, the student weekly *Review* downplayed the issue. It pointed out that a member of the team was president of the college YMCA and would be surprised to hear that "Christianity is incompatible with foot ball."[1]

The achievements of the Oberlin players and those of other schools did not still the arguments against football. The injuries incurred in playing the game continued to be a topic of concern. But when *Nation* magazine pointed out that seven of the twenty-two men in a Yale-Harvard game suffered injuries—a higher percentage of casualties, it said, than in most bloody war battles—the *Oberlin Review* observed defensively that only one of the seven footballers was hurt seriously enough to prevent his playing in the next game five days later. Then, too, it went on, if all the intramural class matches at Oberlin as well as the varsity's games in the fall of 1894 were taken into account, "The foot ball season at Oberlin ought to convince all local critics that reports of injuries are largely exaggerated. There have been during the past season ten or a dozen different elevens composed of Oberlin men, making an aggregate of at least one hundred and fifty men engaged in the dangerous (?) game. And no one is at all the worse. A few sprains and bruises, which are already nearly forgotten, comprise the 'casualties.'"[2]

Oberlin's experience notwithstanding, the issue of serious injuries would not go away. After the 1905 season, the constant criticism leveled at the game reached an uproar when the *Chicago Tribune* reported that eighteen footballers had been killed and 159 others had been seriously injured in games that fall.[3] Many schools, including Columbia, Northwestern, and Stanford, immediately banned the game.

Headmasters at seventy preparatory schools were so dismayed by the violence of mass-momentum plays that they asked the Intercollegiate Football Rules Committee to ban them altogether. One of them, Endicott Peabody of Groton, asked President Theodore Roosevelt to speak directly about the situation to the "Big Three"—Harvard, Yale, and Princeton—which were so influential in the development of college football.

Roosevelt was personally appalled at the brutality of the sport. He was shocked when he saw the photograph of a bloodied Swarthmore player whom opposing players from the University of Pennsylvania had purposely targeted.[4] Then, too, his own son had received a black eye and other bruises in scrimmages with the Harvard freshman squad.[5] He was, however, a fan, and when it was suggested that Harvard abolish the game, he declared that it "would be a real misfortune to lose so manly and vigorous a game."[6]

Coupled with the president's abhorrence of football's violence was his repugnance at the dishonest practices the game had encouraged—special inducements for athletes and the hiring of so-called tramp athletes, among others. "Brutality in playing the game should awaken the heartiest and most plainly shown contempt for the player guilty of it," he declared, "especially if this brutality is coupled with a low cunning."[7]

Urged on by Peabody, Roosevelt summoned representatives of the Big Three to the White House. One was Walter Camp of Yale, an old friend of Roosevelt's when he attended Harvard and the two schools competed. "Brutality and foul play should receive the same summary punishment given to a man who cheats at cards," he told them.[8] One unsubstantiated story has it that the president warned the college representatives that unless they took on the responsibility of making the sport safer, he would issue an executive order and take steps to ban it altogether. Whether Roosevelt actually made such a threat or even had the power to prohibit the sport is a moot point. He did urge the three schools to draw up an agreement that would lead to clean and ethical playing. The influence of his position as president, as well as his reputation as a vocal exponent of Muscular Christianity in general, and football in particular, was enough to spur the formation a few weeks later of what came to be called the Intercollegiate Athletic Association of America.[9]

The association focused on establishing rules to make football less dangerous. It did not, however, address the concerns of critics who saw the sport's other negative aspects. One of them was the noted American historian Frederick Jackson Turner. Turner described football as a "business, carried on too often by professionals, supported by levies on the public, bringing in vast gate receipts, demoralizing student ethics, and confusing the ideals of sport, manliness, and decency."[10]

At many schools, a trend was developing—students were losing control of athletic activities, first to the faculty, then to alumni and their school's governing body. The main reason was money. Football was expensive, and colleges were bending to pressures both to support the rising costs incurred by a team and to reap the revenues that a successful one earned. In full realization of football's status as a moneymaker, Harvard launched a stadium-building craze in 1903 when it constructed the first reinforced concrete arena. With temporary bleachers added for games with Yale, the stadium could seat more than forty thousand spectators.

Oberlin, though, followed its own path. The faculty remained adamant about not underwriting the sport. The professors might have relished Oberlin's new status in the college world that football had wrought, but that didn't mean they wanted to support it financially. As far as they were concerned, the cost of paying a coach, to cite one costly expense, was still the responsibility of the student athletic association.

That was a major blow to the association. It started the 1894 season in debt, and while it took in $1,280.38 that fall and winter, it spent almost the entire amount and was paying a bank seven percent interest on a six-month $350 loan.[11] This was at a time when other schools were already reaping substantial financial rewards from football. A Harvard-Penn game, to cite one example, took in fifty thousand dollars at the gate against twenty thousand dollars in expenses.[12] Professor James Monroe offered to help make up the Oberlin deficit by giving a lecture for the benefit of the coach fund. His topic was Frederick Douglass, the black leader whom Monroe had known personally and with whom he had worked on the antislavery cause before the Civil War.[13]

Despite supporters such as Monroe, the student organization never made a go of financing the school's sports programs. As late as the 1905–6 academic year, athletics were a losing proposition. The surplus from the football season that year was a meager $7.48. The basketball team was the only one to turn a profit; it took in $131.32. Deficits were run up by the baseball and track teams, and an interscholastic track meet ran in the red.[14]

Well aware that the student association was admittedly "deeply in debt,"[15] the faculty ordered the athletic oversight committee to assume stricter control of the total sports program. It was particularly worried about the commercialization fostered by student athletic organizations at other schools. It voted to "recommend" that Oberlin's teams—its football, baseball, and tennis varsities—"shall not contest with teams made up of other than college students or on grounds not under the control of colleges or schools." And, in a reminder that religion was not a dead issue at Oberlin, it made a "request" that the oversight committee "exercise all possible care in regard to the prevention of traveling on the Sabbath."[16]

Oberlin played Baldwin-Wallace and Hiram for the first time in 1895, but because of some cancellations, the team met only four other schools that fall. It compiled a record of four wins, one loss, and one tie (a scoreless game with Kenyon). The record made Oberlin the self-proclaimed champion of Ohio, the only college in the state with a "just claim" to the title because it had defeated every Ohio college it met except Kenyon. There was the added good news that the football games netted several hundred dollars.[17]

The 1895 varsity had an outside coach—W. M. (Billy) Richards, who had been a regular substitute on Yale teams. But Richards demonstrated little talent for shepherding the team, so, while other schools were hiring professional coaches, the association decided to recruit its next coach from the team itself, a throwback to the early days when the captain of the varsity doubled as coach. The man chosen was Clate Fauver, the first in a line of Oberlinites who were to guide the team over the next half century. Fauver also played on the 1896 team, but he was not its captain. That honor went to Jim McMurray. Under Fauver's guidance, Oberlin held its opponents scoreless in its five wins; but the team also lost three games and tied one.[18] Despite the losses, Oberlin again claimed the state championship.

The 1897 varsity won five games. It lost one contest and tied another. Following the 1898 season—during which the team compiled a 7–1 record, losing only to Cornell—Oberlin boasted that it was "everywhere recognized as one of the leading foot-ball colleges of the West," that "very rarely has it failed to win the Ohio state championship and its remarkable record in recent seasons has challenged the respect of foot-ball experts throughout the country. Not less a subject for pride is the dignity and manliness which the team has always shown in hard-fought contests and in all dealing with its rivals. No college has done more than Oberlin to prove that this much-criticised game, when properly managed, is in the highest degree conducive to health of body and to the development of the virtues that especially denote the gentleman."[19]

Ohio newspapers voted Oberlin the champions of Ohio in 1909, 1910, and 1911. It held second place to Ohio State in 1912, and tied OSU for first place in 1913.[20] So it seemed, for a time, that football could thrive with little financial support and with the school's ideals intact. At any other school, victorious season after victorious season would have been the cause for cheers. At Oberlin, though, it provoked a backlash. The faculty fussed and worried. It was leery of the increasing attention football commanded on so many campuses. In 1910, it warned against "the over-emphasis on winning" and what it considered the alarming employment of "high salaried" coaches that make "'amateur' athletics impossible as a profession." Although the faculty did not call for the elimination of football at Oberlin, it suggested that students try playing the less-injury-prone games of rugby or soccer.[21] The suggestion, not unsurprisingly, failed to stir any positive student reaction.

There was some justification for the faculty's growing concern. Across the nation, in the years after 1905, football had become synonymous with big business, thriving especially on the university level. Intent on increasing their student populations, Columbia, Northwestern, and Stanford put aside their earlier reservations and revived their teams, for there was competition

OHIO - 39
OBERLIN - 0

A sign of the times ahead: A successful end run in the 39–0 defeat that Ohio State handed Oberlin at Columbus in a game in 1914. Two years later, again in Columbus, OSU racked up a 128–0 drubbing, the worst loss Oberlin has ever suffered. Courtesy of the Ohio State University Photo Archives.

not only on the football field but in the classroom as well. A football team—especially a winning football team—offered so many ancillary benefits: It increased enrollments, promoted a school's name, won it a reputation that attracted not only students but also teachers. And it brought in revenue. Rule changes, in particular the legalization of the forward pass, made the game more exciting, attracting greater spectator support. At the urging of Walter Camp, Yale, for example, built a stadium that seated more than seventy thousand fans.[22]

In the same year that Camp persuaded Yale to erect the huge stadium, 1913, the Oberlin student association found itself penniless. It had no money to finance any sports activities whatsoever, so the college itself finally took over complete control of all athletic expenses. In a matter of a few years' time, the association was disbanded, its duties and responsibilities completely taken over by the college's department of physical education.[23] By 1919, the department had direct control of both intercollegiate and intramural athletics.[24] Oberlin's sports program would remain within the context of a scholastic environment.

Action in a 1921 game. Players still did not wear identifying numbers.

The college would field a football team, but the game would be played on its terms. Studies still came first. A faculty committee found that Oberlin football teams played, on the average, fewer games each season than other schools. That was fine with the committee, but it was nevertheless concerned that near the middle of the football schedule, the players "were likely to neglect their studies, expecting to make them up after the close of the season." The committee recommended that any student found deficient in classroom work be dropped from intercollegiate play.[25]

Gradually, after the turn of the century, as colleges across the nation expanded into universities, and universities became educational behemoths, their governing boards, composed to a large extent by successful businessmen, took over athletic policy from faculty members. They were the ones who spurred the building of stadiums way out of proportion to the number of students who were enrolled.[26] Colleges that Oberlin had once contested, the ones that had put it on a par with the best in the West, grew rapidly and could afford to mount varsities underwritten by scholarships and other recruitment perks.

Soon Oberlin could no longer field a team that was even competitive with some of its early rivals—Michigan, for example. After 1897, Oberlin did not play Michigan again until 1902. By then, both schools had experienced a decade of steady, almost uninterrupted rise in enrollments. But Michigan's student body, and hence its source of potential football players, was still well over twice the size of Oberlin's.[27] In that year and the next two years, Wolverine teams amassed a total of 180 points against Oberlin, while Oberlin's

Oberlin students rally on the eve of an Ohio State game in the early 1920s.

varsities failed to score a single point. In all, then, in the seven games the two schools played between the years 1891 and 1905, Oberlin won only one—the controversial game in 1892—though Michigan, of course, considers its record with Oberlin unblemished.

Oberlin teams fared better with Ohio State, at least for a time, because OSU remained a small school, on a par with Oberlin, until after the turn of the century. By 1916, however, Ohio State's enrollment began to increase dramatically, and that year its student body was more than three times that of Oberlin's.[28] As with Michigan, the disparagement was visible on the gridiron. Ohio State swamped Oberlin 128–0 that year. In the next two games that the two schools played, in 1917 and 1920, OSU teams racked up 83 points, Oberlin not a one.

A miracle of sorts occurred in 1921, a thrilling 7–6 upset at Columbus engineered by Oberlin's varsity against an Ohio State team that had gone to the Rose Bowl the previous year. Although outweighed twenty-four pounds to a man by OSU players, Oberlin's eleven allowed only one Ohio State touchdown, and that in the first five minutes of the game.[29] It held after that, allowing Ohio State only five first downs. On offense, it drove for nine first downs.[30] Most of them came during a sensational eighty-five-yard march down the field in the third quarter that culminated in a short pass across the goal line for Oberlin's lone, winning touchdown and point-after.

The Ohio State coach was so upset by the loss that he made his squad stay on the field after the game for a special practice session.[31] Oberlin was the

The highlight of Oberlin's undefeated 1921 season was its remarkable 7–6 victory over Ohio State. It merited a two-line, eight-column headline in the *Columbus Citizen*.

last school in the state to defeat OSU in football.[32] Its triumph was, according to the college's theology scholar Kemper Fullerton, both physical and moral: Oberlin's men were "better trained," and there was "the fact they don't smoke and live a fast life as so many men do in other colleges."[33]

The 1921 team was the first Oberlin squad to record an undefeated season since the 1892 varsity did so almost thirty years earlier. But in truth, by then it was evident that Oberlin was, year by year, being totally outclassed by the schools it had once played. In the successful football season of 1921, for instance, Oberlin had an enrollment of 1,758 students.[34] That same fall, once-tiny Ohio State had more than four times as many students: 8,850.[35] Over a thirty-year span between 1892 and 1922, the two schools had played twenty-six games (including Ohio State's second loss to Oberlin in 1892 that OSU does not recognize). Three games—in 1910, 1911, and 1913—were played to scoreless ties. Of the rest, OSU won thirteen, Oberlin ten.

When they parted ways, OSU followed a crowded path marked by dollar signs. "When we beat Wisconsin in the last 50 seconds," an Ohio State halfback said, "I recall $100,000 was raised for the building fund."[36] The money went to build a huge, horseshoe-shaped stadium that seated 85,000 fans. The university dedicated the stadium in the same year it last played Oberlin, 1922.[37] Its attendance that season totaled 162,500 fans.[38] Michigan's stadium, originally built for 72,000 spectators, was completed in 1927.[39] That season, nearly 300,000 fans watched the Wolverines play.[40]

By way of contrast, during that time, the stands on opposite sides of Oberlin's gridiron seated, combined, a total of only 4,280 spectators.[41] Even before Ohio State's enormous stadium was completed, OSU was able to draw 8,415 spectators to its 7–6 loss to Oberlin in 1921. Yet the most Oberlin attracted to a game that fall, a contest against Wooster, was 5,809 fans, and for all four of its home stands that season its total attendance was only 11,395. The Oberlin football team that year showed a net profit of $8,059, an increase of $1,910 over the previous season.[42] Ohio State's athletic association entered the academic year with a $43,532.85 profit; it had made just shy of $160,000 on gate receipts alone.[43] The most Oberlin ever netted from a home game with Case, for example, occurred in 1923 when it took in $3,384.[44] The enormous difference in the revenue-producing potential of football between the two schools was exemplified when Oberlin opened its own new stadium in 1925. It had a seating capacity of only 3,050.[45]

One recurrent bone of contention at Oberlin and many other schools was eligibility. Some teams fielded not only freshmen and graduate students, but also transfer students and, in some cases still, hired ringers. In 1903, the Oberlin faculty, which had ten years earlier voted to bar postgraduates from varsity teams, took up the question of excluding Academy students from them. It realized, however, that a school the size of Oberlin could not field enough athletes to man all the teams now engaged in sports. The exclusion of the Cads, it reported, "would seriously jeopardize" the school's standing in state athletics. So the faculty came up with a compromise. It decided, with regard to football, that as many as three prep students could be eligible to play. However, if two men of equal ability sought a position on the varsity—one a college man, the other a Cad—preference had to be given to the college student.[46]

The appointment in 1906 of Fred Savage, a hero of the victorious 1892 football team, as Oberlin's director of athletics reinforced college policy regarding its sports program and set the tone for the future. Savage fought against the commercialization of football. He campaigned to have the college take over the underwriting of all sports. He also pressed for installing physical education graduates with faculty ranking in every coaching position—a precedent set by the University of Chicago when it hired Amos Alonzo Stagg as an associate professor in 1892. The faculty-status program

Some Oberlin College sign maker got carried away at reunion time in 1908; members of the undefeated team in the fall of 1892 would have been part of the graduating class in 1893, not 1892.

was inaugurated in 1911 when Glenn Gray, captain of the 1909 football team, was appointed head coach.[47] The coaches of all teams were now regular faculty members, unlike the professionals hired on a season-by-season basis at so many other schools.[48]

Savage joined Walter Camp on the rules committee of the newly formed national football association. Its revised regulations, he said, were a "large factor in eliminating the evils of the game." Savage also became a firm supporter of the Ohio Intercollegiate Athletic Association, which the state's "Big Six"—Oberlin, Case, Kenyon, Ohio State, Ohio Wesleyan, and Western Reserve (previously Adelbert)—had formed in 1903. It had devised eligibility rules limiting participation in intercollegiate athletics to undergraduates, barring freshmen—and, by inference, preparatory students—from varsity play, and setting a three-year limit to any student's participation. Savage said all the rules "have proven particularly wise."[49]

Ironically, just at the time Savage was setting a high moral tone for collegiate football, Oberlin faced an embarrassing scandal. After repeated warnings, the college in the fall of 1916 dismissed sixteen male students, suspended two more, and put four others on probation. They were members of four organizations that had started out as cooperative housing ventures. They were accused of violating Oberlin's strict rule against secret, self-perpetuating fraternities. Two of the subrosa frats had closed in 1914, but the other two had promised to disband and hadn't.[50] Of the punished students, ten were men who had played on the 1915 football varsity and were expected to play on the 1916 one. Their loss and the hospitalization of the squad's coach forced postponement of the team's first scheduled game against Heidelberg College. Oberlin scraped up enough men to field an eleven that year, but it was a green team, hopelessly lacking in solid backfield material.[51] They lost all seven games, managing to amass a total of only 16 points in three of them, while allowing their opponents 378. The most humiliating defeat was the 128–0 loss to Ohio State.[52]

Coincidentally, in 1916 Oberlin closed its Academy, and as a result, cut off the breeding ground for many of its players. The result was a marked drop-off in future football candidates. The Oberlin teams that followed in the 1920s compiled respectable records for a number of years—6–1 in 1922, 8–0 in 1924, 7–1 in both 1925 and 1926—but the schools Oberlin played now included institutions such as Hiram, Baldwin-Wallace, Albion, Wooster, and Marietta. Ohio State was already playing schools with growing enrollments and similar football policies: Minnesota, Michigan, Chicago, Purdue, and Illinois.[53] In the summer of 1928, OSU withdrew from the Ohio Conference.[54]

Although Oberlin was playing little-known schools, morale on campus was high. After playing intercollegiate football for thirty-five years, students at a chapel meeting in 1926 at last awarded themselves, and their teams, a nickname. The contest was among "Savages" (after Fred Savage), "Kingbirds" (in honor of the school president, Henry Churchill King), and "Yeomen" (a dehyphenating of "Ye-O-Men"). Yeomen won out. (There was an attempt after World War II to change Yeomen to Crimson Knights, but the new name did not stick.[55] A more recent effort, touted by the *Oberlin Review*, refers to the football team as the Crimson Thunder, but Yeomen is still the nickname in the school media guide. Women engaged in intercollegiate sports such as lacrosse and swimming are called Yeowomen, though the independently minded basketball team calls itself Lady Crimson.)

Oberlin's 1891 flying wedge fifty years later. The reunion, marking the fiftieth anniversary of intercollegiate football at Oberlin in October 1941, brought together surviving members of the college's first varsity squad. The veteran on the far left is unidentified. The others are (from left) Fred Savage, Louis Hart, Clate Fauver, James McCord, Wallace Grosvenor, Carl Semple, Steve Williams, Carl Kinsley, Lynds Jones, and Charles Borican.

The Depression was a watershed of sorts at Oberlin—the beginning of a fundamental demographic change in its student body. More students began coming from major cities and, in general, the urban East. For Oberlin, a non-denominational Christian college—that is, a Protestant school—that meant a dramatic increase in the number of Catholics and Jews. At the same time, the outlook of most faculty members became more secularized. Attendance at chapel—a major opportunity for students and faculty to meet and mingle and a conscientious part of Oberlin's earlier godly bent—was no longer required. That left fewer and fewer events, music recitals in the main, to bring the two groups together.[56] Eventually, in 1966, Oberlin's religious legacy was abandoned when the theological seminary closed its doors and joined the Divinity School at Vanderbilt University in Nashville, Tennessee.

In October 1941, on the eve of World War II, as part of Alumni Homecoming Day, some aging faces with familiar names appeared on the football field. To celebrate the fiftieth anniversary of Oberlin football, members of the team of 1891 gathered for a special reunion. The team's captain, Wallace Grosvenor, was on hand. So, too, were Charles Borican, Clayton Fauver, Louis

Oberlin Varsity Squad, Composed of Veteran
Marine and Bluejacket Fightingmen, Gathers Under
Historic Elm for Trip to Rochester
Score: Oberlin 27—Rochester 12

The reason for Oberlin's success in the 1940s: Military trainees drawn from all across the country during the war. Oberlin went from a washout season before World War II began in 1941, when it lost all seven games, to seven wins and a tie in 1943. Even better, the 1945 team above won all eight games on its schedule, a record never since equaled by Oberlin.

Hart, Lynds Jones, Carl Kinsley, James McCord, Fred Savage, Carl Semple, and Carl Williams. "Grove" was photographed shaking hands with the captain of the 1941 team, whose uniform was in sharp contrast to the outfits worn in the old timers' day. The youth was helmeted and wore shoulder pads and knee and shin guards.[57]

The war that broke out less than two months later ironically provided Oberlin with another rare sports opportunity to celebrate. The college became a center for the education of a navy V-12 unit that each year drew more than 250 young men from across the nation to the school.[58] The football team, made up of a number of the hardy sailors, won all eight of its games. It amassed 231 points, held four of its opponents scoreless, and allowed its four other foes only forty points among them.[59]

The war experience was a fluke. Afterwards, Oberlin's teams were competitive against the kind of schools it was playing, but the game was headed in directions that the school was unequipped to keep up with. New developments—the advent of free substitutions and platooning—added even more excitement to the sport and drew increasing numbers of spectators to games throughout the nation. Between 1953 and 1970, attendance at college football contests skyrocketed from nearly 17 million fans to more than 29 million.[60] But larger squads required much more money.[61] Commercialization of the sport became endemic. Oberlin refused to resort to the kind of recruiting for, and financing of, a football team that was encouraged and customary, particularly on the university level. As early as 1951, a special faculty committee on eligibility reinforced Oberlin's rule against a failing student representing the college in any public event.[62] Two years later, the faculty adopted a statement of policy that was really both a reiteration of the college's long-standing policy and a guidepost for a future fraught with temptations of high-powered, well-financed, income-producing college football: "In no way does the College grant special consideration to the students participating in intercollegiate athletics. All students meet the same standards for admission, scholarship, and graduation; all students qualify under the same standards for scholarship aid, financial assistance, and employment."[63]

Students didn't seem to mind the school's course, even from 1951 through 1962 when Oberlin teams never experienced a season in which they won more games than they lost. Indeed, the 1955 team lost every one of its eight games. "Still," a 1957 grad recalled, "there were moments, especially at halftime, when we scoffed at the opposing college's lower average SAT score and cheered the Oberlin marching band, composed of Conservatory students who played Beethoven and made more body contact in performing their routines than our defense did during the game."[64]

Oberlin's teams deteriorated in the three decades after that, so much so that the exhilaration prompted by the 6–2 record set by the 1963 team—Oberlin's first winning season in thirteen years—was so exciting that, so the story goes, an aging English professor joined in tearing down the goalposts at the final game of the season.[65]

On the surface, the appointment of thirty-one-year-old Jack Scott as athletic director in 1972 reinvigorated the entire sports program at Oberlin. Considered a radical at the time, Scott expanded the school's athletic budget for women, introducing them to cross-country and swimming teams. He hired blacks as coaches, opened the college gymnasium to townspeople, eliminated admission fees at all athletic events, gave teams a major voice in the selection of their coaches, and added classes to the physical education curriculum that dealt with the sociological impact of sports. He cared, said one supporter, as much about the lacrosse team as he did about the football team. But at the same time, Scott's methods antagonized both the faculty and students. He accused one dean of being a racist. His authoritarian ways alienated athletes. Eighteen months after he took command, Scott resigned, leaving behind a legacy of bitterness.

The same year Scott left, 1974, was the last time the football team had a winning record—five wins versus four losses. Barely sixteen men turned out for the 1975 team, which won only two games against four losses.[66] Even after the college was instrumental in the creation of the North Coast Athletic Conference in the 1980s and its teams played against other schools dedicated to similar academic priorities such as Allegheny and Earlham, Oberlin was rarely competitive any more. A major reason was the lack of interest in physical education; the number of phys-ed majors had dwindled to as little as one a year. As a result, a century after it pioneered in physical education training, Oberlin officially dropped it as a major in 1985.

The lack of interest in physical education was reflected in the school's depleted talent pool. Oberlin's prime concern became mustering enough football candidates to field a team, much less win. A 56–0 loss to Allegheny in 1992 left the varsity with only thirteen of its twenty-nine players healthy enough to suit up, forcing Oberlin to forfeit its next game.[67] The Yeomen that year were "unequivocally the worst team in football," according to the cable sports station ESPN.[68]

If that was not bad enough, the 1994 team managed only one touchdown in nine games. At a time when all other schools fielded both offensive and defensive platoons, only nineteen students showed up for Oberlin's season finale that fall, and only its quarterback was spared from playing on both offense and defense. So few students went out for football in the early 1990s, in fact, that it was not unusual at games that the time clock was kept running after it should have been stopped when the ball went out of bounds— "clock management," designed, with a rival's complicity, to shorten the game and thereby cut down on injuries to Oberlin's few players.[69]

Listed as a Division III school, Oberlin by the end of the 1996 season had lost forty straight games. It opened the 1997 season at home with an 18–17 win over Thiel College of Greenville, Pennsylvania, its first victory since the last game of the 1992 season. Jubilation over the triumph momentarily transformed the school's students, ordinarily complacent where football was concerned. The campus rang with celebrations. At the football field, the scoreboard remained lit up for days. But in the ensuing Saturdays, the team reverted to its losing ways, falling at one point to Wittenberg 74–0. It ended the season with nine losses. In the next season, 1998, the Yeomen lost all ten of its games, suffering in particular humiliating losses of 68–0 to Wittenberg and 71–0 to Allegheny. The defeats put Oberlin's record in the six years since 1993 at one victory against fifty-nine losses. "And if that is not frustration," a sports correspondent for the *Oberlin Review* declared, "nothing is, to be sure."[70]

The fall 1999 season held much promise. The Oberlin eleven sported a new nickname—the Crimson Thunder—a new coach and, particularly encouraging, a new schedule. The coach, Jeff Ramsey, made it clear that the season would be a rebuilding one; Oberlin's games would be, in effect, practice scrimmages. The team would not have to face the powerhouse varsities of the North Coast Athletic Conference—Wittenberg and Allegheny. And the conference agreed that, come the fall 2000 season, its members would abide by a so-called power-rated system, with Oberlin on the lowest rung and with the easiest schedule.

Unfortunately, Oberlin could not field more than about thirty players for any one game, so despite their heroics and the relaxed schedule, the 1999 season results were chilling: the Crimson Thunder lost all its ten games, including what was its best hope for a win, a much-heralded game, dubbed the Brain Bowl, against lowly Swarthmore, which took the field with a twenty-six-game losing streak. But Oberlin lost 42–6. And a game against the Pomona-Pitzer Sagehens of California—a contest especially arranged to even the odds for victory—ended in the dismal score of Pomona-Pitzer 65, Oberlin 0.

There were, however, some gratifying notes. For one thing, the number of students attending Oberlin's home games grew appreciably, and to spur the team on, an ad hoc pep band, cheerleaders, and pom-pom girls appeared. Then, too, the determination and grit of the under-strengthed, often-demeaned Oberlin team was epitomized in an unsolicited remark made by the father of the quarterback of the Thiel team, which defeated Oberlin 63–12. The man, himself a career football coach, wrote that, although his son's team won, he was "more encouraged with the spirit" that Oberlin symbolized. "It is all that is great about America: the willingness to strive no matter what the odds, able to pick yourself up and get back in the game, to risk it all for just one more chance at glory. Well, Yeomen of Oberlin, glory was yours on that day, won at the cost of the game, but not at the price of your pride, dedication, or courage."[71]

Fifty-six players turned out for the 2000 season, but despite renewed interest the Yeomen amassed only 47 points to their opponents' 301 and lost all ten contests on their schedule, extending the Oberlin losing streak to thirty-nine games—and raising once more the question of football's viability at the college.

EPILOGUE

Then rally we gladly around it,
That banner to each of us dear,
And bravely we look to the future,
And thrown down the guantlet [sic] to fear. . . .
—Cleveland K. Chase

By college—not university—standards, Oberlin is a large school. Its current total enrollment of twenty-eight hundred students outnumbers the student body of most of its current football opponents. But, if anything, its students—always known as being left of center—have become even more alienated from the side of American culture that promotes commercial high school and college football. They are turned off by the fame—they would say notoriety—that is showered on athletes, and resent the debunking of academic interests. Not surprisingly, in the past, they have not attended Oberlin's football games. Average attendance at home contests in the mid-1990s was 335 spectators, most of whom, it was believed, were the parents of players on the visiting team.[1]

During his early years as director of athletics, Fred Savage fought to have more time devoted to athletics. "I view in considerable alarm," he said in 1913, "the gradual encroachment here at Oberlin of the schedule of classes, seminars, field work and laboratories upon the time of the students."[2] In time, though, Savage put the school's athletic programs into a different perspective and became a proponent of eliminating gate receipts and reducing team schedules. In 1923, the football varsity was reduced to only about seventy-five minutes of intensive practice three days a week, with a light workout on the Friday before a Saturday game and no practice whatsoever on Monday. As little as ninety minutes a week were spent on actual scrimmage. It was a type of football, one observer wrote, that required "little physical strain," depending instead "largely on sound coaching, clever tactics, and the tradition of good fellowship and teamwork."[3]

By then, Savage could say, "Oberlin College has come to be widely recognized for its conduct of sports—sports for sport's sake, for the love of the contest and for the good of the rank and file of the students, and not for any ulterior motives." Its athletic policy, he continued, "has been merely a policy of simple, downright honesty, the acceptance of students as they come to the College and the development and training of them to the best of our ability."[4]

Through the years, a succession of athletic directors from Savage on has reiterated Oberlin's policy. John Herbert Nichols, who succeeded Savage in 1935, believed that the "ONLY REALISTIC APPROACH [his emphasis] for an educational institution is the policy that uses athletics as one of the fine educational opportunities for the complete education of the students." When the program is financed "from the regular academic budget," he said, "the problems of pressure, recruitment, subsidization, sportsmanship, and scholarship standards are solved almost automatically."[5]

Lysle Kendall Butler, a star of the 1925 football team, headed Oberlin's physical education, intramural, and athletics programs after 1955. He echoed his predecessors: "The purpose of athletics," he declared, is "not to entertain or for publicity or to raise money, but simply to educate."[6] Similarly, Oberlin's presidents have all restated, in almost identical terms, the college's view: Academics take priority over athletics. One, Henry Churchill King, who was president from 1903 to 1927, said that "all college so-called sports" have "their most valuable office, it should never be forgotten, not as serious business or money-making enterprises, but simply as PLAY. A relative good becomes a serious evil, when it is allowed to overtop greater values; but in its place it contributes to the sanity and health of all other interests."[7]

Oberlin, said his successor, Ernest Hatch Wilkins, "has never financed athletes directly or indirectly because they were athletes, and has never made it easier for athletes to enter or to stay in college than for non-athletes."[8] His successor in 1947, William Edwards Stevenson—a winner of an Olympic gold medal in track in 1924—insisted that its athletic programs be justified as educational or recreational, "not because they make money or provide public entertainment."[9] *His* successor, Robert Kenneth Carr, made a point of saying that Oberlin took "pride in avoiding over-emphasis of intercollegiate athletics."[10]

Not surprisingly, however, in view of the college's dismal football record, the students, the professors, the college administration, and the school's alumni have, since the 1970s, debated, sometimes heatedly, what the role of football should be at Oberlin. A faculty study in 1970 supported the school's involvement in the sport and commended Oberlin for deciding not to go along with the Ohio Conference's official designation of an annual state champion. Oberlin chose instead to schedule games outside the conference, diversifying its schedule by playing schools such as Carnegie-Mellon and Hamilton, whose athletic policies were comparable to Oberlin's.[11]

The seven faculty members and three students on another study committee in 1978 were evenly divided, five for and five against, over the question of whether the college should continue its football program. (Amazingly, the faculty members were divided four to three in favor of retaining it, the students two to one against.)[12] When, subsequently, the issue of abolishing football was put before the general faculty, those who favored retention stressed the negative consequences of dropping football, chiefly a drop in male admissions and a reduction in alumni financial support.[13] When they finally voted, forty-eight teachers favored abolishing football, but seventy-nine were for retaining it.[14] The support for keeping the football program failed, however, to silence the debate over the sport's future at Oberlin. The issues are familiar to anyone who has followed the team in recent years.

There was a time, a century ago, when football provided a means for exercise for Oberlin's men students, an opportunity to get out into the fresh air and relax from constant studying. It was an outlet for the unspoken sexual urges of the player, their male fans, and their female counterparts in the college. But in a day and age when students have a wide variety of athletic and exercise programs to choose from, when the time for them to do so is available, and the facilities for developing a sound, healthy body are handy, what does football contribute? Then, too, is football relevant to a student body becoming multicultural, with a rising percentage of international students interested in other sports, such as soccer? And how do you justify its costs at a time when the participation of women in all intercollegiate sports except football is now a given?

Why is football important? What are the ramifications if it is dropped? Is the University of Chicago's experience relevant? What is especially fascinating about Chicago's football experience is its connection to Oberlin. Before he became president of Oberlin, Ernest Wilkins was dean of colleges at Chicago. He conducted a survey of the grades of football players on the university's 1923 and 1924 teams, finding that either "the football men are mentally of low grade, or that the conditions under which they live during the football quarter are such as to prevent them from doing their work properly." Wilkins was for drastic reform of Chicago's football poli-cy, but he opposed abolishing the game. However, four years after Wilkins's critical study was written, Chicago had a new president, Robert Maynard Hutchins, who believed that football and extracurricular activities were sec-ondary to an academic education.

Coincidentally, Hutchins had grown up in Oberlin, and the man he brought in to run Chicago's athletic program was a friend of his from the town, Thomas N. Metcalf. An Oberlin student and later its director of athletics, Metcalf had coached the college's football team to its upset victory over Ohio State in 1921. Metcalf was an embodiment of Oberlin's athletic philosophy: "There is no necessity for athletics to be over-emphasized to the extent of interference with academic work." He described recruiting and subsidizing players as the "greatest evil" in college athletics. Chicago's physical education department, he announced, would operate without regard to gate receipts.[15]

Following the 1939 season, Chicago abandoned football. "There is no doubt," declared Hutchins, "that on the whole the game has been a major handicap to education in the United States." In Chicago's case, he explained, many of the universities on its schedule were now much larger than they were only fifteen years ago, and as many as half of the football players in the Big Ten were physical education majors. "If you win," Hutchins declared, "you must keep on winning." Moreover, he continued, football had done much to confirm popular misconceptions of a university as either a kindergarten or a country club. "Other sports develop cooperation, team spirit, sportsman-ship, and fair play just as well as football," he added.[16]

Did Chicago benefit from the abolition of football? Many people didn't think so. "The loss for the university was and remains real," William H. McNeill, a distinguished historian who had been editor of the college news-paper in the 1930s, wrote in 1991. "Hutchins muffed a chance to continue [the] tradition of pioneering in sports and cashing in on the public atten-tion football commanded; and the student body lost the chance of supple-menting their superior intellectual prowess with a more visceral but very valuable sort of collective identity, based on association with famous ath-letes and cheering them on—thus associating themselves and the whole university with another, quite genuine kind of excellence."[17]

No major university followed Chicago's lead. Indeed, in more recent times, spurred in great measure by the promise of huge television fees, the opposite has been true. The trustees of Ohio State voted in November 1997 to ex-pand their already monster-size football stadium to accommodate ninety-eight thousand fans by adding more seats and luxury boxes. At the same time, the Universities of Virginia and Alabama and the State University of New York at Buffalo were engaged in multimillion-dollar expansion programs.[18]

Another example of football's impact on educational policy was experienced at Rutgers, which had played Princeton in the first football game in 1869. In 1994, Rutgers opened a $30 million, 40,500-seat stadium with high hopes of generating a sizeable annual revenue for the university. "A successful athletic program," said the school's president, Francis L. Lawrence, "underlines the university's academic reputation in an especially compelling way."[19] Rutgers' team, however, suffered a string of losing seasons, failing to win even one game in 1997. At best, the stadium was never more than half filled, and ticket sales fell off precipitously. The school's entire athletic program had by then lost $31.5 million in the past decade.[20] New Jersey's governor Christine Todd Whitman and state legislators of both parties found the situation intolerable. All across the nation, other state-supported institutions were pouring money into intercollegiate sports, making headlines and hefty profits. So in January 1998 Whitman took the unprecedented step of intervening in university affairs and proposed her own candidate to run the school's athletic program—a marketing specialist who was head of the state's Sports and Exposition Authority. "High profile, winning athletic teams attract attention to the school," a spokesperson for the governor said. "They attract resources and they attract prestige." One critic, alumnus Milton Friedman, a Nobel Prize–winning economist, pleaded for the school to turn away from big-time sports and return to academic and intellectual values. "As long as athletes are admitted on lower standards than other students," he said, "sports is a corruptive influence on higher education."[21] But much to the chagrin of Friedman and many faculty members, who wanted more money spent on hiring professors and reducing class sizes, Lawrence agreed with the governor. "Sports takes up one whole section in the newspaper," the Rutgers president declared. "We want athletics to complement the university and develop its stature to the point where we are as successful as our peer institutions."[22]

It is a dilemma, and there is no easy answer to whether football is a worthwhile educational experience. It is an exhilarating game, fun to watch. It does bolster school spirit, and it can certainly contribute to school income. On the other hand, it is a sport limited to physically adept men and, unlike other sports, few of its participants continue to play it after graduation. It also lends itself to corrupt practices, influenced by the need to win: relaxed educational standards for players, coddling them with special perks, ignoring incidents of their antisocial behavior.

A century ago, Oberlin chose, and stuck to, a different course than schools such as Michigan and Ohio State took. It was, is, commendable. But is it practical today? A century ago, the football team did wonders for student morale and promoted Oberlin's name throughout the country. But in recent years the school has become the butt of jokes. How do you make the team competitive? Some proponents of maintaining Oberlin's football program have suggested starting another conference that would include schools attuned to Oberlin's academic standards—for example, including in its roster Swarthmore, Carleton, and Grinnell—but travel costs and travel time are so prohibitive that the idea is impractical. So how do you make the team competitive? Recruit more football candidates? Provide athletic scholarships unrelated to academic standards?

Oberlin's current president, Nancy S. Dye, is committed to continuing an intercollegiate athletics program, but it "must strive," she wrote in a broad overview of Oberlin's future, "to achieve a competitive" one. Dye's remarks were made in conjunction with a special study issued in April 1997 by a school committee devoted to long-range planning. Its conclusions recalled what all of Oberlin's presidents have expressed for the past century and a half. The committee called for a "renewed commitment" to athletics. "We value achievement, but worry about overwork," it declared. Then, the committee added, in what would have been taken in the nineteenth century as an argument for the Muscular Christianity movement: "For the value of sports resides in addressing the needs of a person for wholeness and a sense of physical and mental well-being; and it contributes to such life skills as tolerance for difference, the building of self-discipline, the celebration of collective achievement, and a healthy respect for the body as well as the mind."[23]

What are Dye and the committee saying about Oberlin? By competitive, Dye apparently means that, as far as football is concerned, the team ought to be able to win some of its games. Yet how that can be accomplished is one of the unresolved questions that has been argued over for years.

A century ago, Oberlin wrestled with the issue of whether football had a place in a serious college setting. It decided to permit the sport, but placed it, and all athletics, secondary to academic achievement. It—and a number of schools that faced the same issue—made peace with that. The problem it wrestles with now is how to balance the desire to field a team with the reality of what it means, in terms of money and recruiting, to have one that has the chance to win at least sometimes.

Or, to put it another way, can Oberlin, as it enters the twenty-first century, afford to have a football team?

In the past two decades, in an attempt to add elan to and stimulate a ground-swell of support for what had become Oberlin's "disintegrating football program," members of the alumni and friends of Oberlin organized the Heisman Club. Its chief aim, when it was created in 1978—in the midst of a string of losing seasons and the recurring debate about the sport's future—was to provide a quarter of a million dollars to endow the football program as well as the college's athletic program in general. The club's first project was the establishment of the Heisman Room located in a newly built gymnasium.[24] A tinted enlargement of a photograph of Heisman in uniform when he played for the University of Pennsylvania occupies a dominant place on one of its walls.

Heisman's spirit and winning ways are also recalled every year at Oberlin. At first, a home game each fall was especially denoted as Heisman Day. Now a commemoration coincides with Oberlin's commencement exercises in the spring. The resurrecting of Heisman's spirit at a time when the college is an anachronism in modern football is a poignant reminder of a time long ago when, in truth, Oberlin was a prince, if not king, of the gridiron, and the game itself was a sport played just for the fun of it.

APPENDIX A

ROSTERS

Here's to the Oberlin boys
With their jolly good spirits and noise....
—Louise Pond, Class of '90

1890

Wallace F. Grosvenor	James B. McCord
Paul A. Gulick	Edward W. Pinkham
Thomas W. Johnson	Howard K. Regal
Lynds Jones	Henry W. Sperry
Carl Kinsley	Harry W. Sumner
John W. Wright	

Substitutes: Willard L. Beard, George A. Lawrence, Seabury C. Mastick, James W. Raine, Charles W. Savage.

Mastick was originally elected captain. He resigned because of an injury sustained during the summer prior to the football season. Sperry was elected his successor.[1] As captain, Sperry was expected to coach the team. Only one game, against Adelbert, was scheduled, but it was cancelled because of a snowstorm.

1891[2]

Carlton Aylard	William H. Merriam
George R. Berry	Howard K. Regal
Wallace F. Grosvenor	David P. Simpson
Louis E. Hart	Carl S. Williams
William J. Jacobs	Stephen R. Williams
Lynds Jones	John H. Wise

176

Substitutes: Charles H. Borican, Paul A. Gulick, Charles W. Savage, Carl Y. Semple, Henry W. Sperry, George D. Wilder.

Grosvenor was captain, and thus coach, of the team. Bert M. Hogen was its manager.

Four games were played, with the following results: Michigan 26, Oberlin 6; Oberlin 12, Adelbert 6; Oberlin 10, Case 0; Adelbert 18, Oberlin 8.

1892[3]

George R. Berry	William H. Merriam
Clayton K. Fauver	Max F. Millikan
Louis E. Hart	Charles F. Savage
Thomas W. Johnson	Josiah C. Teeters
Lynds Jones	Ellsworth B. Westcott
Andrew B. Kell	John W. White
Miles E. Marsh	Carl S. Williams
John H. Wise	

Substitutes: Orin W. Ensworth, Louis B. Fauver, Washington Irving Squire, Harry Zimmerman.

John Heisman was coach of the team. He missed the fifth game of the season against Kenyon. Carl S. Williams was the captain, Bert M. Hogen the manager.

Seven games were played, with the following results: Oberlin 40, Ohio State 0; Oberlin 38, Adelbert 8; Oberlin 56, Ohio Wesleyan 0; Oberlin 50, Ohio State 0 (Ohio State does not acknowledge having played this game); Oberlin 38, Kenyon 0; Oberlin 16, Adelbert 0; Oberlin 24, Michigan 22 (disputed by Michigan, which claims it won).

1893[4]

Ernest H. Boothman	John W. Mott
Clayton K. Fauver	Howard K. Regal
Elmer B. Fitch	Clyde H. Shields
Solomon S. Lee	Frank N. Spindler
James H. McMurray	Newell C. Stewart
William H. Merriam	John W. White

Substitutes: Frederick C. Ballard, Percy C. Cole, Robert H. Cowley, Orin W. Ensworth, Lynds Jones, Andrew B. Kell, John W. Price, Charles V. Streator, Arthur G. Thatcher.

E. B. (Jake) Camp coached the team's first four games. John Heisman coached subsequent games against Chicago and Illinois. There was no coach for the final game of the season against Case. Charles C. Brackin was the team's manager, Fauver the captain.

Seven games were played, with the following results: Oberlin 6, Kenyon 0; Oberlin 38, Ohio State 10; Oberlin 30, Kenyon 8; Oberlin 40, Adelbert 4; Oberlin 33, Chicago 12; Oberlin 34, Illinois 24; Case 22, Oberlin 8.

1894[5]

Floyd H. Bogrand	William H. Merriam
Ernest H. Boothman	William R. Miller
Percy C. Cole	Charles G. McDonald
Robert H. Cowley	James H. McMurray
Clayton K. Fauver	John F. Rudolph
Elmer B. Fitch	Charles V. Streator
Henry A. Young	

Substitutes: William H. Baer, John H. Behr, Rae S. Dorsett, Walter Y. Durand, Willis J. Miller, Samuel David Miller, Royal C. Peirce, Daniel H. V. Purnell, Ira D. Shaw, Henry B. Voorhees.

John Heisman coached the team. John T. Ellis resigned as manager of the team early in October because of unspecified "circumstances."[6] His place was taken by Alvan W. Sherrill. Merriam was elected captain, but refused the position. He was replaced by Fauver, captain also of the 1893 team.

Eight games were played, with the following results: Oberlin 67, Mount Union 0; Oberlin 12, Wittenberg 0; Oberlin 0, Washington and Jefferson 0; Oberlin 20, Case 4; Adelbert 22, Oberlin 4; Michigan 14, Oberlin 6; Penn State 9, Oberlin 6. (Oberlin was originally declared the winner. Walter Camp decided a disputed call in Penn State's favor.)

APPENDIX B

THE BOYS OF AUTUMN

Here's to our Oberlin days
Soon we part and go various ways;
Time may pass ne'er so fleet, echo still will repeat,
All hail to old Oberlin days.
—Louise Pond, Class of '90

Ten of the sixty-eight Oberlin students who were on teams between 1890 and 1894 lived into their sixties, sixteen into their seventies, another fourteen into their eighties, and three were nonagenarians. The youngest to die was only twenty years old (**Clyde Shields**, drowned). The oldest was ninety-eight (Seabury Cone Mastick). Two, both varsity captains—Wallace Grosvenor and Clayton Fauver—died on the same day, March 3, 1942, only a few months after they participated in the fiftieth-anniversary reunion of the 1891 squad. Six of the football players remained closely attached to the college all their lives. Twenty of them, incidentally, married Oberlin coeds, a testament perhaps to the attraction between sexes that football engendered.[1]

There was one suicide: **Ernest Howard (Boothie) Boothman**. A few days after the 1894 football season closed, the speedy Boothman, a mainstay of the varsity, was elected captain of the team for the coming year.[2] His photograph appeared in *Spalding's Foot Ball Guide*, as did that of a former Oberlin football mainstay, Carl Williams, who had transferred to the University of Pennsylvania.

Because of injuries, Boothman missed a number of games in the fall of 1895. After his graduation the following spring, Boothman read law with his father, former congressman Melvin M. Boothman of Bryan, Ohio. He subsequently went to the Klondike as a representative of the Ohio Gold Prospecting Company. Boothman committed suicide on January 4, 1901 while living in Hutchinson, Kansas. He destroyed everything that would have divulged his identity, then ingested strychnine-based rodent poison. It is not known why he took his life, nor is it clear how his identity was determined. Boothman was twenty-eight years old at the time of his death.[3]

Clayton (Clate) King Fauver, who played on the 1892, 1893, 1894, and 1895 teams with Boothman, was elected to Phi Beta Kappa and graduated in 1897. Like him, his two younger twin brothers, Edgar Fauver and Edwin Fauver, played for and coached the Oberlin varsity. Clayton studied law at Western Reserve University and, while a student there, pitched for the Cleveland baseball team of the American League. He practiced law in Cleveland until 1916, when he moved to New York, where he remained until 1923. Fauver was a member of the Oberlin Board of Trustees from 1920 until his death in 1942. He became the college's investment executive in 1932 and moved the following year to Oberlin, where he became president of the Oberlin Savings Bank. He died suddenly, a victim of coronary thrombosis, in Chatsworth, Georgia, while traveling by car to Florida. He was sixty-nine years old.

Barely three weeks earlier, Fauver's brother Louis (Lou) Benjamin Fauver died in Elyria, Ohio, after a long illness marked by arthritis and heart trouble. Louis, who had graduated in 1896, first studied abroad at the University of Heidelberg before returning to the United States and studying law in the office of a judge. He was admitted to the bar in 1899 and practiced as a corporation lawyer in Elyria. In 1928, he became the attorney for Oberlin College. He was seventy-three years old when he died.

Like Clayton Fauver, Henry Bert (Cy) Voorhees was a major league pitcher after leaving Oberlin. Voorhees, a sub on the 1894 varsity, was a Conservatory student who did not graduate. He pitched in both leagues, for Philadelphia of the National League and Washington of the American League in 1902. He married an Oberlin student, Emma Uhler. Voorhees responded to an alumni questionnaire in 1906, when he was thirty-two years old. What happened to him after that is not known.

Upon graduation in 1892, Wallace Fahnestock (Grove) Grosvenor attended the Chicago Homeopathic College and Rush Medical College, receiving medical degrees from both. A specialist in obstetrics, he practiced medicine in Chicago all his life. He was seventy-two when he died of heart trouble in 1942.

Grosvenor's teammates on the 1890 varsity that was snowed out of what would have been Oberlin's inaugural football game had diversified careers.

Seabury Cone Mastick, who was on the three-man student committee appointed to persuade the faculty to permit the game with Adelbert and who would have captained the team except for an injury he suffered, spoke at commencement exercises in June 1891 on the "Indirect Influence of Law."[4] He went on to study at the Hastings Law College of the University of California. In 1896, he married Oberlin coed Agnes Eliza Warner, whose parents had donated the building that housed the school's Conservatory of Music. During World War I, Mastick was a lieutenant commander in the U.S. Navy. Afterwards, he studied chemistry at Columbia University, and over a period of more than thirty-five years was an officer and later director of the Warner Chemical Company. During that time, he also served as the president of a bank in Pleasantville, New York, and as a state senator in Albany. The Masticks were major benefactors of Oberlin. She died in 1963, after they had been married sixty-seven years. Mastick's second wife, Kathrin Cawein, had also attended Oberlin. He died while vacationing with her in Wales in 1969. He was ninety-eight years old.

Another member of the student committee, classmate **George Addison Lawrence,** received a bachelor of divinity degree from McCormick Seminary in 1894. A Presbyterian, he had pastorates in Wisconsin, Ohio, and Illinois before being forced by ill health to give up preaching in 1908 when he was in his early forties. He returned to Oberlin and made his home in Talcott, a college boarding hall, where his wife, Carrie Turner Memmott, also an 1891 graduate, served as director. Lawrence died of arteriosclerosis in 1940 when he was seventy-four years old.

The third member of the student committee and a member of the 1891 varsity as well, **David Peter Simpson,** was elected to Phi Beta Kappa and graduated in 1892. He studied abroad at the Universities of Heidelberg, Leipzig, and Paris, and subsequently he taught at West High School in Cleveland, which he had attended as a teenager. He was principal of the school at his retirement in 1935, when he was sixty-five years old. He died in Cleveland in 1961 at the age of ninety-one.

Henry Walter Sperry, who replaced the injured Mastick as captain of the 1890 team, was a member of the class of '92 but evidently did not graduate with it. He worked in the hardware business for a time in Denver, returned home to Sherman, New York, after that, and later went into the mortgage-loan and insurance business in Los Angeles. He died in 1922 at the age of fifty-three.

Little is known about **Paul A. Gulick,** a member of the 1890 team and a substitute on the 1891 squad. He left Oberlin in 1892, returned briefly at the turn of the century, and was reported to be living in the Far East and engaged in business. When last heard of in 1942, he would have been in his seventies.

Howard (Howie) Krum Regal, who got to play on the 1891 and 1893 teams and had worked for the *Oberlin News* while in college, landed a job on the *Springfield (Massachusetts) Republican* after his graduation in 1894. He spent the rest of his life on the newspaper, rising eventually to become its managing editor and a major journalistic figure in New England. The only break in his career came with the discovery of gold in the Yukon in 1896, when he took a leave of absence to go prospecting. He died suddenly, apparently of a heart attack, in 1936 while backing his car from the yard of his home. He was sixty-three years old.

Another member of the 1890 team, Carl Kinsley, received a bachelor's degree from Oberlin in 1893 and a master's in 1896. He subsequently earned a degree in electrical engineering from Cornell and taught for several years at Washington University in St. Louis. As a major during World War I, he was chief of military intelligence for radio, telegraph, and telephone operations for the Army General Staff. A pioneer in electronics—he had installed the first radio station in the United States on Fire Island, New York—Kinsley joined the U.S. Steel Corporation in 1931. He died of a heart attack in Falls Church, Virginia, in 1959, when he was eighty-eight years old.

Like Grosvenor, two other members of the 1890 varsity also became doctors. One was James Bennett McCord. After his graduation in 1891, he studied at Northwestern University and practiced until 1899 in Lake City, Iowa. He then served as a Congregational medical missionary for more than forty years, founding the first hospital for Africans in Natal Province, the McCord Zulu Hospital in Durban. He was a captain in the British Army during the Zulu Rebellion of 1908, continued in its Medical Corps until 1917, then transferred to the U.S. Army Medical Corps. McCord was married to Margaret Caroline Lucy Mellen, Oberlin 1893. He died in Oakham, Massachusetts, in 1950 of a cardiac condition following an operation on his knee. He was eighty years old. Five of his six children and a grandson attended Oberlin.

The other doctor was Edward Warrick Pinkham. Pinkham, who also graduated in 1891, received his medical degree from Harvard Medical School in 1895. He was awarded two silver stars for gallantry while serving with the U.S. Army in the Philippines during the Spanish-American War.[5] A gynecologist, he was attending physician at the Metropolitan Opera House in New York from 1925 to his retirement in 1934. He returned to active duty in World War II, when he was seventy-one years old, with the rank of colonel, taking charge of a hospital center in France. Pinkham died in Sarasota, Florida, in 1960, when he was ninety.

Although they couldn't have known each other at Oberlin, Pinkham must have met **Charles Victor (Ole) Streator** in New York City. Streator, a sub on the 1893 team and a member of the 1894 varsity, didn't enter the Conservatory until the spring of 1893, two years after Pinkham graduated. But for many years Streator, who graduated in 1899, worked as a voice coach at the Metropolitan Opera, where Pinkham was attending physician. Streator had moved to New York and studied there after Oberlin, and returned to New York in 1907 after a stint of teaching in Wisconsin. A personal friend of tenor Enrico Caruso, Streator died in 1951 at the Ohio Masonic home in Springfield. He was seventy-nine years old.

Four other members of the 1890 team also enjoyed varied careers. After graduating from Oberlin in 1891, **Willard Livingstone Beard** studied further at the Hartford Theological Seminary. He returned to Oberlin to receive a doctor of divinity in 1916 after spending nearly twenty years in China as a missionary, YMCA official, and then president of Foochow College. He went back to China, engaging in general missionary work, between 1927 and 1936. At the outbreak of World War II in 1941, Beard returned to his boyhood home in Birmingham, Connecticut. Beard was married to an Oberlin student, Ellen Lucy Kinney. All six of their children attended the college. He died at the age of eighty-two in 1947 in Jacksonville, Florida.

James Watt Raine, a native of England, also went into the ministry. He attended both Berea College and Union Theological Seminary after his graduation from Oberlin. Raine later returned to the Oberlin Theological Seminary as a postgraduate student. Over the years, Raine, a Congregationalist, had pastorates in Ohio and New York and also taught English at Berea College in Kentucky. During World War I, he had charge of religious work at several Army camps. Raine married an Oberlin graduate, Harriet May, who died a year after their marriage in 1894. When last heard from in 1935, he was sixty-five years old.

Another member of the 1890 squad, **John Wells Wright,** returned to his home state of Wisconsin immediately upon graduation from Oberlin in 1891 and went into partnership in a Ripon drug firm. Three years later, he joined a knitting manufactory, eventually becoming its president. He also was a vice president of a Ripon bank and both a trustee and the treasurer of Ripon College. Wright died of heart trouble at the age of sixty-nine in 1937.

A fourth member, **Harry W. Sumner,** never graduated. He was briefly heard from in 1931, when he was living in Seattle and engaged in the manufacture of diesel engines. Sumner died there in 1949. He was seventy-eight years old.

William J. Jacobs, a theologian who was on the 1891 varsity and had been elected to Phi Beta Kappa at Western Reserve before attending Oberlin, subsequently received a doctorate at Wooster and spent half a century as a Congregational preacher. He was pastor of a Detroit church for more than twenty-three years. Jacobs suffered a sudden heart attack and died in Long Beach, California, while vacationing there with a daughter. Seventy-four years old, he had planned to return to Michigan that day.

Another theolog who was on the 1891 varsity, George Durand Wilder, transferred to Yale University in 1893, receiving a bachelor of divinity degree from there the following year. Wilder went to China as a missionary. He was stationed in Peking during the Boxer Rebellion, when he lost virtually all his possessions. Wilder spent forty-four years in China as a Congregational church aide. An expert on bees and bird lore, he was in 1925 the first president of the Peking Society of Natural History. Wilder retired in 1939 when seventy years old but continued to teach Chinese studies in Peking. The Chinese government decorated him for his work for famine relief in China and Manchuria. He and his wife, Oberlin graduate Gertrude Williams Stanley, were imprisoned for seven months when Japan invaded China just prior to World War II. They were repatriated in 1943. All four of their children attended Oberlin College. Wilder died in Oberlin following a heart attack in 1946. He was seventy-six years old.

Little is known about Thomas Winder Johnson, who played on the 1892 varsity while he was still an Academy student. He apparently left Oberlin after the academic year 1892–93 ended. At one point he managed a lumber company, and at times he lived in both Arizona and Florida. He died in the latter state in 1952 at the age of eighty-one.

Carlton Aylard of the 1891 team graduated in 1892 and married an Oberlin student, Margaret Goshen, the next year. With the exception of two years when he was in business at the turn of the century and a year overseas with the YMCA during World War I, Aylard spent his entire life teaching in Minnesota and Colorado. He died in Denver in 1941 of a blood infection when he was seventy-three years old.

Louis Edward Hart, who was on the football varsities of 1891 and 1892, played as a substitute for the Chicago Athletic Association while working in a law office. He got into two games, he wrote in December 1893, and came off the field "with the usual amount of gory noses, sprained ankles, etc."[6] Hart was admitted to the Illinois bar in 1895 and practiced law in Chicago all his life. He was a special state attorney for a time, and president of the Oberlin Alumni Association in the late 1920s. After the death of his first wife, he married a former Oberlin student, Karen Michelson Hartwick. Hart died of a stroke in West Chicago in 1957, when he was eighty-six.

Lynds Jones played on both the 1891 and 1892 teams and was a substitute in 1893, when he got into one game after graduating from the college and entering the Theological Seminary. In all, counting his time as an emeritus professor, Jones compiled a record of fifty-eight years on the Oberlin faculty. He first taught geology, then zoology and ornithology, as well as animal ecology. His course in the study of birds was the first such recognized college course in the nation. Jones retired in 1930, when he was sixty-five, but he continued as curator of the Oberlin Museum. He was eighty-six when he died, in 1951.

Carl Sheldon (Cap) Williams, the quarterback who was captain in 1892 of the first of the teams that John Heisman coached and who subsequently transferred to the University of Pennsylvania, was unanimously elected captain of Penn's 1895 team and was an All-American. He received a bachelor of science degree from Penn in 1894 and a medical degree in 1897. An oculist by profession, Williams studied in Heidelberg and London before settling in Philadelphia. He returned to the University of Pennsylvania in 1902 to coach the football team, and in his six years there compiled an overall winning record that included two undefeated seasons.[7] It is not known what he did after that, or when and where he died.

The other Williams who played for Oberlin, Stephen (Steve) Riggs Williams received a master's degree and later a doctorate from Harvard. He taught zoology, botany, and geology at Miami University of Ohio for forty years, until his retirement in 1940. A past president of the Ohio Academy of Science, he died in Oxford, Ohio, in 1954, aged eighty-three.

Josiah (Joe) Cattell Teeters, a 1893 postgraduate and one of the oldest students ever to play football, had a varied career after leaving Oberlin. At first he became a teacher and taught mathematics at, among other places, the Idaho Industrial Institute. After 1908, he was variously engaged in the sheep-raising business and as a merchant, a miner, and a draftsman. He died in Spokane in 1935 following a major operation. He was seventy-two years old.

Less is known about Carl Young Semple, the youngest member of the 1891 team. He left Oberlin soon after his misadventure with the stolen chicken, returning only for the fiftieth-anniversary celebration of Oberlin football in the fall of 1941. Semple became involved in mining investments in Baxter Springs, Kansas, where he died in 1959 at the age of eighty-six. The only other reference to him in the alumni files of the Oberlin College Archives is an interview he gave to the *Cleveland Plain Dealer* in 1953 that dealt with his father, a surgeon-dentist who patented the first chewing gum.

William (Will) Harvey Merriam, who was almost as young as Semple when he first played for Oberlin on the 1891 team, played varsity football for all four years he spent in the college. For a while after his graduation, he coached a football team in Ripon, Wisconsin. He worked briefly as a clerk in both a mercantile agency and for a railroad, then returned to school, receiving a medical degree from the University of Pennsylvania in 1902. He served as a doctor for an insurance company and for a number of hospitals in Massachusetts and Ohio. During World War I, he was a surgeon at Army hospitals in Kansas and at other posts. Troubled for some time by a brain tumor, he died, however, of pneumonia in Walter Reed Hospital, Washington, D.C., in 1928 when he was fifty-five years old.

Perhaps one of the most adventuresome of lives was led by Hawaiian-born **John Henry Wise.** Upon graduation from the Theological Seminary in 1893, Wise returned home and two years later participated in an unsuccessful attempt to restore Queen Liliuokalani to the Hawaiian throne. He was tried for treason by a military commission and sentenced to prison. Apparently Wise served only one year of a three-year sentence. Upon his release, he engaged in a number of different businesses—fishing and building, to name two—and then, his past indiscretion pardoned, served as an interpreter and clerk in the Hawaiian legislature. An authority on the local language and legends, he was Hawaii's commissioner to the Panama-Pacific International Exposition before World War I, and during the war he was superintendent of Kapiolani Park. A member of the Territorial Senate in 1919 and 1921, Wise served on the legislative commission to Washington. He was subsequently prohibition director of the territory. Before dying of pneumonia at the age of sixty-eight in 1937, Wise spent his last years farming and teaching.

Miles Eugene Marsh earned a master's degree from Harvard after graduating from Oberlin in 1893. He served as principal of a high school in Nebraska before accepting the principalship of the preparatory department at Berea College. From 1909 to 1914 he was instrumental in founding and was dean of Berea's well-known vocational schools. During World War I, Marsh worked briefly for the YMCA at a military base outside Washington, D.C. He left Berea in 1918 to teach in high schools in North Carolina. Marsh died of pneumonia in 1937. He was seventy-one years old.

Max Frank Millikan, who was on the 1892 varsity and refereed during the 1893 season, worked as a bookkeeper in a Minneapolis grain business after his graduation in 1894. While studying law in New York, he did clerical work. He practiced law the rest of his life, and from 1916 on he was also vice president of a gas and electric company. One of his two brothers who also attended Oberlin was Robert A. Millikan, winner of the Noble Prize for physics. Mary Grace Millikan, a teacher in Oberlin High School and one of his three sisters who also were Oberlin graduates, married John Hinckley Behr, a sub on the 1894 varsity. Max Millikan died at his country place in Easton, Maryland, in 1940 after a heart attack. He was seventy years old.

Millikan's brother-in-law **John Hinckley Behr** spent two more years at Oberlin but never went out for the football varsity after the fall of 1892. Upon graduation, he studied law at Western Reserve University, earned his law degree there in 1900, and subsequently began to practice in Cleveland. However, failing health compelled him to move to the milder climate of Albuquerque, New Mexico, in 1901. He died there the following year after being married to Mary Grace Millikan for only ten months. He was twenty-nine.

John W. White also died young. White had played on the 1892 and 1893 teams. Although a member of the class of '99, he did not graduate. He was working as a brakeman for the Chicago, Milwaukee & St. Paul Railway in August 1907 when he was fatally struck by a switch engine in the Muskegan Yards. His age was thirty-three.

A little more is known about **George Robin Berry,** who also died at a relatively young age. A theolog who was on the 1891 and 1892 squads, Berry preached in towns in Ohio until 1901, when he turned to business ventures—gold mining in Alaska, running a mahogany company, and later working for a life-insurance agency in Cincinnati. Berry moved to Spokane in April 1910. Two months later, he died there of apoplexy at the age of forty-six.

Almost nothing is known about two other players on the 1892 team: **Andrew Bertram Kell** and **Ellsworth Burnett Westcott.** The only note in Kell's alumni file gives his address as Coles Ferry, West Virginia, but there is no indication of when he lived there. Similarly, a card in Westcott's file gives his address as River Falls, Wisconsin.

On the other hand, a great deal is known about **Charles Winfred (Fred) Savage,** who had been halfback on the 1890 varsity that didn't play, a sub on the 1891 team, and a regular on the 1892 team. Upon graduation in 1893, Savage taught Latin and coached athletics at Oberlin Academy until 1896, then went to Harvard for a master's degree; after that he taught Latin in Pittsburgh between 1898 and 1904. Savage planned on becoming a dentist.[8] He took graduate studies in medicine and physical education at Columbia. However, his career plans changed when he was asked to take over coaching and physical training at Oberlin. He became an associate professor in 1906 and a full professor in 1908. He was director of athletics at Oberlin from 1906 to 1935, when he became popularly known as "Doc" Savage. During that time, he was a member of the rules committee of the American Intercollegiate Football Association, and served on the United States Olympic Committee in 1924 and 1928. A strong advocate of strict rules regarding the amateur status of college athletes, Savage was president of the Ohio Athletic Conference in the early 1930s. He died at home in Cleveland in 1957 when he was eighty-seven years old.

Orin Wayne Ensworth, who was a sub on both the 1892 and 1893 teams, worked for a year or so as a traveling salesman after graduating in 1894. In 1898, he married a former Conservatory student, Gertrude Aurilla Dalrymple. Ensworth held a variety of jobs—as a high-school teacher, a machinist, with a motor company, and later with a gas and electric firm. He was secretary of the Board of Education of Warren, Pennsylvania, from 1905 to 1911. Ensworth died of a cerebral hemorrhage in Albion, New York, in 1938, when he was sixty-six years old.

Another 1892 sub, the inventive Harry Zimmerman, received mechanical and electrical engineering degrees from Cornell after graduating from Oberlin in 1893. He devised a platform binder for harvesting wheat, invented shutter fasteners, and manufactured working gloves and cutlery. For a time in the mid-1920s, he was in the real estate business in Florida, and later he was a manufacturer in Toronto. Zimmerman married an Oberlin graduate, Beulah Belle Johnson, in 1899. It is not known when and where he died.

What happened to Alabaman Washington Irving Squire, a sub on the 1892 team, is unknown, too. Squire was a member of the class of '97 but never graduated. He tried to enlist in the Army during World War I but was rejected as not being physically fit, and afterward he tore the ligaments of his back. He volunteered for YMCA work overseas but was deemed not fit to work abroad. He was working for the YMCA's national war work council in New York when last heard from in 1919, just before his forty-eighth birthday.

Ordinarily, when any of the team members wrote to classmates or to the school itself, they recalled with nostalgia their years spent at Oberlin and expressed gratitude for the moral values they had absorbed. The only exception was Newell Coe Stewart, who, despite poor vision, played end in every game during the 1893 season. He complained that the physical examination he was given by Dr. Fred Leonard was inadequate. Stewart, who was "considered as one more interested in athletics than studies," was told, he said in responding to an alumni questionnaire in 1922, "which muscles to develop, but no thought seemed to have been given to the reason why I was not a good student as well as athlete." Stewart said that he discovered "that I should have had glasses years before. I have always blamed Oberlin for not finding that out and giving me a better chance for scholarship." According to that same questionnaire, Stewart never graduated from Oberlin and never attended any other school. He gave his present occupation as an electrical engineer, saying he had started his apprenticeship with a Cleveland company in 1894. Stewart died in New Scotland, New York, in 1932. He was sixty years old.

Three teammates on the 1893 varsity chose the medical profession. While still a senior in 1896, **Robert (Bob) Henry Cowley** was excused from classes at Oberlin and permitted to take courses at the Western Reserve Medical School.[9] He received his medical degree from there in 1901. Later studies took him to England, Germany, and Austria. Cowley practiced in Lorain, Ohio, for two years, before moving to Berea, Kentucky, where he established the student health service at Berea College. He later practiced medicine in California and Oregon. Together with a New York physician, he developed a serum for the prevention of complications from measles. Cowley had married an Oberlin student, Anna Perry, class of '97, in 1902. Upon retirement, he made his home in Berea, dying there in 1948 when he was seventy-six years old.

Solomon S. Lee, who studied medicine at the University of Michigan, became a physician and surgeon at the Osceola mine in Calumet, Michigan. He was last heard from in 1908, when he was thirty-five years old.

Arthur Gilbert Thatcher became a dental surgeon. After receiving his degree in that field from the University of Pennsylvania in 1900, he practiced in Fremont, Ohio, until his retirement. He was also active in Boy Scout work and as an elder and superintendent of the Presbyterian Church Sunday School in Fremont. He died there of a heart attack in 1951 at the age of seventy-nine.

John W. Mott, Oberlin's quarterback in 1893, worked as a gymnast instructor in Wisconsin after his graduation in 1894. He subsequently studied law in a Cleveland law office and practiced in that city for thirteen years. He moved to San Diego in 1911 and went into the real estate business for five years before returning to the practice of law. Mott was active in the YMCA and the San Diego Goodwill Industries, serving as president of the latter in the mid-1930s. He died in San Diego in 1950, aged eighty-one.

Frank Nicholas (Spin) Spindler was astonished when he did postgraduate study at Harvard following his graduation from Oberlin in 1894. Spindler, who had played in every game of the 1893 football season, met numerous Oberlin graduates in Cambridge, though, unfortunately for him, they did not get together often. He had a difficult time adjusting to a life without friends, "especially whether it depends on the presence of women friends, as we felt it did in Oberlin."[10] At first, he wrote back to his classmates that "since leaving Oberlin I have withdrawn entirely from the sentimental arena."[11] But after another year at Harvard, he realized, he said, "It takes a man about two years to outgrow the Arcadian co-educational life that we led in Oberlin and become used to the more independent, Bohemian, but monastic life that students lead here."[12] Spindler, who received two degrees from Harvard, became a professor of both psychology and Latin and taught in a number of colleges in the Midwest. He died accidentally at the age of seventy in 1935 when he fell down a flight of stairs and fractured his skull while on a visit to a niece in Cleveland.

Another victim of an accident was **Frederick C. Ballard,** who also played on the 1893 team. Ballard had gone on to the University of Michigan after graduating from Oberlin in 1897. He practiced law in Sandusky, Ohio, until 1904, when he moved to North Branch and became a bank president. Ballard died at the age of eighty-three in 1958 as the result of a fall from a ladder while cleaning the eaves trough of his home.

Like Spindler, after his graduation in 1897, **James (Jim) Henry McMurray** studied at Harvard and took up teaching. McMurray, the captain of Oberlin's varsity under Clate Fauver's coaching in 1896, earned his doctorate at James Millikin University in Decatur, Illinois. He was a professor of science and later president of Central College in Indiana. And before he joined the Red Cross as a field director during World War I, he also served as president of Lincoln College in Illinois. After the war, he resumed teaching as head of the department of social sciences at Maryville College in Tennessee. McMurray died of meningitis in Maryville in 1938. He was sixty-seven years old. He had married an Oberlin student, Kathryn Belle Romig, in 1897.

Percy (Perce) Cochran Cole, who also married an Oberlin student, Lucile [*sic*] Maud White, enjoyed a dual career as a lumber salesman and, every fall, a football umpire. Cole, who was a sub in 1893 and a regular in 1894, coached the Berea College team in 1895. He subsequently lived in various cities, including Houston and Cincinnati. He died in the latter in 1963, eighty-six years old.

Only the barest of information is available about two other members of the 1893 team, both of whom had religious careers. **Elmer Brown Fitch Jr.,** class of '96, became a clergyman, but where he ministered and when and where he died is unknown. **John W. Price,** who never graduated from Oberlin, studied for the pastorate in Cleveland and for missionary work in New

York before going to Brazil as a missionary. He died in Denver in 1951, at the age of eighty-one.

William H. Baer was the only member of the 1894 varsity to serve in the Spanish-American War. He was a corporal in a New York infantry regiment and served in Cuba. Baer had enlisted shortly after graduating in 1898. Upon his return, he worked for a number of railroads in the Midwest until 1907, when he entered the real estate business. In 1926, when he was fifty-two years old, he was living in Cleveland. What happened to him after that is not known.

Oddly enough, a little more is known about Floyd H. Bogrand, who attended Oberlin for only the 1894–95 academic year. He afterward attended Allegheny College in western Pennsylvania, then returned to the school that he had left to play for Heisman and Oberlin, Hiram College. He graduated from there in 1896. He afterward taught school, was a traveling salesman, and then a broker. In an undated alumni questionnaire, he gave his current occupation as a hotelkeeper in Cleveland and said he was about to purchase another establishment.

Three teammates on the 1894 squad became doctors. One, Henry Alfred Young, received his medical degree from Ohio Wesleyan University in 1901. While studying there, he acted as physical director of several church gymnasiums. Young practiced medicine for thirteen years in Cleveland. He then moved to Dayton for three years and, finally, settled in Chicago. During a serious flood in Dayton in 1913, Young headed a relief train to aid flood victims. Two years later, he made his way alone to Montenegro on the Adriatic coast with typhus serum during an epidemic there. Young died in Chicago in 1930 of cardio-renal complications induced by an "athletic heart." He was fifty-six years old.

John Francis (Rudey) Rudolph received his medical degree from Western Reserve in 1903. He had served as a physical instructor in Wisconsin following his graduation from Oberlin in 1898. Rudolph practiced medicine in New Mexico, and Kansas, and from 1919 on, in Warren, Ohio. During World War I he was a captain in the Medical Corps. Rudolph retired in 1942 because of ill health. He died in Cleveland seven years later of Parkinson's disease and arteriosclerosis. He was seventy-six years old.

Rae Shepard Dorsett attended the medical school of the University of Pennsylvania after his graduation in 1896. He practiced in Philadelphia, where he was also on the faculty of Temple University. A specialist in both internal medicine and orthopedics, Dorsett served in the Medical Corps in France during World War I. He suffered a nervous breakdown in 1935, dying two years later in his summer home in Blain, Pennsylvania. He was sixty-two years old.

Charles Gilman (Mac) McDonald, who, like Merriam, played on the Oberlin varsity for four years, graduated from Oberlin in June 1898, just shy of his twenty-third birthday. His interest in the game continued even after he earned a law degree at the University of Michigan. He moved to Omaha and in 1903 coached the Creighton University team there. One day in February 1918, in Omaha, McDonald complained of stomach pains. He was on his way to seek medical help when he collapsed and died in the doorway of a doctor's office. He was forty-one years old. McDonald had married an Oberlin student, Charlotte May Clark.

A teammate from the 1894 team who also married an Oberlin coed was **Walter Yale Durand.** Durand, who was a sub on the team and also one of three students on the newly created advisory board on athletics, graduated in 1896. He was a Latin tutor at Oberlin Academy for a year, then taught in an upstate New York academy. He subsequently did graduate work at Harvard, receiving a master's degree, and for the next seven years taught in the prestigious Phillips Academy, Andover, Massachusetts. Durand returned to Oberlin in 1907 as an associate professor of English, but he was forced to resign the following spring because of eye trouble. He then accepted a position as a special agent for the United States Department of Commerce, directing investigations of the lumber, coal, meat-packing, and other industries. The classmate he married was Sara Ellen Watson. Durand died of Bright's disease while living in Washington in 1926. He was fifty-one years old.

Ira Dennison Shaw, who married Conservatory student Grace Eleanor Prince, devoted his entire life to teaching. Upon graduation in the spring of 1898, he became superintendent of schools in Randolph, Vermont. Following graduate work at Columbia, during which he played center on the university's 1901 team, Shaw was educational director of the YMCA in New York, then in Philadelphia. He worked for the international committee of the YMCA from 1909 to 1919. The last two years of his service were spent in wartime France, where his duties with American servicemen ranged, he said, "from blacking boots to burying the dead."[13] Upon his return from abroad, Shaw worked for a soldier rehabilitation agency in Cleveland, and in 1924 he joined Berea College as an associate professor of education. He retired in 1939, but during World War II he became a munitions-factory inspector and at its conclusion in 1945 worked as a substitute teacher at Oberlin High School. There is no indication of when he died. Shaw was ninety-two years old when he gave an interview in July 1961 to the local Oberlin newspaper. He claimed at the time that he was the oldest living football player.[14]

Charles Henry Borican, who was three days older than Shaw, actually was, as far as can be ascertained, the oldest living football player. Borican lived until January 1964, dying when he was ninety-four years old. Borican, the first black to play football for Oberlin, taught in several states following his graduation in 1894. "I am in the land of cotton and tobacco," he wrote his classmates from a Warrenton, North Carolina, institute. "This district is the only one represented by a negro in Congress. I think I shall aspire in that direction. Strange things happen now and then."[15] However, discrimination, apparently, intervened to block his career. A native of New Jersey, Borican returned there after eight years of teaching in North Carolina and Kentucky. He taught for seven more years in New Jersey and would have continued teaching "but for one thing—The last place in which I taught I could find no house suitable for my family so had to leave them and go home every other week."[16] Finally, Borican quit and became a rural mailman, a job he held until his retirement twenty-nine years later in 1934, when he was sixty-five years old. He worked subsequently as a bricklayer and paper hanger. Meanwhile, one of his three sons, John Borican, a Columbia University postgraduate student, became a track star, both pentathlon and decathlon champion, with six world records as a middle-distance runner.

The only other black on Oberlin's first teams, **Daniel H. V. Purnell,** a sub in 1894, spent the greater part of his life after graduating from Oberlin in 1897 as pastor in African Methodist Episcopal churches in Ohio, Illinois, Indiana, and Kentucky. From 1906 to 1909, he was superintendent of the Amanda Smith Industrial Home in Harvey, Illinois. For a time he was editor of the *Ohio Standard and Observer* in Xenia. Purnell died of organic heart disease in Columbus in 1936. He was sixty-eight years old.

The little that is known about another 1894 sub, **Royal Chauncy Peirce,** deals with his death in 1904 when he was killed in an accident in the Akron yards of the Pennsylvania Railroad, for whom he worked. He was thirty-three years old.

The three Millers, all unrelated, who played with the 1894 team, enjoyed different careers. **Samuel David (Dave) Miller** went from the Oberlin Theological Seminary in 1895 to Albany Medical College in New York State. While he studied there, Dave, who held a bachelor of divinity degree from Oberlin, had pastorates in several towns in New York State. Upon receiving his medical degree, he practiced in upstate New York until 1907, when he moved to Jacksonville, Florida. He conducted a sanitarium there until his death from heart failure in 1930. He was just shy of sixty years old when he died.

Willis Jay Miller, a theolog, class of '97, was in the Congregational ministry in Kansas following his graduation. But he switched to the YMCA after a year, working until retirement as general secretary of various YMCA offices in Ohio, Indiana, Maine, Kentucky, and Tennessee. Willis was married to Oberlin student Joanna Adell Jenney Allen. He died in 1945 of heart disease in Gilroy, California, where he had gone to retire. He was eighty years old.

William (Billy) Raymond Miller, who graduated in 1898, received a degree in mechanical engineering from Cornell the following year. He was an official of a manufacturing company in Doylestown in 1908, when he returned an alumni questionnaire. He was thirty-three years old at the time. What happened to him after that is not known.

Information exists about four of the varsity team managers. **Bert Miley Hogen,** the team manager in 1892, graduated in the spring of 1893 and worked for a time for the Ohio YMCA in Cleveland. He graduated from the Chicago Theological Seminary in 1898, and from then to 1900 was pastor of a Congregational church in Utah. He subsequently switched to a career in both business and education. In all, he preached three years, taught three years, was in the mining business two years, and represented an insurance company for seventeen. Although retired from the ministry, he kept active in church affairs. Hogen died in Salt Lake City of chronic myocarditis and arteriosclerosis shortly after his sixty-eighth birthday in 1936.

Charles (Charley) Clark Brackin, the 1893 team manager, graduated in 1894, whereupon he studied law at Western Reserve. He entered the real estate business after 1895 and then studied mining. He subsequently worked for the Gold Leaf Mining Company in California. At one point, a classmate ran into Brackin in Mexico, where he had been trapped and had taken part in a revolution. "Charley," the classmate said, "was the only member of our class except myself who knew well (and came to love it) that early West that was so lusty, so turbulent, and so enchanting."[17] Brackin died of old age in Kinsman, Ohio, in 1959. He was ninety years old.

John Tenney Ellis, who set up the team's 1894 schedule but resigned as manager at the start of the season for unexplained personal reasons, graduated in the spring of 1894 and remained in Oberlin while working as a traveling agent for a Youngstown creamery and cold-storage company. Ellis, the son of Oberlin professor John M. Ellis, subsequently became engaged in journalism in New York and Washington. He was attending a meeting of the Christian Endeavor Society in Boston in mid-July 1895 when he slipped while leaving his hotel. He struck his head on the marble steps, fracturing his skull. Ellis, who was a few months shy of his twenty-fifth birthday, never regained consciousness. He died some thirty or forty hours later. His body was brought back to Oberlin for burial.

Alvan Woodward Sherrill, who managed the 1894 varsity in Ellis's place, earned a medical degree from the University of Pennsylvania four years after his graduation from Oberlin in 1897. His career included service in several hospitals and a sanatorium in Pennsylvania. He was on the faculty of the Pittsburgh Medical School and served twice as president of the Academy of Medicine. Sherrill was with the Army Medical Corps for a time during World War I, then transferred to the Coast Guard. He died in Pittsburgh in 1963, age ninety-one.

In addition, **William Cleland (Bib) Clancy,** who covered the team for the *Oberlin Review* in 1894, became one of the greatest athletes in Oberlin's history. He played third base for the college's baseball team, and he made the football varsity as a halfback in both the 1895 and 1896 seasons. Between studies and athletics, Clancy was able to find time to work in the book and wallpaper store of Oberlin's mayor, A. G. Comings. For a time after his graduation in 1897, he played infield with the Detroit Tigers. Clancy subsequently became a cashier at a local Oberlin bank, but his health required an outdoor life. He studied with tree surgeons and for a while worked in various parts of New York State and then Cleveland. In 1925, Oberlin College hired him to care for the campus trees, which he did for the rest of his life, becoming a well-known figure around the school. Accustomed to spending his winters in the South, Clancy died in 1941, when he was sixty-nine years old, while he was caring for trees on a large estate in Sumter, South Carolina.

NOTES

Once again we stand amid the shadows,
Once again we gather here to sing;
Once again we linger in the twilight,
And wonder what the coming day will bring.
—*Margery Strong, Class of '02, "Senior Farewell Song,"*
to music by Annie Mayhew, Class of '02

The following abbreviations are used on second reference to citations in the notes:

Danzig   Allison Danzig. *Oh, How They Played the Game: The Early Days of Football and Heroes Who Made It Great.* New York: Macmillan, 1968.

DeSpain   Raymond E. DeSpain Jr. *An Historical Analysis of the Life and Professional Career of John William Heisman, 1869–1936.* Ph.D. dissertation, Texas A&M University, 1991.

OAM   *Oberlin Alumni Magazine.*

OCA   Oberlin College Archives.

ON   *Oberlin News.*

OR   *Oberlin Review.*

Putney   Clifford Putney. *Muscular Christianity: The Strenuous Mood in American Protestantism, 1880–1920.* Ph.D. diss., Brandeis University, 1995. Draft form of the manuscript.

Shults   Fredrick D. Shults. *The History and Philosophy of Athletics for Men at Oberlin College.* Ph.D. diss., Indiana University, 1967.

Umphlett   Wiley Lee Umphlett. *Creating the Big Game: John W. Heisman and the Invention of American Football.* Westport, Connecticut: Greenwood Press, 1992.

Weyand   A. M. Weyand. *American Football: Its History and Development.* New York: D. Appleton, 1926.

1. In the Beginning

Epigraph taken from Raymond E. DeSpain Jr., *An Historical Analysis of the Life and Professional Career of John William Heisman, 1869–1936* (Ph.D. diss., Texas A&M University, 1991), 162–63.

1. David P. Simpson, "Historical Sketches of Athletics at Oberlin (In the Nineties)," *Oberlin Alumni Magazine* (March 1914): 161–62.

2. Book 15, Office of the Registrar, 1859–1995, Oberlin College Archives, 235. Heisman is listed under the heading "Post Graduate Class of '92" with another graduate student whose marks in English, German et al., are given for the fall term, but no entry follows "J. William Heisman." Heisman is also listed on page 141 of the *Catalogue of Oberlin College for 1892–93*, together with four other graduate students. One of the others is Stephen R. Williams, who played on the 1892 football team.

3. Clifford Putney, *Muscular Christianity: The Strenuous Mood in American Protestantism, 1880–1920* (Ph.D. diss., Brandeis University, 1995), 4. Although the page (4) and the chapter (1) are indicated on the manuscript page, the rough draft of the uncorrected dissertation loaned to me by the author varies in being sometimes paginated and sometimes not. This and other such Putney citations that follow are therefore tentative.

4. Ibid., 1:20.

5. Ronald A. Smith, *Sports and Freedom: The Rise of Big-Time College Athletics* (New York: Oxford University Press, 1988), 72.

6. Putney, 2:20.

7. Ibid., 3:13.

8. Ibid., 3:14

9. Ibid., 2:24–25.

10. Ibid., 1:31.

11. Smith, *Sports and Freedom*, 95.

12. Putney, 3:69. The college president was Henry Churchill King, who served from 1902 to 1927.

13. Ibid., 1:59.

14. Parke H. Davis, *Football: The American Intercollegiate Game* (New York: Scribner's Sons, 1911), 93.

15. This and other quotes by the Rev. Dr. John Bigham that follow are from an unpaginated reprint of his article, "This Foot-ball Question," which appeared in the *DePauw Palladium*, November 1, 1897.

16. A. M. Weyand, *American Football: Its History and Development* (New York: D. Appleton, 1926), 2–3. The chief justice was William S. Gummere, the clergyman William J. Leggett.

17. Ibid., 16.

18. Ibid., 17. The mayor was P. C. Fuller.

19. Ibid., 24. The banking official was E. L. Richards.

20. Ibid., 13. The congressman was L. N. Littauer.

21. Ibid., 17–18.

22. Ibid., 15. The missionary was T. M. McNair, the congressman Blair Lee.

23. Ibid., 21. The Pennsylvania attorney general was John C. Bell.

24. Ibid., 29. The U.S. senator was George W. Pepper.

25. Ibid., 29–30. The railroad executives were Fred P. Gutelius, general superintendent of the Canadian Pacific; Rush N. Harry, treasurer of the Big Four System; and Charles S. Krick, general manager of the Pennsylvania System.

26. DeSpain, 162–63. Heisman's book, *Principles of Football*, was published in 1922.

27. *ON*, November 1, 1894. The newspaper quotes a story in the *Cleveland Leader and Herald* reporting on the death of Barton N. Silliman of Warren, Ohio.

28. *OR*, November 2, 1892. Purdue won the game, played on October 24, 22–0.

29. Charles W. Savage, *OAM* (October 1941): 5.

30. Alexander Johnston, "The American Game of Foot-ball," *Century Magazine* (October 1887): 895.

31. Ibid., 897.

32. John W. Heisman, "Fast and Loose," *Collier's* (October 20, 1928): 14.

33. Nicholas Mason, *Football: The Story of All the World's Football Games* (New York: Drake, 1975), 60.

34. Hal D. Sears, "The Moral Threat of Intercollegiate Sports: An 1893 Poll of Ten College Presidents, and the End of the Champion Football Team of the Great West," *Journal of Sport History* (Winter 1992): 211.

35. *ON*, December 12, 1894.

36. Ibid., November 15, 1894.

37. Robin Lester, *Stagg's University: The Rise, Decline, and Fall of Big-Time Football at Chicago* (Urbana: University of Illinois Press, 1995), xix.

38. Warren Taylor, "The Achievement of Oberlin College, 1833–1933," *OAM* (December 1969): 12.

39. W. C. Cochran, "Antiquity of Football," *OAM* (February 1906): 158–59.

2. THE SPORT

Epigraph taken from "All Hail! Our Alma Mater," words by Clara Little Simpson, 1892, music by Geo. W. Andrews. From Anna Louise Strong and Edna Barrows, *Songs of Oberlin* (n.p., n.d.), 14. Both Ms. Strong and Ms. Barrows were members of the Class of 1905.

1. Frank G. Menke, *The Encyclopedia of Sports* (New York: A. S. Barnes, 1953), 412.

2. Weyand, 4.

3. Ibid., 5.

4. In its first encounter with Yale, played at New Haven, Harvard won, four goals to none.

5. Davis, *Football*, 92.

6. Smith, *Sports and Freedom*, 75.

7. Allison Danzig, *Oh, How They Played the Game: The Early Days of Football and the Heroes Who Made It Great* (New York: Macmillan, 1968), 10.

8. Davis, *Football*, 68.

9. Weyand, 11.

10. Davis, *Football*, 113.

11. Weyand, 18.

12. Smith, *Sports and Freedom*, 86.

13. *OR*, November 17, 1891.

14. John W. Heisman, "Hold 'em!" *Collier's* (October 27, 1928): 12.

15. Heisman, "Fast and Loose," 14.

16. Heisman, "Hold 'em!" 13.

17. John W. Heisman, "Signals," *Collier's* (October 6, 1928): 13.

18. Weyand, 12.

19. Danzig, 17.

20. Weyand, 28.

21. John W. Heisman, "Their Weight in Gold," *Collier's* (November 24, 1928): 55.

3. The Faculty Concedes

Epigraph taken from Strong and Barrows, *Songs of Oberlin*, 33. This ditty, one of two "Football Songs," was sung to the tune of "Oh, the Grand Old Duke of York."

1. W. C. Cochran, "Historical Sketches of Athletics at Oberlin (In the Sixties)," *OAM* (February 1914): 129. An Oberlin College trustee, Cochran was a member of the Class of 1869.

2. Robert J. Keefe. *Physical Education at Oberlin College: A Report of a Type C Project* (Ph.D. diss., Teachers College, Columbia University, 1952).

3. W. S. Cochran, "Some Facts on the New Athletic Field Project," *OAM* (April 1914): 200.

4. *Oberlin College: Historical and Descriptive, 1899* (Columbus, Ohio: Champlin Press, 1899), in Miscellaneous Publications and Printed Materials, 1834–1996, College General, OCA, 3–4.

5. Ibid., 4.

6. Ibid., 3.

7. Keefe, *Physical Education*, 33.

8. Ibid., 28.

9. Fredrick D. Shults, *The History and Philosophy of Athletics for Men at Oberlin College* (Ph.D. diss., Indiana University, 1967), 64.

10. W. C. Cochran, "Historical Sketches," 130.

11. Shults, 216.

12. Stewart I. Edelstein, "Mens Sana in Corpore Sano," *OAM* (April 1970): 5.

13. W. C. Cochran, "Historical Sketches," 130.

14. Shults, 158–59.

15. Geoffrey Blodgett, "The Meaning of Peters Hall," *OAM* (Fall 1997): 20.

16. John Barnard, *From Evangelicalism to Progressivism at Oberlin College, 1866–1917* (Columbus: Ohio State University Press, 1969), 79–81.

17. John Mark Tucker, "Wide Awakening: Political and Theological Impulses for Reading and Libraries at Oberlin College, 1883–1908," *Occasional Papers* (February 1997): 62.

18. Barnard, *Evangelicalism*, 3.

19. Tucker, "Wide Awakening," 54.

20. Harlan F. Burket, "Historical Sketches of Athletics at Oberlin (In the Eighties)," *OAM* (February 1914): 135. Burket attended Oberlin from September 1877 to June 1882. He became a prominent lawyer and a judge of the Supreme Court of Ohio.

21. Edelstein, "Mens Sana," 6. Weldy Walker played right field for Oberlin.

22. *OR*, June 3, 1882.

23. Ibid., June 2, 1891.

24. Harvard graduated several students in a special four-year course, but the degree was not called a physical education degree.

25. W. C. Cochran, "Historical Sketches," 130–31.

26. *OR*, October 7, 1874.

27. Ibid., September. 23, 1874.

28. Daniel C. Kinsey. *The History of Physical Education in Oberlin College, 1833–1890* (Master's thesis, Oberlin College, 1935), 138.

29. Shults, 72.

30. Burket, "Historical Sketches," 136. Burket played on the baseball varsity with the Walker brothers. He pitched the last game, a class contest, that was played on the old Campus field, then the first game played on the field in back of Peters Hall and also the first game on what he termed the "present" grounds on North Professor Street. Also, see David W. Zang, *Fleet Walker's Divided Heart: The Life of Baseball's First Black Major Leaguer* (Lincoln: University of Nebraska Press, 1995), 21–22.

31. *OR*, December 15, 1883.

32. Ibid., December 20, 1884.

33. Ibid., November 22, 1877.

34. Minnie L. Lynn, "Fifty Years of Physical Education—1885–1935," *OAM* (April 1935): 204.

35. *OR*, December 10, 1889.

36. Michael Oriard, *Reading Football: How the Popular Press Created an American Spectacle* (Chapel Hill: University of North Carolina Press, 1993), 90–91.

37. Kinsey, *Physical Education,* 144.

38. Student folder of Frederick Bushnell Ryder, Alumni Records, OCA. Ryder used the pen name of Jack Ryder in writing baseball news for the *Cincinnati Enquirer* for thirty-one years. I am assuming he went by that name while a student, as well, which seems likely.

39. Kinsey, *Physical Education,* 145.

40. *OR*, October 22, 1889.

41. Ibid., December 3, 1889.

42. Shults, 74.

43. *OR*, January 7, 1890.

44. Ibid., November 18, 1889.

45. *OR*, December 10, 1889. The game between juniors and sophomores was for the school championship. It ended in a scoreless tie.

46. Kinsey, *Physical Education,* 146.

47. *OR*, November 18, 1889.

48. Ibid., December 15, 1891.

49. Ibid., December 17, 1889.

50. Ibid., January 7, 1890.

51. Cash Book, Cash Account of Athletic Association, 1889–90, Office of the Secretary, OCA, 2.

52. *OR*, March 11, 1890. The lumber dealer was Edmund Hall of Detroit. According to the Cash Book, p. 3, the lumber for the grandstand ran to $426.54.

53. *OR*, February 18, 1890.

54. Ibid., February 25, 1890.

55. Shults, 233.

56. *OR*, March 18, 1890.

57. Ibid., July 1, 1890.

58. Ibid., March 5, 1889. The village is identified as Waldersbach in the October 31, 1930, issue.

59. *Hi-O-Hi*, 1890, OCA, 4.

60. "A Sketch Book of the Class of '89 Oberlin College," Class Files, OCA. From an anonymous typed account.

61. *OR*, November 4, 1890.

62. One of the three-man committee, Seabury Cone Mastick, was chosen to replace Ryder. Mastick, a senior from California, had played halfback on the junior team the previous season. He was, in fact, one of the heroes in its win over a senior team in the school's first intramural game. But during the summer Mastick injured himself and had to resign as captain. Replacing him was the quarterback on the previous season's sophomore team, Henry Walter Sperry. Because the varsity had no coach, Sperry would assume a triple role: quarterback, team captain, and coach.

63. The second member of the three-man committee, George Addison Lawrence, was, like Mastick, a senior and a halfback. Lawrence had excelled in Latin and ethics in the Preparatory Department and was headed for a career in the ministry.

64. Student folder of David Peter Simpson, Alumni Records.

65. Simpson, "Historical Sketches," 161–62.

66. *OR*, December 15, 1891.

67. A placard borne in the team photograph of the 1890 varsity reads "167 lbs."

68. Howard Krum Regal, letter to editor of *Oberlin News*, April 27, 1926. From student folder of H. K. Regal, Alumni Records.

69. Charles Winfred Savage, *OAM* (October 1941): 5.

4. GAME TIME

Epigraph taken from "Young Field Day," *Oberlin Annual 1889*, 105.

1. *Hi-O-Hi*, 1890, OCA, 36–37.

2. Student folder of Charles Henry Borican, Alumni Records.

3. Nat Brandt, *The Town That Started the Civil War* (Syracuse: Syracuse University Press, 1990), 261–62.

4. *Oberlin College Alumni Catalogue . . . 1833–1936* (Oberlin, 1937), Int. 77.

5. "Report of the President," *Oberlin College Annual Reports for 1892*, 5. Five years earlier, there had been only eighteen regular professors. Total faculty then totalled forty-eight teachers. There had been only seven elective courses seven years earlier.

6. Student folder of George Robin Berry, Alumni Records. One of the other two theologs, in addition to Berry and Wise, was William J. Jacobs, a Phi Beta Kappa student at Adelbert College who had then gone on to Lane Seminary in Cincinnati before matriculating at Oberlin as a postgraduate. Jacobs celebrated his twenty-sixth birthday as the fall term began. (Student folder of W. J. Jacobs, Alumni Records.) The fourth theolog was George Durand Wilder, both of whose parents were Oberlin graduates. A popular, handsome student, Wilder had transferred from Yankton College in South Dakota as a junior in 1889. He was twenty-two years old. (Student folder of G. D. Wilder, Alumni Records.)

7. Student folder of John Henry Wise, Alumni Records.

8. Student folder of Stephen Riggs Williams, Alumni Records.

9. Stephen R. Williams to Dr. J. H. Nichols, December 23, 1941, S. R. Williams folder, Alumni Records, OCA. Williams was living in Oxford, Ohio, at the time.

10. Student folder of William Harvey Merriam, Alumni Records.

11. Student folder of Carl Young Semple, Alumni Records.

12. Carl Semple, *OAM* (March 1942): 13.

13. Shults, 235.

14. *OR*, December 15, 1891.

15. Ibid., June 10, 1941, clipping in Geoffrey Blodgett Papers, 1945–1996, OCA.

16. "President's Report for the year 1920–21," 99, in Annual Reports, Bentley Historical Library, University of Michigan. Michigan's total enrollment in 1891–92 was 2,692 students.

17. Will Perry, *The Wolverines: A Story of Michigan Football* (Huntsville, Ala.: Strode, 1974), 23. Michigan had scored one touchdown and one goal, but the game was officially recorded as a 1–0 victory over Racine.

18. Perry, *Wolverines*, 28.

19. Christy Walsh, ed., *Intercollegiate Football: A Complete Pictorial and Statistical Review from 1869 to 1934* (New York: Doubleday, Doran, 1934), 211.

20. Perry, *Wolverines*, 29.

21. Both *OR*, October 12, 1892, and the *Cleveland Leader and Herald*, November 1, 1891, describe the team's uniform.

22. Unless otherwise noted, the description of the Oberlin-Michigan game is from *OR*, October 27, 1891.

23. Perry, *Wolverines*, 32.

24. *OR*, December 15, 1891.

25. *ON*, November 5, 1891.

26. *The Oberlin College (1996) Football Media Guide*, 34, incorrectly gives the score of the game as 20–0.

27. *ON*, October 29, 1891.

28. *OR*, November 3, 1891.

29. Ibid., December 13, 1891.

30. Danzig, 132.

31. Oriard, *Reading Football*, 57–58.

32. Unless otherwise noted, the description of the Oberlin-Adelbert game is from *OR*, November 3, 1891.

33. *ON*, November 5, 1891.

34. Ibid.

35. Ibid.

36. *Cleveland Leader and Herald*, November 1, 1891.

37. The description of the Oberlin-CAC game is from *OR*, November 17, 1891.

38. Unless otherwise noted, the description of the Oberlin-Case game is from *OR*, November 17, 1891.

39. *Cleveland Leader and Herald*, November 15, 1891. The newspaper identifies Steve Williams as scoring both touchdowns.

40. *Cleveland Leader and Herald*, November 22, 1891.

41. Ibid.

42. Ibid.

43. Ibid.

44. *OR*, December 1, 1891.

45. *OR*, December. 15, 1891.

46. Ibid.

47. Ibid

5. THE COACH

Epigraph taken from "Heisman: The almost-forgotten football genius whose first memory of Brown was–a football game," *Brown Alumni Monthly* (December 1972): 34.

1. Bruce Kostic, "John Heisman," a 1970s student term paper, in John W. Heisman student folder, Alumni Records, 1–2.

2. *OR*, December 19, 1901.

3. John McCullum and Charles H. Pearson, *College Football U.S.A., 1869 . . . 1972* (Greenwich, Conn.: Hall of Fame Publishing, 1972), 88.

4. Cash Book, Cash Account of Athletic Association, 1889–90, Office of the Secretary, 12.

5. DeSpain, 43.

6. Umphlett, 3.

7. DeSpain, 17.

8. John W. Heisman, "Look Sharp Now!" *Collier's* (November 3, 1928): 19.

9. John W. Heisman, "Rules Rush In," *Collier's* (November 10, 1928): 12.

10. John W. Heisman, "Signals," *Collier's* (October 6, 1928): 12.

11. Ibid., 12. Unless otherwise noted, Heisman's experiences at Titusville, enroute to Providence, at Brown, and at the University of Pennsylvania are from his article, "Signals," 12–13, 31–32.

12. DeSpain, 49.

13. Umphlett, 17. Penn beat Rutgers in the indoor game, 13–10.

14. Heisman, "Signals," 13.

15. Heisman, "Fast and Loose," 54.

16. Heisman, "Hold 'em!" 12.

17. Ibid., 13.

18. Edwin Pope, *Football's Greatest Coaches* (Atlanta: Tupper and Love, 1956), 119.

19. Heisman, "Look Sharp Now!" 32.

20. John W. Heisman, "The Thundering Herd," *Collier's* (October 13, 1928).

21. Danzig, 133.

22. Heisman, "Thundering Herd," 12.

23. Ibid., 59.

24. Pope, *Football's Greatest*, 50.

25. Umphlett, 30–31, and *Elyria Chronicle-Telegram*, January 14, 1979.

26. John T. Brady, *The Heisman: A Symbol of Excellence* (New York: Atheneum, 1984), 7.

27. DeSpain, 52.

28. Brady, *The Heisman*, 21.

29. John W. Heisman, "Little Giants of the Gridiron," in Walsh, *Intercollegiate Football*, 20.

6. The Team

Epigraph taken from DeSpain, 163.

1. "Report of the President," *Oberlin College Annual Reports for 1893*, 5–6.

2. *OR*, September 20, 1892.

3. Ibid., September 28, 1892. The eight-day lapse between editions of the *Oberlin Review* was due to the fact that the publication changed its publication date from a Tuesday to a Wednesday.

4. "Report of the President," *Oberlin College Annual Reports for 1893*, 5.

5. Ibid., 6.

6. *OR*, September 20, 1892.

7. John H. Wise to "Dear boys," November 17, 1890, Student Letters (John H. Wise), Oberlin File, OCA.

8. Carl Y. Semple, *OAM* (March 1942): 5. The chicken was stolen from Prof. John Millot Ellis, professor of mental and moral philosophy. Prof. John Fisher Peck, an associate professor of Greek, was principal of the Academy.

9. Student folder of Louis Edward Hart, Alumni Records.

10. *OR*, September 20, 1892.

11. Ibid., September 28, 1892.

12. Ibid., September 20, 1892.

13. Ibid., October 2, 1895, gives Williams's nickname as "Capp."

14. *ON*, September 29, 1892.

15. *OR*, October 5, 1892.

16. Minutes of the Athletic Association, September 29, 1892, Athletics and Athletic Association Files, Office of the Secretary.

17. *OR*, September 20, 1892.

18. Student folder of Josiah Cattell Teeters, Alumni Records. Teeters was twenty-nine years and one month old. Others on the 1892 team who were older than Heisman were Berry, Louis Fauver, Jones, Marsh, Savage, Wise, and Zimmerman. In the case of Wise and Zimmerman, they were older by only a matter of a month or two. Wise was born in July 1869, Zimmerman in September of that year. As for Teeters, he is outranked in age by Willis Jay Miller, a theolog, who was nearly twenty-nine and one-half years old when he played on the 1894 varsity.

19. John W. Heisman, "Between Halves," *Collier's* (November 17, 1928): 18.

20. Heisman, "Hold 'em!" 12.

21. *Hi-O-Hi*, 1890, OCA, 66.

22. Student folder of Louis Benjamin Fauver, Alumni Records.

23. Student folder of Clayton King Fauver, Alumni Records.

24. *OR*, October 4, 1893.

25. Ibid., November 24, 1891.

26. Ibid., September 28, 1892.

27. *ON*, October 13, 1892.

28. "Heisman: The almost-forgotten football genius," 34.

29. Simpson, "Historical Sketches," 161–62.

30. Heisman, "Look Sharp Now!" 32.

31. *OR*, October 24, 1941, Geoffrey Blodgett Papers, 1945–1996, OCA.

32. Student folder of John W. White, Alumni Records.

33. DeSpain, 55.

34. C. W. Savage Scrapbook, 1887–1894, Scrapbooks and Diaries Collection, OCA.

35. Heisman, "Signals," 31.

36. Heisman, "Thundering Herd," 60.

37. David Reisman and Reuel Denney, "Football in America: A Study in Culture Diffusion," *American Quarterly* (May 1952): 319.

38. DeSpain, 80. Later, at Georgia Tech, Heisman's diet banned alcohol and smoking, too, but he allowed a bottle of beer and a cigar after a victory. He also restricted his players to cold showers only, except after a game, and no sex. At the time at Oberlin, such restrictions—against alcohol, smoking, and sex—were standard in every phase of student life.

39. Charles W. Savage, *OAM* (October 1941): 5.

40. *OR*, October 24, 1941, clipping in Geoffrey Blodgett Papers, 1945–1996.

41. Charles W. Savage, *OAM* (October 1941): 5.

42. *OAM* (February 1923): 26.

43. *OR*, October 19, 1892.

44. *ON*, October 13, 1892.

45. The lineup devised by Hogen and Carl Williams is from *ON*, September 29, 1892. It was tacked to the bulletin board at Peters Hall, the main classroom and faculty office building on campus. The roster of the first game against Ohio State University that Heisman went with is from *OR*, October 19, 1892.

46. Student folder of Thomas Winder Johnson, Alumni Records.

47. Student folder of Max Frank Millikan, Alumni Records.

48. *OR*, October 19, 1892.

7. HEISMAN BALL

Epigraph taken from Heisman, "Fast and Loose," 55.

1. *OR*, October 13, 1892.

2. Wilbur Snypp, *The Buckeyes: A Story of Ohio State Football* (Huntsville, Alabama: Strode, 1974), 18.

3. Snypp, *Buckeyes*, 24–25.

4. *Ohio Guide* (New York: Oxford University Press, 1962), 259.

5. *Annual Report of the Registrar and University Examiner* Columbus: Ohio State University Press, 1962), 64.

6. *Record of Proceedings of the Board of Trustees of the Ohio State University from November 18, 1890, to June 30, 1900* (Columbus: Hann & Adair, 1900), 5–6.

7. Student folder of Frederick Bushnell Ryder, Alumni Records. Ryder, who was instrumental in convincing the faculty to permit intercollegiate play, made a career in athletics. He had left Oberlin for Williams College, where he played football, and subsequently was the coach of the Ohio State University team when Oberlin played it in 1892. OSU compiled a 5–2 record that year. Ryder was teaching in Columbus at the time, and later became proprietor of Columbus Academy. He saw brief service with an Ohio cavalry unit in the Spanish-American War, then returned to Columbus and coached OSU's 1898 team, which lost five games and won three. Ryder then landed a job on the staff of the *Ohio State Journal* and later the *Cincinnati Commercial-Tribune*. He subsequently joined that city's *Enquirer* and was its baseball editor for thirty-one years. Ryder died of a heart attack there in 1936 when he was sixty-four years old.

8. Unless otherwise noted, the description of the Oberlin-OSU game is from *OR*, October 19, 1892. Interestingly, in one article, Heisman is identified as "Heeseman." Such misspellings were present in several issues. He was called "Heissman" in the account of the first Adelbert game in 1892.

9. *ON*, October 20, 1892.

10. Ibid.

11. Heisman, "Thundering Herd," 59.

12. *ON*, November 3, 1892.

13. DeSpain, 45–47. An older brother, Daniel, who worked in a barrel factory, was killed in May 1892 when a runaway freight car collided with another freight car. He was caught between the bumpers of the two colliding cars.

14. Heisman, "Look Sharp Now!" 19.

15. Unless otherwise noted, the description of the first Oberlin-Adelbert game is from *OR*, October 26, 1892.

16. Student folder of Miles Eugene Marsh, Alumni Records.

17. I am guessing that Andrew Bertram Kell and another footballer, Ellsworth Burnett Westcott, were Academy students. There is virtually nothing in their alumni

files to indicate when they arrived in Oberlin or where they were from or how old they were. I have assumed the lack of information means they entered the Academy early on and dropped out after a year or two.

18. Heisman, "Thundering Herd," 13.

19. *OR,* November 23, 1892.

20. Ibid., November 2, 1892.

21. The description of the Oberlin–Ohio Wesleyan game is from *OR,* November 9, 1892.

22. Heisman switched Thomas Johnson from left halfback to left end, put Lynds Jones into Johnson's place in the backfield, and in moving Teeters to Jones's spot at right tackle, had John White take over for Teeters at right guard. Neither Johnson, Jones, nor White had ever played their newly assigned positions before.

23. Student folder of Washington Irving Squire, Alumni Records.

24. Unless otherwise noted, the description of the second Oberlin-OSU game is from *ON,* November 10, 1892.

25. *OR,* November 16, 1892.

26. *Buckeye Football* 1996, 276.

27. Cash Book, Cash Account of Athletic Association, 1889–90, Office of the Secretary, 12.

28. Unless otherwise noted, the description of the Oberlin-Kenyon game is from *OR,* November 16, 1892.

29. *Ohio Guide,* 481.

30. *ON,* November 24, 1892, quotes the *Elyria Democrat,* November 16, 1892.

31. *OR,* November 16, 1892.

32. The description of the second Oberlin-Adelbert game is from *OR,* November 23, 1892.

33. Ibid., November 16, 1892.

34. Ibid.

35. Perry, *Wolverines,* 30.

36. *ON,* November 24, 1892.

8. "Unblushing Effrontery"

Epigraph taken from DeSpain, 162–63.

1. The description of the Oberlin-Michigan game is based, with some exceptions, on *OR,* November 23, 1892.

2. Umphlett, 34. Umphlett implies that Westcott held onto the ball and then handed it to an end, but the *OR* account contradicts this, saying Westcott carried it himself. Nevertheless, the idea of the fake pass was born, and Heisman used it for ten years until rules eventually outlawed it by demanding that the center hike the ball at once.

3. *OR,* November 23, 1892, incorrectly gives the score at this point in the game as 16–10.

4. *ON,* November 24, 1892.

5. *University of Michigan Daily,* November 21, 1892, Geoffrey Blodgett Papers, 1945–1996.

6. *ON,* November 24, 1892.

7. *University of Michigan Daily,* November 21, 1892, Geoffrey Blodgett Papers, 1945–1996.

8. *Detroit Tribune,* November 20, 1892, Geoffrey Blodgett Papers, 1945–1996.

9. *OR,* November 23, 1892.

10. Ibid., November 30, 1892.

11. Walsh, *Intercollegiate Football,* 211.

12. *Oberlin College (1996) Football Media Guide,* 34.

13. *OR,* November 30, 1892.

14. Ibid., November 23, 1892. The local insurance agent was Frank E. Sherrill, employed by the Northwestern Mutual Life Insurance Company.

15. C. W. Savage Scrapbook, 1887–1894.

16. *OR,* March 8, 1893.

17. Ibid., December 1, 1892.

9. The Winning Spirit

Epigraph taken from *OR,* December 19, 1901. Corbin's poem is entitled "Football in Paradise."

1. The description of the Oberlin booth at the Columbian Exposition is based on accounts in *OR,* February 15, November 8, 1893.

2. Minutes of the Class of 1894, Class files, College General, OCA. At a meeting of the class in chapel on October 3, 1893, members voted 60–20 for cap and gown.

3. Ibid., October 11, 1893.

4. Ibid., October 31, 1894.

5. Ballantine's objections to cap and gown were enumerated at a class meeting on October 9, 1893, Minutes of Class of 1894.

6. *OR,* November 30, 1892.

7. Ibid., May 3, 1893.

8. Ibid., November 23, 1892.

9. *Hi-O-Hi,* 1894, OCA.

10. *Oberlin College Annual Reports for 1893,* 23–24.

11. Cash Book, Cash Account of Athletic Association, 1889–90, Office of the Secretary, 13, 18–21.

12. Minutes of the Athletic Association, Athletics and Athletic Association Files, OCA, 54. The board voted to increase the admission to 35 cents at a meeting on September 26, 1893.

13. *Oberlin College Annual Reports for 1894,* 4–5.

14. Umphlett, 33.

15. *OR,* October 4, 1893.

16. Student folder of Charles Clark Brackin, Alumni Records.

17. E. B. Camp is identified as "Jake" in *OR,* December 19, 1901.

18. Ibid., September 27, 1893.

19. Ibid.

20. Ibid., December 19, 1901.

21. Ibid., September 27, 1893.

22. Stephen R. Williams to Dr. J. H. Nichols, December 23, 1941, student folder of Stephen R. Williams, Alumni Records.

23. *OR*, September 27, 1893.

24. Ibid., October 9, 1895. According to the November 28, 1894, issue, Boothman was also known as Boozie.

25. Ibid., September 27, 1893.

26. Shults, 238.

27. *OR*, November 1, 1893.

28. *ON*, October 5, 1893.

29. *OR*, October 4, 1893.

10. CAMP TIME

Epigraph taken from "Tribute to Oberlin's High Standing Kicker," *Hi-O-Hi*, 1890, OCA, 143.

1. *OR*, October 18, 1893.

2. Unless otherwise noted, the description of the Oberlin-Kenyon game is from *OR*, October 11, 1893.

3. J. H. Nichols, "50 Years of Football," *OAM* (October 1941): 4.

4. *OR*, November, 22, 1893.

5. *ON*, October 12, 1893.

6. Unless otherwise noted, the description of the Oberlin-OSU game is from *OR*, October 25, 1893. The account says Clate Fauver captained the team in Merriam's absence, but Merriam had already resigned, and Fauver had been elected in his place. Ergo, it is likely that the writer, Washington Irving Squire, was unaware of this.

7. Oddly, Ryder is not listed in the OSU's football media guide as being the team's coach in 1893. He is for 1892. But no coach is listed for 1893. Presumably then, he did not coach the entire season.

8. *ON*, October 23, 1893.

9. Ibid.

10. Ibid., November 1, 1893. *ON*, November 2, 1893, carries most of the *Lantern*'s quote.

11. *ON*, October 26, 1893.

12. The description of the second Oberlin-Kenyon game is from *OR*, October 25, 1893.

13. Ibid., December 13, 1893.

14. Ibid., October 25, 1893.

15. Bert M. Hogen to "Dear People of '93," undated letter, Class Notes, 1893, Class Files, OCA, 102.

16. Cash Book, Cash Account of Athletic Association, 1889–90, Office of the Secretary, 27.

11. Westward Ho!

Epigraph taken from Strong and Barrows, *Songs of Oberlin*, 24. The song is entitled "The Crimson and Gold."

1. DeSpain, 60–61.
2. Ibid., 63.
3. John W. Heisman, "Inventions in Football," *Baseball* (October 1908): 40.
4. DeSpain, 63.
5. Unless otherwise noted, the description of the Oberlin-Chicago game is from *OR*, November 8, 1893.
6. Smith, *Sports and Freedom*, 189.
7. Ibid., 22.
8. Lester, *Stagg's University*, 19.
9. Ibid., 15.
10. Ibid., xix.
11. *OR*, December 13, 1893.
12. Danzig, 108.
13. Student folder of Benjamin Markley Nyce, Alumni Records. Nyce attended Oberlin 1884–90. A member of the Class of '91, he left Oberlin before graduating and subsequently graduated from Princeton and the McCormick Theological Seminary in Chicago. A Presbyterian minister, he at one time was president of Talladega College in Alabama. He died two days after Christmas in 1934, shortly after his sixty-fifth birthday.
14. Minutes of the Athletic Association, Office of the Secretary, 56, 59. The association adopted a resolution disapproving of the fire-alarm incident during the "recent jollification" over the Chicago victory.
15. Heisman, "Thundering Herd," 13.
16. *OR*, November 8, 1893.
17. Unless otherwise noted, the description of the Oberlin-Illinois game is from *OR*, November 8, 1893.
18. *OR*, November 15, 1893, quotes the *Chicago Tribune* remarks.
19. Heisman, "Thundering Herd," 13.
20. *OR*, November 15, 1893.
21. Cash Book, Cash Account of Athletic Association, 1889–90, Office of the Secretary, 27.
22. *OR*, October 3, 1894, carries the report of the treasurer of the Athletic Association, who happened then to be Boothman.
23. Cash Book, Cash Account of Athletic Association, 1889–90, Office of the Secretary, OCA, 29.
24. *OR*, November 14, 1894.
25. Unless otherwise noted, the description of the Oberlin-Case game is from *OR*, November 25, 1893.
26. *OR*, December 6, 1893, quotes the *Integral*.
27. Ibid., December 13, 1893.
28. Ibid.

29. *Oberlin College Annual Reports for 1894*, 6.

30. Student folder of Frederick Green, Alumni Records.

31. *OR*, December 13, 1893.

32. Ibid., November 29, 1893.

33. Ibid., December 6, 1893.

12. Pros and Cons

Epigraph taken from DeSpain, 162.

1. *OR*, January 17, 1894.

2. Ibid., April 11, 1894.

3. Ibid., September 26, 1894.

4. Sears, "Moral Threat," 218. The president of Allegheny College quoted was D. H. Wheeler.

5. Ibid., 320. The college presidents cited are J. W. Brashford of Ohio Wesleyan and J. W. H. Wilder of Illinois Wesleyan.

6. *ON*, November 15, 22, 1894.

7. Ibid., December 6, 1894.

8. Ibid.

9. Walter Camp, *Football Facts and Figures* (New York: Harper, 1894), 2.

10. Ibid., 4.

11. Ibid., 5.

12. Ibid., 210.

13. Ibid., 127.

14. Ibid., 127.

15. Ibid., 20.

16. Ibid., 21.

17. Ibid., 43–44.

18. Ibid., 28.

19. Ibid., 9.

20. Ibid., 236–37.

21. Kenyon, Wittenberg, and Miami also participated in the tournament.

22. DeSpain, 62–63. The *Ohio State University 1996 Media Guide* gives the score as *Akron* 12, OSU 6.

23. Smith, *Sports and Freedom*, 184.

24. Minutes of the Athletic Association, Office of the Secretary, 15.

25. Meeting of June 11, 1894, Minutes of the Advisory Board of Athletics, Athletics and Athletic Association Files, OCA, 37.

26. *OR*, December 13, 1893.

27. Shults, 241.

28. *Oberlin College Alumni Catalogue 1833–1936* (Oberlin, 1937), Int. 77.

29. *OR*, October 10, 1894.

30. Unless otherwise noted, the preseason account of Oberlin's team and its prospects are from *OR*, September 26, 1894.

31. Lester, *Stagg's University*, 25.

32. Student folder of Henry Bert Voorhees, Alumni Records.

33. *OR*, October 9, 1895.

34. Ibid., December 13, 1893.

35. Ibid., October 2, 1895.

36. Student folder of Clyde Harold Shields, Alumni Records.

37. Student folder of Rae Shepard Dorsett, Alumni Records.

38. Student folder of Floyd Henry Bogrand, Alumni Records.

39. *OR*, September 26, 1894.

13. Play by Play

Epigraph taken from Heisman, "Fast and Loose," 55.

1. *OR*, December 12, 1894.

2. Ibid., December 13, 1893.

3. Ibid., December 12, 1894. The gymnast was Charles T. Tinker.

4. Student folder of Henry Alfred Young, Alumni Records.

5. Heisman, "Inventions in Football," 41.

6. Student folder of Rae Shepard Dorsett, Alumni Records.

7. *Ohio Guide*, 393.

8. Unless otherwise noted, the description of the Oberlin–Mount Union game is from *OR*, October 3, 1894.

9. Student folder of William Raymond Miller, Alumni Records.

10. *ON*, October 4, 1894. The account says that Bogrand made nine out of *ten* goals, but there were eleven touchdowns in all and no indication that anyone else made a kick after a touchdown.

11. *OR*, October 3, 1894.

12. Ibid., October 17, 1894.

13. Ibid., October 10, 1894.

14. Ibid.

15. Unless otherwise noted, the description of the Oberlin-Kenyon game is from *OR*, October 17, 1894.

16. *ON*, October 18, 1894. The Kenyon captain was a man named Williams.

17. *OR*, December 12, 1894.

18. Unless otherwise noted, the description of the Oberlin-Washington and Jefferson game is from *OR*, October 31, 1894.

19. *OR*, November 7, 1894. Bennett was writing to his father in Oberlin.

20. *ON*, November 1, 1894.

21. *OR*, November 7, 1894.

22. Ibid.

23. *ON*, November 1, 1894.

24. *OR*, November 7, 1894.

25. Ibid., October 31, 1894.

26. Ibid., November 7, 1894.

27. Ibid., October. 31, 1894.

28. Ibid., October 24, 1894.

29. Ibid., November 8, 1894.

30. Ibid., October 31, 1894.

31. *ON*, November 8, 1894.

32. Unless otherwise noted, the description of the Oberlin-Case game is from *OR*, November 7, 1894.

33. Heisman, "Between Halves," 18.

34. Ibid.

35. *OR*, November 14, 1894.

36. *ON*, November 8, 1894.

37. Heisman, "Between Halves," 18.

14. Downs

Epigraph taken from John W. Heisman, "Here Are Men," *Collier's* (November 16, 1929): 46.

1. Smith, *Sports and Freedom*, 216.

2. *OR*, November 14, 1894.

3. Unless otherwise noted, the description of the Oberlin-Adelbert game is from *OR*, November 14, 1894.

4. *OR*, December 12, 1894.

5. *ON*, November 8, 1894.

6. *OR*, November, 14, 1894.

7. Perry, *Wolverines*, 31–32.

8. *ON*, November 22, 1894.

9. *OR*, October 10, 1894.

10. Walsh, *Intercollegiate Football*, 214. On the same day three weeks earlier when Oberlin played a scoreless tie with Washington and Jefferson, Michigan was defeating Case 18–8. The Wolverines thanked Oberlin alumnus Charles Browning, who refereed the first half, for its first touchdown "as well as many gains," which the *Cleveland Plain Dealer* sarcastically commented, "he must have figured by an entirely new system of measurement."

11. Unless otherwise noted, the description of the Oberlin-Michigan game is from *OR*, November 21, 1894.

12. *ON*, November 22, 1894.

13. Perry, *Wolverines*, 33.

14. *Ann Arbor Courier*, November 19, 1894.

15. Ibid.

16. *Elyria Chronicle-Telegram*, January 14, 1979.

17. *Ann Arbor Courier*, November 19, 1894.

18. *ON*, November 29, 1894.

19. *OR*, November 21, 1894.

20. Ibid., October 24, 1894.

21. Ibid., November 28, 1894.

22. Ibid.

23. Ibid.

24. Ibid., November 21, 1894.

25. Unless otherwise noted, the description of the Oberlin–Penn State game is from *OR*, November 28, 1894.

26. *Centre Daily Times*, State College, Pennsylvania., October 25, 1967. An account of Atherton's role identifies him as "Charlie" and says White was the referee.

27. *ON*, November 29, 1894.

28. *OR*, December 12, 1894.

29. Perry, *Wolverines*, 34.

30. Walsh, *Intercollegiate Football*, 214.

31. *OR*, December 12, 1894.

32. *ON*, November 29, 1894.

15. End Runs

Epigraph taken from Heisman, "Fast and Loose," 55.

1. *ON*, November 29, 1894.

2. *General Catalogue of Oberlin College 1833–1908*, 124.

3. *Owl*, December 1, 1894.

4. *General Catalogue of Oberlin College 1833–1908*, 124.

5. *ON*, November 29, 1894.

6. Ibid., December 6, 1894.

7. *General Catalogue of Oberlin College 1833–1908*, 124.

8. Lester, *Stagg's University*, 246f.

9. Student folder of John W. Heisman, Alumni Records. The alumni questionnaire he returned is dated April 15, 1908.

10. DeSpain, 77.

11. Umphlett, 255.

12. DeSpain, 119.

13. Ibid., 120.

14. Ibid., 148.

15. Ibid., 138.

16. Umphlett, 243. Heisman was buried in Rhinelander, Wisconsin, after his death on October 3, 1936. His second wife survived until 1964.

17. DeSpain, 69.

18. Heisman, "Rules Rush In," 12.

19. DeSpain, 76.

20. Danzig, 91.

21. Heisman, "Rules Rush In," 38.

22. DeSpain, 106–7.

23. Ibid., 109.

24. Umphlett, 255–56.

25. DeSpain, 146.

26. Umphlett, 236–38.

27. DeSpain, 199–201.

16. Over Time

Epigraph taken from *OR*, December 19, 1901. Corbin's poem is entitled "Football in Parenthesis."

1. *OR*, December 12, 1894.
2. Ibid.
3. Danzig, 29.
4. Robert Treat, *The Official Encyclopedia of Football* (New York: A. S. Barnes, 1968), 17.
5. *New York Times*, October 10, 1905.
6. Lester, *Stagg's University*, 75.
7. Smith, *Sports and Freedom*, 193.
8. Danzig, 29.
9. Weyand, 180–81.
10. Smith, *Sports and Freedom*, 214.
11. Cash Book, Cash Account of Athletic Association, 1889–90, Office of the Secretary, 34–35.
12. *OR*, December 12, 1894.
13. Ibid., October 16, 1895. Also, see Frederick J. Blue, "Oberlin's James Monroe: Forgotten Abolitionist," *Civil War History* 35 (December 1989): 286–89.
14. *Oberlin College Annual Reports . . . December 5, 1906*, 159.
15. *OR*, October 9, 1895.
16. Shults, 242.
17. *OR*, December 5, 1895.
18. *Oberlin College (1996) Football Media Guide*, 34. There appears to be some discrepancy. According to the Record Book kept by the Athletic Department, Oberlin lost to Chicago 30–0, to Illinois 22–6, and to Michigan 10–0. It says one of Oberlin's wins was against Case by a score of 34–0. But the media guide gives the Chicago game score as 0–0, and the Case score 16–10.
19. *Oberlin College: Historical and Descriptive, 1899*, Miscellaneous Publications, College General, 31–32.
20. George M. Jones, "Oberlin Athletics in Recent Years," *OAM* (April 1914): 193.
21. Shults, 270.
22. Mason, *Football*, 60.
23. Shults, 152.
24. Ibid., 73.
25. Ibid., 283.
26. Smith, *Sports and Freedom*, 98.
27. Michigan had 3,792 students in the fall of 1902. By the fall of 1905, it had 4,571. *President's Report for the Year 1920–1921*, University of Michigan, Bentley Historical Library. According to the *Oberlin College Alumni Catalogue 1833–1936*, Int. 77, Oberlin's enrollment in the 1902–3 academic year was 1,509.
28. According to the *Annual Report of the Registrar and University Examiner for 1961–62* (Columbus: Ohio State University, 1962), 64, Ohio State had 6,188 students in the 1916–17 academic year.

29. *Oberlin 1833–1923*, Office of the Secretary.

30. *Hi-O-Hi*, 1922, OCA, 102.

31. Snypp, *Buckeyes*, 73.

32. *Sports Illustrated*, June 17, 1996. The letter to the editor was written by John Kingdon.

33. Geoffrey Blodgett, "Oberlin Football Celebrates Long History," *OR*, October 4, 1991, 23.

34. *Oberlin College Alumni Catalogue 1833–1936*, Int. 79.

35. *Annual Report of the Registrar and University Examiner, for 1961–62* (Columbus: Ohio State University, 1962), 64.

36. Snypp, *Buckeyes*, 64. The player quoted is Gerald R. (Pete) Stinchcomb, an All-American halfback in 1920.

37. Ibid., 72.

38. *Buckeye Football 1996*, 239.

39. Perry, *Wolverines*, 127–28.

40. *Michigan Football ('96) Media Guide*, 261.

41. Sale of seats pamphlet, Intercollegiate Sports, Records of the Department of Physical Education for Men, OCA.

42. *OR*, November 23, 1921.

43. *Ohio State University Athletic Association, Treasurer Report for Year Ending August 31, 1921* (Athletic Board: Minutes, 1912–23, Records of the Athletic Board, Ohio State University Archives).

44. Football Settlements, College of Arts and Sciences, Physical Education, Intercollegiate Sports, OCA.

45. *Description of Oberlin Buildings*, Printed Materials, Int. 33.

46. Shults, 255–56.

47. Jones, "Oberlin Athletics," 197. Gray was unfortunately killed in a hunting accident in Utah in October 1911.

48. Shults, 118.

49. *Oberlin College Annual Reports . . . for 1906–7*, 275.

50. "The Secret Fraternity Cases—Dean Cole: Statement made to the faculty," *OAM* (October 1916): 20.

51. *OR*, September 12, 1916.

52. Record Book, 1891–1969, Oberlin Department of Physical Education and Athletics.

53. *Buckeye Football 1996*, 278.

54. Shults, 306.

55. Blodgett, "Oberlin football," 23.

56. Geoffrey Blodgett to Nat Brandt, August 8, 1997.

57. Cover, *OAM* (November 1941).

58. *Oberlin College Annual Report of the President 1945–1946*, 26.

59. Record Book, Oberlin Department of Physical Education and Athletics.

60. Danzig, xvii.

61. Geoffrey Blodgett Papers, 1945–1996, OCA.

62. Shults, 331.

63. Ibid., 333–34.

64. *Sports Illustrated,* October 7, 1996. The letter to the editor was written by Harry I. Subin.

65. Blodgett, "Oberlin football," 23.

66. *OR,* November 18, 1975.

67. *USA Today,* October 29, 1992.

68. *OR,* September 27, 1996.

69. *College Football '96,* August 26, 1996, 106.

70. *OR,* November 20, 1998.

71. The football coach/father was John B. Wiley. *Oberlin News-Tribune,* September 21, 1999.

17. EPILOGUE

Epigraph taken from Strong and Barrows, *Songs of Oberlin,* 3–4. The song is entitled "Oberlin Reunion Song."

1. *Columbus Dispatch,* April 21, 1996.

2. *ON,* June 25, 1913, clipping in Geoffrey Blodgett Papers, 1945–1996, OCA.

3. "Thirty-one Years of Football," *OAM* (February 1923): 26.

4. Shults, 172.

5. Ibid., 174.

6. Ibid., 177.

7. Ibid., 162–63.

8. Ibid., 165.

9. Ibid.

10. Ibid., 167.

11. "Certain Aspects of Intercollegiate Football at Oberlin College." This "confidential" report was found in folder "100 Years of Football," Geoffrey Blodgett Papers, 1945–1996, OCA.

12. The breakdown of the faculty-student vote tally is from Geoffrey Blodgett to Nat Brandt, August 8, 1997. Blodgett chaired the committee that drew up the report, which was entitled "Report in favor of retaining intercollegiate football."

13. Ibid.

14. Minutes of General Faculty, February 28, 1978, Office of the Secretary. There were two abstentions among the 129 faculty members who voted.

15. Lester, *Stagg's University,* 152–53.

16. *Chicago Tribune,* January 13, 1940.

17. Lester, *Stagg's University,* 197.

18. *New York Times,* December 26, 1997.

19. Ibid., April 12, 1998.

20. Ibid., February 5, 1998.

21. Ibid., April 12, 1998.

22. Ibid., January 10, 1998.

23. "Broad Directions for Oberlin's Future: Reports on the Oberlin College Planning Process 1996–97," Miscellaneous Publications, 1834–1997, OCA, 81.

24. Heisman Club brochure.

APPENDIX A: ROSTERS

Epigraph taken from Strong and Barrows, *Songs*, 22. The title of the song is "Oberlin."

1. *OR*, November 4, 1890.

2. The 1891 roster is based on the *Hi-O-Hi* of 1892, OCA, 158, and the Record Book maintained by the Oberlin Department of Physical Education and Athletics.

3. The 1892 roster is based on the Record Book of the Oberlin Department of Physical Education and Athletics and the team photograph.

4. The 1893 roster is based on the Record Book of the Oberlin Department of Physical Education and Athletics.

5. The 1894 roster is based on the Record Book of the Oberlin Department of Physical Education and Athletics and two team photographs, one of which appeared in *OR*, December 19, 1894.

6. *OR*, October 11, 1894.

APPENDIX B: THE BOYS OF AUTUMN

Epigraph taken from Strong and Barrows, *Songs*, 23. The title of the song is "Oberlin."

1. Unless otherwise noted, details that follow regarding the Oberlin football players are from their respective student folders in Alumni Records.

2. *OR*, December 12, 1894.

3. *Cleveland Leader*, January 8, 1901.

4. Commencement program, 1891, Commencement Files, 1834–1997, College General.

5. *New York Times*, August 31, 1960.

6. Class Letter, Louis Edward Hart, December 6, 1893, Class Files, OCA.

7. Umphlett, 33.

8. *Cleveland Plain Dealer*, January 18, 1957.

9. Book 16, Office of the Registrar, 1859–1995, OCA, 406.

10. Class Letter, Frank Nicholas Spindler, April 13, 1896, Class Files, OCA.

11. Class Letter, Frank Nicholas Spindler, May 10, 1895, Class Files, OCA.

12. Class Letter, Frank Nicholas Spindler, April 13, 1896.

13. *ON*, August 14, 1918.

14. *Oberlin News-Tribune*, July 20, 1961.

15. Class Letter, Charles Henry Borican, May 9, 1896, Class Files, OCA.

16. Charles Henry Borican to Dr. Arthur T. Laird, July 15, 1956, student folder of Charles H. Borican, Alumni Records.

17. William Raine, undated note with photograph, received in Oberlin March 21, 1954, student folder of Charles C. Brackin, Alumni Records.

BIBLIOGRAPHY

They all deserve a glory for the title they redeem,
When we wish to tell the story of Ohio's Champion team.
It is love for Alma Mater; oh, forever may it last,
As the voices of the present join the echoes of the past.
—M. B. Jewett, Class of '00, "Oberlin Victorious,"
Oberlin Review, *Dec. 19, 1901*

ARCHIVES AND MANUSCRIPT SOURCES

Bentley Historical Library, University of Michigan
    Annual Reports of the Board of Intercollegiate Athletics
    Annual Reports of the President
    Board of Regents Exhibits
Oberlin College Archives
    Institutional Records:
        Alumni Association Records, 1839–(1920–85)–1996
            Class Files, 1922–1989
            Oberlin Alumni Magazine, 1904 to present
        Alumni and Development Records, 1833–1995
        College of Arts and Sciences, 1872–1997
            Department of Physical Education, 1886–1997
        College General
            Class Files, 1834–1995
            Commencement Files, 1884–1997
            Miscellaneous Publications and Printed Materials, 1834–1997
        Office of the Secretary, 1834–1989
            Athletics and Athletic Association Files
            Oberlin College Athletic Association Files
            Ohio Atlantic Conference Files
        Office of the Registrar, 1859–1995
        Photographic Collections, 1848–1995
        Presidential Assistants (William F. Bohn, 1912–52)

Student Files and Grade Books, 1833–1996
Scrapbooks and Diaries Collection (Charles W. Savage, 1887–1894)
Noninstitutional Records:
Oberlin File
Personal Papers:
Geoffrey Blodgett Papers, 1945–1996
John H. Nichols Papers, 1890–1979
Fredrick Shults Papers, 1959–1988
S. Frederick Starr Papers, 1983–1994
Ohio State University Archives
Records of the Athletic Board
Records of Proceedings of the Board of Trustees

BOOKS

Annual Report of the Registrar and University Examiner. Columbus: Ohio State University Press, 1962.

Barnard, John. *From Evangelicalism to Progressivism at Oberlin College, 1866–1917*. Columbus: Ohio State University Press, 1969.

Brady, John T. *The Heisman: A Symbol of Excellence*. New York: Atheneum, 1984.

Brandt, Nat. *The Town That Started the Civil War*. Syracuse, N.Y.: Syracuse University Press, 1990.

Butkus, Dick. Introduction. *Seventy-Five Seasons: The Complete Story of the National Football League*. Atlanta: Turner Publishing, 1986.

Camp, Walter. *American Football*. New York: Harper & Bros., 1896.

———. *The Book of Foot-ball*. New York: Century, 1910.

———. *Football Facts and Figures*. New York: Harper, 1894.

Clary, Jack. *Great College Football Coaches*. New York: Gallery, 1990.

Danzig, Allison. *Oh, How They Played the Game: The Early Days of Football and the Heroes Who Made It Great*. New York: Macmillan, 1968.

———. *The History of American Football: Its Great Teams, Players, and Coaches*. Englewood Cliffs, N.J.: Prentice-Hall, 1956.

Davis, Parke H. *Football: The American Intercollegiate Game*. New York: Scribner's Sons, 1911.

Hansen, Harry, ed. *Illinois: A Descriptive and Historical Guide*. New York: Hastings House, 1974.

Hartson, Louis D., ed. *Alumni Register: Graduates and Former Students, Teaching and Administrative Staff, 1833–1960*. Oberlin, Ohio: Oberlin College, 1960.

Larson, Melissa. *College Football*. New York: Gallery, 1989.

Lester, Robin. *Stagg's University: The Rise, Decline, and Fall of Big-Time Football at Chicago*. Urbana: University of Illinois Press, 1995.

Mason, Nicholas. *Football: The Story of All the World's Football Games*. New York: Drake, 1975.

McCullum, John, and Charles H. Pearson. *College Football U.S.A., 1869 . . . 1972*. Greenwich, Conn.: Hall of Fame Publishing, 1972.

Menke, Frank G. *The Encyclopedia of Sports*. New York: A. S. Barnes, 1953.

Michigan Football ('96) Media Guide. Ann Arbor: University of Michigan Athletic Department, 1996.

Oberlin College (1996) Football Media Guide. Oberlin, Ohio: Oberlin College Department of Athletics and Physical Education, 1996.

Ohio Guide. New York: Oxford University Press, 1962.

Oriard, Michael. *Reading Football: How the Popular Press Created an American Spectacle*. Chapel Hill: University of North Carolina Press, 1993.

Perrin, Tom. *Football: A College History*. Jefferson, N.C.: McFarland, 1987.

Perry, Will. *The Wolverines: A Story of Michigan Football*. Huntsville, Ala.: Strode, 1974.

Pollard, James E. *Ohio State Athletics, 1879–1959*. Columbus: Ohio State University Press, 1959.

Pope, Edwin. *Football's Greatest Coaches*. Atlanta: Tupper and Love, 1956.

Robertson, James O. *American Myth, American Reality*. New York: Hill & Wang, 1980.

Smith, Ronald A. *Sports and Freedom: The Rise of Big-Time College Athletics*. New York: Oxford University Press, 1988.

Snypp, Wilbur. *The Buckeyes: A Story of Ohio State Football*. Huntsville, Ala.: Strode, 1974.

Stevens, Marvin A., and Winthrop M. Phelps. *The Control of Football Injuries*. New York: A. S. Barnes, 1933.

Strong, Anna Louise, and Edna Barrows. *Songs of Oberlin*. n.p., n.d.

Treat, Robert. *The Official Encyclopedia of Football*. New York: A. S. Barnes, 1968.

Umphlett, Wiley Lee. *Creating the Big Game: John W. Heisman and the Invention of American Football*. Westport, Conn.: Greenwood Press, 1992.

Valenzi, Kathleen D. *Champion of Sport: The Life of Walter Camp*. Charlottesville, Va.: Howell, 1990.

Walsh, Christy, ed. *Intercollegiate Football: A Complete Pictorial and Statistical Review from 1869 to 1934*. New York: Doubleday, Doran & Co., 1934.

Weyand, A. M. *American Football: Its History and Development*. New York: D. Appleton, 1926.

Woodward, C. Vann. *The Strange Career of Jim Crow*. New York: Oxford University Press, 1957.

Zang, David W. *Fleet Walker's Divided Heart: The Life of Baseball's First Black Major Leaguer*. Lincoln: University of Nebraska Press, 1995.

ARTICLES

Bigglestone, W. E. "Oberlin College and the Negro Student, 1865–1940." *Journal of Negro History* (July 1971): 198–219.

Bigham, John. "This Foot-ball Question." *Depauw Palladium* 1:3 (November 1, 1897): reprint unpaginated.

Blodgett, Geoffrey. "The Meaning of Peters Hall." *Oberlin Alumni Magazine* (Fall 1997): 10–18, 20–21.

———. "Oberlin Football Celebrates Long History." *Oberlin Review*, October 4, 1994, 23.

Blue, Frederick J. "Oberlin's James Monroe: Forgotten Abolitionist." *Civil War History* 35 (December 1989): 286–89.

Brown, Gwilym S. "Jeepers! Peepers Is in Charge Now." *Sports Illustrated* (October 23, 1972): 40–46, 49.

Burket, Harlan F. "Historical Sketches of Athletics at Oberlin (In the Eighties)." *Oberlin Alumni Magazine* 10:5 (February 1914): 134–36.

Camp, Walter. "Kicking and Its Future." *Baseball* 2:3 (January 1909): 23–24.

———. "New Rules and College Football." *Baseball* 1:6 (October 1908): 36–39.

———. "Recent Changes in Football Tactics." *Baseball* 2:1 (November 1908): 46–48.

———. "The Increased Value of the Kicking Game." *Baseball* 2:2 (December 1908): 39–40.

Cochran, W. C. "Antiquity of Football." *Oberlin Alumni Magazine* 2:5 (February 1906): 158–59.

———. "Historical Sketches of Athletics at Oberlin (In the Sixties)." *Oberlin Alumni Magazine* 10:5 (February 1914): 129–34.

Cochran, W. S. "Some Facts on the New Athletic Field Project." *Oberlin Alumni Magazine* 10:7 (April 1914): 200–204.

Edelstein, Stewart I. "Mens Sana in Corpore Sano." *Oberlin Alumni Magazine* 63:5 (April 1970): 4–13.

Ford, Jackie. "The Heisman Spirit—It's Still Spreading." *Oberlin Alumni Magazine* 81:3 (Spring 1985): 29–31.

"Heisman: The Almost-forgotten Football Genius Whose First Memory of Brown Was a Football Game." *Brown Alumni Magazine* (December 1972): 32–35.

Heisman, John W. "Between Halves." *Collier's* (November 17, 1928): 18, 53–55.

———. "Fast and Loose." *Collier's* (October 20, 1928): 14–15, 54–55.

———. "Here Are Men." *Collier's* (November 16, 1929): 25, 44, 46.

———. "Hero Stuff." *Collier's* (November 2, 1929): 18–19, 72–73.

———. "Hold 'em!" *Collier's* (October 27, 1928): 12–13, 50–51.

———. "Inventions in Football." *Baseball* 1:6 (October 1908): 40–42.

———. "Look Sharp Now!" *Collier's* (November 3, 1928): 18–19, 52.

———. "Rough Humor." *Collier's* (November 9, 1929): 21, 47–48.

———. "Rules Rush In." *Collier's* (November 10, 1928): 12–13, 38, 42.

———. "Signals." *Collier's* (October 6, 1928): 12–13, 31–32.

———. "The Thundering Herd." *Collier's* (October 13, 1928): 12–13, 59–60.

———. "Their Weight in Gold." *Collier's* (November 24, 1928): 28, 55–57.

Hoover, Earl R. "Why There's a Bit of the Western Reserve in Every Game of Football." *Western Reserve Magazine* (January–February 1981): 50–51.

Horger, Marc. "Basketball and Athletic Control at Oberlin College, 1896–1915." *Journal of Sport History* (Fall 1996): 257–83.

Johnston, Alexander. "The American Game of Foot-ball." *Century Magazine* 34:6 (October 1887): 888–98.

Jones, George M. "Oberlin Athletics in Recent Years." *Oberlin Alumni Magazine* 10:7 (April 1914): 193–99.

Judson, William J. "Athletics." *Oberlin Alumni Magazine* 40:1 (November 1946): 26–27.

Lynn, Minnie L. "Fifty Years of Physical Education—1885–1935." *Oberlin Alumni Magazine* 31:7 (April 1935): 204–6.

Nichols, J. H. "50 Years of Football." *Oberlin Alumni Magazine* 20:10 (October 1941): 2–5.

Patsko, Scott. "Thirty Minutes to Play—A Lifetime to Remember." *Oberlin Alumni Magazine* (Fall 1997): 28–30.

Reisman, David, and Reuel Denney. "Football in America: A Study in Culture Diffusion." *American Quarterly* (May 1952): 309–25.

Sears, Hal D. "The Moral Threat of Intercollegiate Sports: An 1893 Poll of Ten College Presidents, and the End of the Champion Football Team of the Great West." *Journal of Sport History* 19:3 (Winter 1992): 211–26.

Shults, Fredrick D. "A Philosophy for Educational Athletics." *Oberlin Alumni Magazine* 78:3 (Summer 1982): 20–25.

Simpson, David P. "Historical Sketches of Athletics at Oberlin (In the Nineties)." *Oberlin Alumni Magazine* 10:6 (March 1914): 161–62.

Sperber, Murray. "In Praise of Student-Athletes: The NCAA Is Haunted by Its Past." *Chronicle of Higher Education* (January 8, 1999): A76.

———. "Point of View: College Sports' Disheartening Pattern of Failed Reform." *Chronicle of Higher Education* (November 3, 1993): A52.

Stone, Christian. "Lost Glory." *Sports Illustrated* (August 26, 1996): 106–7.

Taylor, Warren. "The Achievement of Oberlin College, 1833–1933." *Oberlin Alumni Magazine* 62:1 (December 1969): 5–25, 53.

"The Secret Fraternity Cases—Dean Cole: Statement made to the faculty." *Oberlin Alumni Magazine* 13:1 (October 1916): 9–20.

"Thirty-one Years of Football." *Oberlin Alumni Magazine* (February 1923): 26.

Tucker, John Mark. "Wide Awakening: Political and Theological Impulses for Reading and Libraries at Oberlin College, 1883–1908." *Occasional Papers* (February 1997): 43–70.

In addition, the following publications were employed extensively in writing this book: *Hi-O-Hi* (Oberlin College yearbook), *New York Times*, *Oberlin News-Tribune*, *Oberlin Review*.

Theses and Dissertations

DeSpain, Raymond E., Jr. *An Historical Analysis of the Life and Professional Career of John William Heisman, 1869–1936*. Ph.D. diss., Texas A&M University, 1991.

Keefe, Robert J. *Physical Education at Oberlin College: A Report of a Type C Project*. Ph.D. diss., Teachers College, Columbia University, 1952.

Kinsey, Daniel C. *The History of Physical Education in Oberlin College, 1833–1890*. Master's thesis, Oberlin College, 1935.

Kostic, Bruce. "John Heisman." Undated senior term paper [1974], Oberlin College.

Putney, Clifford. *Muscular Christianity: The Strenuous Mood in American Protestantism, 1880–1920*. Ph.D. diss., Brandeis University, 1995.

Shults, Fredrick Davis. *The History and Philosophy of Athletics for Men at Oberlin College*. Ph.D. diss., Indiana University, June 1967.

INDEX